MW01199533

NOT MY TYPE

ALSO BY E. JEAN CARROLL

What Do We Need Men For?

E. JEAN CARROLL

NOT
MY
TYPE

One Woman vs. a President

ST. MARTIN'S PRESS

New York

First published in the United States by St. Martin's Press, an imprint of St. Martin's Publishing Group

NOT MY TYPE. Copyright © 2025 by E. Jean Carroll. All rights reserved. Printed in the United States of America. For information, address St. Martin's Publishing Group, 120 Broadway, New York, NY 10271.

www.stmartins.com

The Library of Congress Cataloging-in-Publication Data is available upon request.

ISBN 978-1-250-38168-2 (hardcover)

ISBN 978-1-250-38181-1 (ebook)

Our books may be purchased in bulk for promotional, educational, or business use. Please contact your local bookseller or the Macmillan Corporate and Premium Sales Department at 1-800-221-7945, extension 5442, or by email at MacmillanSpecialMarkets@macmillan.com.

First Edition: 2025

10 9 8 7 6 5 4 3 2 1

June 24, 2019

The White House

"She's not my type."

October 19, 2022

Mar-a-Lago

"That's Marla, yeah. That's my wife."

This book is for Robbie Kaplan

CONTENTS

NOT MY TYPE

*Friends, there will be no introduction.
From the beginning I want you to feel as
discombobulated as I do as I go to trial.*

I
———

THE DIAMOND AS BIG AS THE RITZ

Q. I hate to ask you this, but—approximately—how many people do you think you've slept with?

A. Eight.

Q. Eight? Could you list me those people?

A. Yes.

Q. Would you mind doing so?

A. Do you **really** want to hear?

Q. I do.

A. I lost my virginity with the star of the swim team after I graduated from Indiana University. Fred Schmidt. The Olympic gold medal winner.

This excerpt is from testimony I'm giving under oath in a confidential videotaped deposition conducted by Alina Habba, Esq., Donald Trump's most beautiful attorney.

We are in the Ruth Bader Ginsburg Conference Room of Kaplan Hecker & Fink, my attorney's offices on the sixty-third floor of the Empire State Building. The question Alina Habba, Esq. "hates" to "ask" me is part of discovery for the approaching trial. The trial that is approaching is commonly known in newspapers as "The Trump Rape Trial," and sixty-three floors is extremely high up. If I look out the windows, I can see the gray-green slivers of six states, the sun glittering and shuttering on skyscrapers, shiny silver planes flying through the air—but I am not looking out the windows. I am looking Alina Habba, Esq.

She is stupendous! Dark, with a broad forehead, cheekbones like pickleball paddles, wide-set eyes as lovely as a baby seal's. I like her immediately. "Good morning, Miss Carroll!" she says, opening up with a gorgeous contemptuous smile.

*   *   *

Alina Habba, Esq. is sitting a little down from me at the long, long white table. My attorney has told me not to trust Alina Habba, Esq. My attorney argues *Windsor* before the Supreme Court. My attorney opens the way for gay rights in America. My attorney trounces the Nazis and White supremacists in Charlottesville. My attorney is "Litigator of the Year."

"Just listen to her questions," says my attorney, Robbie Kaplan. "Tell the truth. Keep it short. Very, *very* short." I receive the impression that saying nothing at all would be best.

Q. How old were you when you lost your virginity?
A. 22.
Q. Okay.

Fred Schmidt is the world record holder in the men's hundred-meter butterfly. Although Fred has terrible eyesight, he and I lose it together in the Le Méridien hotel in Indianapolis, Indiana. Fred's eyes are so bad he must ask United States Senate Minority Leader Everett Dirksen, or Senator Chuck Percy, I can't remember which, to *petition* the United States Navy to let Fred join so he can go fight in Vietnam. Senator Dirksen or Senator

Percy *do* get Fred in, and Fred becomes a Navy Seal, jumps out of planes in Vietnam, and Walter Cronkite—I'm not a hundred percent certain about Cronkite—may wipe away a tear when Fred opens the hatch of *Apollo 11* and recovers Neal Armstrong, Buzz Aldrin, and Michael Collins when they splash down after being the first men on the moon.

I do not tell any of this to Alina Habba, Esq.

I am keeping my answers short. I am telling the truth. I am admiring Alina Habba, Esq.'s green Chanel jacket, more emerald than Granny Smith, with black piping. She is wearing it with very cut (pardon me, Friends, I said *cut*, not cute—Alina Habba, Esq. is never cute), very sleek, very chic black trousers, and heels so high they cause me to wobble, even though I am seated, when I look at them.

Afterward in the Kaplan Hecker & Fink kitchen, my attorneys and I discuss the green Chanel jacket. I say it is a genuine Chanel. Three of my attorneys, Robbie Kaplan, Shawn G. Crowley, and Rachel Tuchman, say it is a knock off. Matt Craig, an unfailingly kind young man, is busy making a sandwich out of string cheese and does not answer.

When I am finished listing Fred Schmidt, I glance at Robbie Kaplan. She is the most famous civil rights attorney in America. She is *very* busy looking down and writing a note, but I can see her left neck muscle is grinning. I know what she's thinking.

She's thinking, "Ha! Donald Trump! *You* never won an Olympic medal!"

*   *   *

As I list the people I "think I've slept with" for the woman I am supposed not to trust, my left eyebrow is itching. This is odd because I have no left eyebrow. Dr. Lance Brown removed it a few days ago. He had discovered a congregation of basal cell carcinomas above my left eye, and had said to me, after making me sit down, "You should *not* wait, E. Jean," and then he had explained what Mohs surgery is. Mohs surgery turns out to be Dr. Lance Brown cutting away layers of skin above my eye—examining the layers under a microscope for signs of cancer, and going on cutting like he's dining on an artichoke until the last layer he examines has zero cancer. And then, I guess, he mops up the blood and slaps on a bandage.

I had agreed to scheduling the "cancer surgery" on one condition:

"What about the scar?" I had said.

"It should be minimal," Dr. Lance Brown had said.

"No! I have a trial coming up!"

Dr. Lance (*lance*!) Brown had been wearing his special magnifying goggles up on his forehead, so I am looking into four eyes as he had started to reassure me.

"No!" I had cried. "The trial is against Donald Trump!"

"I realize that—"

Finally, I almost shout:

"No! I *want* to look like a pirate! I *want* the scar! I want to look *rrrrRRRRR!*"

*   *   *

Perhaps someone can make sense of this cancer narrative. The decision to deal with it before depositions and trial strikes even *me* as strange. I am generally a person who would not love a big scar on her face, so I will simply tell you this:

I have the surgery. The surgery is not painful. It is meticulous and lasts from 9:40 a.m. to 12:50 p.m. Dr. Lance Brown asks me to rest out on his resting sofa after the surgery, and, because caffeine is never good after being cut open, and because I have been shouting with glee about how "long" and "terrifying" the "wound" looks, he adds: "No coffee!"

After "resting" I am driving home to my cabin in upstate New York through torrents of rain and I call my friend Carol Martin.

"I look brilliant!" I shout into the phone. "I'm a pirate! I got a three-inch-long scar that will scare the crap out of you!"

"Jeanie," says Carol, "are you *driving*?"

"I'm on the West Side Highway! You should have seen the blood!"

"Pull over!" cries Carol.

"Can't, Caroly! Almost to the George Washington Bridge."

"You can*not* drive after surgery!"

"I never felt sharper!"

"Stop driving!"

And so on.

And this is one of the reasons why every single one of my attorneys advises me not to drink coffee before I arrive for my deposition with Alina Habba, Esq., detour me from the coffee urn in the Ruth Bader Ginsburg Conference Room, and supply me with packets of horrible chamomile tea. Any frightening event—surgery, breaking my arm, an attack in a dressing room, a deposition for a trial—causes my spirits to *rise*, a great rush of life flows through my veins, and I start laughing and jabbering.

*   *   *

To continue.

Stephen Byers. Number Two. Editor-in-chief of *Outdoor Life*. We live on a ranch in Montana, on the Madison River. I ride my horse, Miss Hot. Steve fights forest fires. We learn to be writers together and are married fourteen years.

Number Three. The dashing English chap, George Butler. Director (*Pumping Iron, The Endurance: Shackleton's Legendary Antarctic Expedition*, etc., etc.). I meet George when I come to New York on assignment for *Outside* magazine to "take Fran Lebowitz camping."

Fran wears her loafers, her Shetland, and her long camel hair coat when we go camping in the Shawangunk Mountains.

George Butler took this photo of Fran not in the Shawangunk Mountains, but in Tompkins Square Park in Manhattan after we returned from camping.

We cook over the fire. We all sleep in the little tent in the forest. It has two exits. Fran is vastly pleased with the two exits, especially the one in the back with the zipper. "In case of a raid," says Fran. When we return to New York, I crash like a felled timber for George Butler and burst into tears when we make love, it is so extraordinary, but Alina Habba, Esq. is too busy trying to make me tell her the *year* I meet George Butler and have the "sex," than to ask questions about the sex, so I pause.

*   *   *

Much of the transcript at the beginning of this chapter does not reflect the pauses. My attorneys tell me over and over: "Pause before you speak." Matt Craig, the attorney in charge of preparing me for this deposition, tells me, "Pause, E. Jean" seventeen times in one prep session. (I count them.) My attorneys believe that if I pause before I speak I will consider what I will say, and if I consider what I will say, I will tell the truth, and if I tell the truth, it will be impossible for me to blather like a halfwit. But, in fact, it is almost impossible for me to pause and consider what I will say before I speak because during most of Alina's six-hour interrogation she is asking me questions I do not want to think about, let alone pause and consider, like—

Q. And did you recall at any point him [Trump] taking his pants off?

I do not care to "consider" at what point Donald Trump takes his pants off. I have trained myself for years not to think of Donald Trump. I am still learning to bat images of Donald Trump away when the flashbacks kidnap my brain. And, in fact, he does not take his pants all the way off, and no matter how many questions Alina Habba, Esq. asks about how it is possible he doesn't take his pants off, the answer is still, he does not remove his pants. So no. When I pause, I am not considering what I will say when I answer Alina Habba, Esq. I am considering how long I am supposed to pause, if I have paused enough, and if I think I have paused enough, I give an answer with absolutely no consideration or forethought whatsoever.

And now I can tell you another fact. Just after Alina Habba, Esq. asks, *"I hate to ask you this but—approximately—how many people do you think you've slept with?"* a strange thing occurs. A perfect silence descends upon the Ruth Bader Ginsburg Conference Room because I am not only pausing to beat the band, but I am also looking down and actually considering who I have slept with. I count on my fingers. I arrive at a total. I double-check it by counting on my fingers again. I look up. I answer.

How long do I pause?

Friends, how long would it take *you* to count up your lovers?

At any rate, Alina Habba, Esq. asks the question about the "number" of my lovers to shame me. But as I am excessively fond of my lovers, my answers to her question give me several minutes of happiness, indeed, some of the only tolerable moments of the entire deposition.

*   *   *

Number Four. Bob Datilla, the literary agent. Number Five. Anthony Haden-Guest, who should be dead. In the 1980s, '90s, and aughts Anthony is out EVERY night, at EVERY party, downing EVERY glass of wine, and—miraculously!—appears EVERY morning at his desk at nine-thirty. When Anthony dances—well, just let me say, when Sir William Lucas compliments Mr. Darcy's dancing and says:

> "I have been most highly gratified indeed, my dear Sir. Such very superior dancing is not often seen."

Sir William has *not* seen Anthony Haden-Guest on a dance floor. He is like a giraffe in battle with a baobab. Tom Wolfe bases the character of the journalist Peter Fallow on Anthony Haden-Guest in *Bonfire of the Vanities.* Bruce Willis plays him in the movie, and it is at this point I mention Number Six. My one and only one-night stand:

"Ben Vereen."

Robbie Kaplan rocks in her chair, recovers, bends forward, and *beams* at her notebook—and everyone else? From Alina Habba, Esq., not a peep. Just the loud glare of her ring, a diamond as big as a Ritz cracker. Her associates, Michael Madaio and a guy named Peter, Ms. English, the court transcriber, and the video camera operators, they are all too young to possess the slightest notion of the Tony-winning star of *Pippin* and *Jesus Christ Superstar, Wicked,* and *Hair,* never heard of Chicken George of *Roots,* or *Tenspeed and Brown Shoe.* Such, I am sorry to say, are the barren lives being lived within the Ruth Bader Ginsburg Conference Room, though Ruth, of course, probably dated Ben herself.

*   *   *

Number Eight. My husband, John Johnson, the incredibly handsome New York anchorman. I do not mention how John would break down my office door in our little house, pick me up, carry me outside to the lawn, and ravish me among the day lilies. And then I add:

"Number Seven is Richard Harris."

I.e., *Gladiator, Unforgiven, A Man Called Horse,* Academy Award nominee for Best Actor for *This Sporting Life* and *The Field,* the Cannes Film Festival Best Actor for I can't remember, *Camelot* on Broadway, Grammy Best Male Pop Vocal nominee ("MacArthur Park"), and the *Harry Potter* films. I meet Richard Harris when I pass him a note at Barbra Streisand's New York premier of *Yentl.*

*   *   *

That is the background, Friends. Now here is the full and complete transcript of our exchange. If you feel sick reading it, you are supposed to. Alina Habba, Esq. designs this series of questions to humiliate me.

A. Do you really want to hear?

Q. I do.

A. I lost my virginity with the star of the swim team after I graduated from Indiana University. Fred Schmidt. The Olympic gold medal winner.

Q. How old were you when you lost your virginity?

A. 22.

Q. Okay. How old were you when you met Steve Byers?

A. Well, we went to school together. I knew him well. He was at Indiana.

Q. How old were you at that time?

A. We were both 25 when we got married.

Q. So—you lost your virginity at 22 to Fred Schmidt. How long were you with him? Or was it just that one time?

A. That was a real romance. Right up to nearly the time I started with Steve.

Q. Okay. And then Steve Byers, 25?

A. (*Witness nods.*)

Q. Okay, who was next?

A. George Butler, the director.

Q. Do you know when that was?

A. When I came to New York to take Fran Lebowitz camping.

Q. Do you have any idea what year that was?

A. 1982, '81 or '82. It's on the cover of the magazine. The date would be on it.

Q. Okay. And after that?

A. Oh, boy. Anthony Haden-Guest. Ben Vereen.

Q. And how do you spell that?

A. V-E-R-E-E-N. How many is that?

Q. We're at five.

A. John would be—who would be—Bob Dattila, longtime boyfriend.

Q. After Ben Vereen, it was Bob—

A. Yes, actually, yes.

Q. Bob?

A. Bob Dattila, literary agent.

Q. D-I-T-T-I-L-L-A?

A. How many is that?

Q. Six.

A. I'm going to have to haul somebody out. John is eight and number seven is Richard Harris.

Q. Richard Harris was before John?

A. Yeah.

Q. Richard Harris?

WITNESS: (*Turning to Robbie Kaplan*) Who did he play?

MS. KAPLAN: (*Googling*) I'm looking right now.

Q. So John, and then—John's your husband?

A. Yes.

Q. And then, that's it?

A. Isn't that enough?

Q. I'm not going to answer that question. I don't judge. So if we have—

RACHEL TUCHMAN: (*My attorney, also googling*) Dumbledore.

MS. KAPLAN: Dumbledore.

Q. So Fred Schmidt, 22. So what year was that?

A. '66.

Q. '66. Steve Byers you said was three years later, so '69?

A. Yes.

Q. George Butler?

A. '82.

Q. So between '69 and '82 you were married to Steve?

A. (*Witness nods.*)

Q. Were there any gaps there where you **didn't** sleep with anyone, I mean when you weren't in a consistent relationship?

A. No.

Q. Anthony Haden-Guest?

A. Yeah.

Q. When was that?

A. Sometime before John Johnson and coming to New York.

Q. How long were you with George Butler?

A. Off and on for a year.

Q. Anthony Guest, how long were you with him?

A. Brief, brief. We would go to parties together.

Q. How many times did you sleep with him, do you know?

A. I have no idea.

Q. Ben Vereen?

A. That was a one-night stand.

Q. One-night stand. Do you know what year that was?

A. '80—I do not know. I do not know. It was a memorable night though.

Q. Is there a reason you didn't sleep with him again?

A. He was on—he was leaving to go west but he had just gotten off Broadway doing something, and he had to leave town.

Q. Okay. Bob Dattila?

A. Long romance.

Q. When did you meet him?

A. Oh, boy, probably—as soon as I arrived, '81, '82.

Q. How long were you with him?

A. Off and on until I met John.

Q. And when was that?

A. I believe it was '84 or '85.

Q. And Richard Harris was before John—correct?

A. Yes.

WITNESS: (*Turning to Robbie*) They have no idea who Richard Harris is.

MS. HABBA: I have no idea who Richard Harris is.

Q. Richard Harris is what year?

A. I'm not sure.

MS. KAPLAN: Just so the record is clear, he played Dumbledore in the Harry Potter movies, and Ben Vereen was the star in *Pippin*, which was the first Broadway show I ever saw.

*   *   *

The deposition starts at 10:15 a.m. and ends at 4:19 p.m. What else can I tell you about Fred, Steve, George, Anthony, Ben, Bob, Richard, and John? I ran into Anthony Haden-Guest last month at a reading I gave at KGB, and do we laugh! He is the same Anthony, as beguiling as ever. His brother Christopher Guest has inherited the title and is now the Fifth Baron Hayden-Guest. Chris's wife, Jamie Lee Curtis, is the Right Honorable Lady Haden-Guest, and after the first trial, Jamie takes me and Lisa Birnbach and Lisa's daughter, Boco, and Lisa's daughter-in-law, Star, to lunch at the Polo Lounge.

Barbra Streisand—who directs and stars in *Yentl*, the premier of which I attend and where I meet Richard Harris—received the Genesis Award from Robbie Kaplan last week in Malibu, and Barbra and I have a wonderful few moments together.

But nobody in the Ruth Bader Ginsburg Conference Room speaks up and names the last man I "have sex" with. Even the person in this room who is suing him for rape and can still hear his breathing on her neck, remains silent.

2

THE GOLD DIGGER

D o you know why I have never seen a therapist in my life?
Because I get over things. Do you know how I get over
things? I do not dwell. You know how I do not dwell?
I forget it.

When therapists write to me during the twenty-seven years
that I have the "Ask E. Jean" column in *Elle* magazine—and,
oddly, *many* therapists write to me—and ask my advice about
their problems, I write back to the therapists and say: "Stop pondering! Move on!"

So, to move on as quickly as possible through this less-than-
shining part of the trial, to talk about the things I do not want
to talk about, it comes as quite a stunner to see that the "conclusions" of the two opposing forensic psychologists paid to "assess"
me before we reach the courtroom—agree on one fact:

I have not "gotten over things."

Thus, as much as I hate proceeding further, I want to take a
look at these "evaluations."

*   *   *

"Do you have problems with alcohol?"

"No."

"What about recreational drugs?"

"No."

"What medications you are taking?"

"Zero medications."

"How often do you drink?"

Do not try to picture Dr. Edgar P. Nace and me at Bemelmans Bar with the $32 martinis. I try; it is impossible. Dr. Edgar P. Nace is in an office in Dallas, Texas, and I am on the sixty-third floor of the Empire State Building in a Kaplan Hecker & Fink technologically advanced conference room, sitting alone at a round table as big as a kiddy pool with a plastic bottle of watermelon-flavored water.

At trial, Trump's attorneys will argue to the jury that I made the "whole story up," and they hire Dr. Nace to help them prove that I am a perjuring gold digger.

Robbie Kaplan will put eleven witnesses on the stand and tell the jury that Trump attacks me in the dressing room, then defames me, and she hires Dr. Leslie Lebowitz, the trauma specialist, the very woman who creates the Sexual Assault Response protocol for the United States Air Force, to assess if I am telling the truth—and, if I am telling the truth, to find out if I suffer any "harms."

Dr. Leslie Lebowitz has completed her assessment and has turned in her report. And now Dr. Edgar P. Nace of Dallas, Texas, is plumbing my depths.

*   *   *

My depths were supposed to be plumbed *yesterday* by two different Trump doctors, Dr. Jill Hayes, of Rockford, Tennessee, a psychologist who specializes in forensic psychological and neuropsychological assessment; and Dr. Ian C. Lamoureux of Scottsdale, Arizona, a psychiatrist who specializes in "complicated criminal and civil cases," but they both drop out the day before they are supposed to plumb my depths, and Robbie Kaplan calls me and says:

"I've just taken a shower and had hot water banging down my head, and I now know why Trump's psychiatrists suddenly withdrew from the case."

"Why, Robbie?" I say.

"Because," says Robbie, "they just read the Leslie Lebowitz report, and it is *impossible* to refute."

So here I am with Dr. Edgar P. Nace.

He seems a nice fellow. Slim, sandy haired, wearing a calm dark tie and brown tweed jacket, he is an even-tempered, literature-loving, bird-watching Methodist (I looked him up)—a board-certified psychiatrist, a graduate of the University of Pennsylvania School of Medicine, an eighty-three-year-old "pillar in the field of addiction," who cannot figure out how to turn on his computer's camera to do our Zoom. But Nace is Trump's ace! Out of all the thousands and *thousands* of psychiatrists in America, many of whom are sexual assault experts—amazingly—Dr. Edgar P. Nace is the only shrink who is brave enough to take $750 an hour off Donald Trump to rebut Dr. Leslie Lebowitz and her Duke PhD, her famous Harvard rape studies, and her United States Air Force protocols—to plumb my depths and to report back on (1) how clinically insane I am, and (2) how big a "malingerer" (i.e., liar) I am, and (3) what harms I am faking when Donald Trump NEVER attacks me.

Dr. Nace is so calm he seems depressed, and I try to lift his spirits by telling him that Hunter S. Thompson once fed me a white tablet sent to him, as Hunter explained to me as we were sitting in the front seat of his fire-apple red convertible, by secret envoy from "Chief of Staff of the US Army, Alexander Haig." "What is it?" I said. It looked like blotter paper with perforated tablets on it. "I don't know," Hunter said. "I've never seen anything like it," I whispered. "Neither have I," Hunter whispered, and he tore off two tablets from the blotter paper, put one in his mouth and handed me the other. "Take yours," he said. "What is it?" I said. "Trust me," Hunter said. "Then tell me what it is," I said. "Acid," Hunter said. "ACID!" I screamed. "Now, don't swallow it," Hunter said, smiling, "just chew it."

I tell Dr. Nace it had "no effect on me, except I believed for several hours that I was Elizabeth Taylor."

It is February 22, 2023, two months before trial, and Dr. Nace administers the following tests to me:

The Michigan Alcoholism Screening Test
The Beck Anxiety Inventory
The Beck Depression Inventory
The Adverse Childhood Experiences from ACE Study
The Posttraumatic Stress Disorder Symptom Scale

Am I crazy if I select "mildly unable to relax," when taking the Beck Anxiety Inventory? Because for the last several weeks I have been mildly unable to relax on account of my hair. Its length. Its color. Its style. I worry it is all wrong for trial. I have been so absolutely mildly unable to relax, in fact, that I watch my old TV show, *Ask E. Jean*, capture several screenshots, and tell Robbie Kaplan and Reiko Hasuike, Robbie's jury consultant, that

"Nobody's gonna believe an eighty-year-old woman was *ever* attractive enough to assault."

I suggest that I cut my hair into the bob I wear in 1996, the year Trump attacks me in the Bergdorf dressing room. "I should do the bob," I say.

To which Robbie replies:

"Don't worry. We will show the jury photos of you from 1996."

"I should cut my hair!"

"Leave it alone."

"I look old."

"You're fine."

"Ancient."

"Just tell the truth!" cries Robbie. "The jury will believe you."

*   *   *

Dr. Nace, does not mention my hair in the enticing opening of his report[*]:

> Ms. Carroll was appropriately dressed and well-groomed . . . She was oriented to person, place, time, and situation. She demonstrated good attention and concentration. She was able to subtract serial sevens without difficulty. Her affect was positive, and when asked how she was feeling, she stated, "fabulous."

The strange thing about Dr. Nace, other than the fact he's getting $750 an hour from Trump, which strikes me as anti-Methodist, is that most of his questions are not about me. Who Dr. Nace is *really* interested in is Dr. Leslie Lebowitz.

*   *   *

Report by Dr. Leslie Lebowitz:

> I interviewed Ms. Carroll for approximately 22 hours: 16 hours in person in New York City with follow-up inter-

---

[*] I score an *8* on the Beck Anxiety Inventory, with scores of 0–21 being "indicative of low anxiety."

views conducted over Zoom for an additional 6 hours. An unstructured clinical interview format was used to facilitate the emergence of unprepared reflection and to allow for a more complete evaluation of emotional and psychological processes.

SUMMARY OF EXPERT OPINIONS

Ms. Carroll's evaluation provided evidence of significant and enduring damage emanating from the assault that allegedly occurred at the hands of Mr. Trump. The nature and pattern of the symptoms fit within what has been documented in the literature on the aftermath of rape. They also fit within what is known about response to trauma more generally.

*   *   *

The "significant and enduring damage" Dr. Leslie Lebowitz is talking about here is that, after Trump attacks me, I never have sex again.

Between Dr. Leslie Lebowitz and me, on the white, oblong table, is a terrifying box of Kleenex. Nobody at Kaplan Hecker is to disturb us. The door is closed. The blinds are drawn.

An imposing selection of legal pads, pencils, pens, and possibly paper clips is also on the table. I cannot recall if there actually *are* paper clips because Dr. Lebowitz is setting up her computer, and I am feeling very vulnerable.

*   *   *

First question:

"Where'd you get that jacket?" I say.

"This . . . ?"

Dr. Lebowitz glances down and smiles in surprise.

"It's twenty years old!"

Let me tell you, Friends, Dr. Lebowitz has no problem with *her* hair. It is a salt-and-peppered glorious downpour of loose waves and elephantine curls. And talking about clothes is as good a way as any to begin an examination.

*   *   *

If you are standing outside the Deprivation Chamber, which is what I call this saltine-and-oyster-soup conference room on the sixty-third floor of the Empire State Building where Dr. Lebowitz is unwinding my life story—the Scots-Irish Carroll family has three settings, (**A**) Upbeat, (**B**) Very Upbeat, and (**C**) Delirious—you hear yips, snorts. Shouts. Whoops. Not all of them mine. By lunchtime the first day, a few things are obvious: I am raised to be tough. There is no crying in the Carroll family. I am fabulous.

A thing that is not obvious: It takes Dr. Lebowitz only another half day to break through my bullshit.

*   *   *

And Dr. Nace? He plumbs my depths again. Two days after he spends most of our first session trying to get the camera on his computer to work and asking piercing questions about Dr. Leslie Lebowitz, today he is loaded for bear. It is February 24, 2023. Two days closer to trial.

"I have been doing some thinking," he says.

Like an actor receiving a callback, he is wearing the same brown tweed jacket, the better to remember him.

"Oh! Good," I say.

I have a big bowl of pretzels in front of me.

"Nice to see you again," I say. I have Sharpied a note to myself to steer Dr. Nace to the facts and not let him go off his rocker on Dr. Leslie Lebowitz.

"Tell me," he says. "I can't figure out how Dr. Lebowitz spent three full days talking to you."

"Plus, six hours of Zooms," I say, just to get *that* out of the way. He shakes his head.

"I can't imagine it."

"The time flew by," I say.

I look down at my notes. I see "HARMS."

"I can't imagine what would take *three* days," says Dr. Nace.

"She asked questions about maybe I was hurt."

"I can't imagine how *anything* could take three days," says Dr. Nace.

I take a pretzel.

"What did you talk about?" says Dr. Nace.

I smile.

"Why would it take three days?"

I eat the pretzel and smile.

"What did she *say*?"

I chew. I take another pretzel.

Silence.

"Your marriage to John Johnson," says Dr. Nace, "when did you divorce?"

*   *   *

Forty-five minutes later:

"The lawyers are not going to like this," says Dr. Nace. "But I have no more questions."

"Well," I say. I'm thinking, "I could ask *you* questions."

I laugh.

"I just can't imagine," he says, "what Dr. Lebowitz finds to talk about that takes three *days*!"

*   *   *

By the end of the three days, Dr. Leslie Lebowitz has found so much to talk about that I am doubled over with a stomach pain. I will let her explain:

> As long as painful, unresolved feelings and intolerable meanings persist, they will drive avoidant behaviors. Avoidance contributes significantly to anchoring the posttraumatic condition, essentially freezing it in place while enacting an ongoing price in terms of lost opportunity and freedom in one's thoughts and behaviors. . . . Ms. Carroll's self-blame and her efforts to avoid ever being in a similarly dangerous situation have had far-reaching consequences for her life, most notably in the area of intimate relationships with men.

In other words:

I flirted with Trump. The flirting led to the assault. I blame myself.

And because I blame myself for the assault, I never flirt with an eligible man again. And because I never flirt with an available man again, I shut down any chance of sparking a romance, and for the next twenty-eight years I miss out on the romps, the sweetness, the tenderness, the delicacy, and the wild erotic pleasures of being with a man.

Is that enough, Friends? The report is forty-nine pages.

> The process by which she avoids engaging with men her own age is automatic, and it illustrates how her traumatic fear triggers involuntary behaviors intended to maintain safety:
> "I can feel the shut-down. It's like when shopkeepers pull

down the metal grate to secure the store. I can feel it when it happens. It is a physical sensation of closing up shop. And boy, do I close up shop. There is a way that when you are interested in someone, you communicate it [in] a million little physical ways, and when you like them, you pursue them in some way. I haven't done that since then. I shut it down, shut it all down. I haven't 'called a boy' since Trump. Something really was killed, no doubt about it. Little Jeanie who was so boy crazy her whole life just shut it down."

Is *that* enough? Or would you like to hear what the advice columnist says? The *Elle* writer who for twenty-seven years advises women that the only reason they are on this earth is to enjoy themselves?

"It costs [me] everything: the joy, the elation of sharing a life, going for a swim with your lover, cuddling, fixing dinner, making bets, playing Scrabble. . . . And then there is that yearning—when your lover walks through the door and there is that feeling in your body like you stepped on a live wire and the feeling shoots through your body from your feet to your head, and then you are in each other's arms. I remember coming home unexpectedly and each of my husbands, their faces would just light up. You lose that. You lose all of it. It's too bad. He did a bad thing. If I had a boyfriend, I would leave here and he and I would go out to dinner and I would tell him everything we had talked about, and he would hold my hand and then we would go to a hotel room and we would make love. And none of that is possible now. I have lost the impetus. I lack the desire to desire. And I totally lack the drive to be desirable."

*   *   *

Now let's see what Dr. Edgar P. Nace's report says:

> Her reported diminished interest in and avoidance of a romantic or sexual relationship with males is not attributable to the alleged sexual assault of the defendant.

Dr. Nace attributes my "avoidance of romantic or sexual relationship with males" to the breakup of my marriage with John Johnson. But he also says that it is beyond his $750-an-hour probe to say whether or not Trump attacks me, but if Trump does *not* attack me, then I am malingering.

> If the alleged assault did not occur (the determination of which is outside the scope of this report), then her complaints would be in the realm of malingering. Finally, if the plaintiff and defendant did have an encounter that did not rise to a level of sexual assault or rape but was other than consensual, a classification of partial malingering may apply; with partial malingering referring to the effects or elements of the traumatic event being exaggerated.

What is fascinating about Dr. Nace's report is that he foresees a problem with our case before anyone one else does.

3

THE COMEUPPANCE

Robbie Kaplan
Shawn G. Crowley
Mike Ferrara
Matt Craig
Joshua Matz
Trevor Morrison
Lawrence Tribe
Kate Harris
Rachel Tuchman
Helen Andrews
Donya Khadem
Emma DeCourcy
Adam Bresgi

This is a list of the attorneys on the Carroll Team. They go to Harvard, Yale, Stanford, clerk for Supreme Court justices, teach law to Barack Obama and John Roberts, are dean of New York University School of Law, and so on.

When I hear what idiots they are, I am in Lafayette, a restaurant in SoHo, standing at the top of a long flight of stairs at the entrance to the private dining room which has a tableful of enough uncorked and breathing wines to float the USNS *Earl Warren*.

I am waiting for the people on the list. They are on their way from a downtown hotel ballroom where they have been secretly presenting our case to twenty-seven "typical New Yorkers." What goes on in the ballroom is called "jury exercises," and this is what happens:

Shawn G. Crowley delivers a ringing opening argument for our side, and calls the first witness to the stand. The way Shawn calls the first witness is she turns and points to large movie screen at the front the ballroom, and a seventy-nine-year-old woman in a sensational gold-and-silver Armani blazer and a bandage above her left eye appears on screen and starts telling her story.

The way the old lady tells her story is through clips edited from a deposition with Alina Habba, Esq.

MS. HABBA: What did he do after that?
WITNESS: He pulled down my tights.

The test trial lasts all day.

*　　*　　*

A portrait of Shawn G. Crowley, the lawyer who presents our case in jury exercises, hangs in the Daniel Patrick Moynihan United States Courthouse. It does not hang in the courthouse because she's a beautiful woman. She is, yes. *Very.* No, it hangs in the courthouse because she is the former co-chief of the Narcotics Unit and the Terrorist and International Narcotics Unit of the U.S Attorney's Office for the Southern District of New York, and as the Carroll Team is the smartest, most ambitious bunch of lawyers in the country, she puts on the movie screen five additional witnesses.

Next up—for the defense—is "the most hated lawyer in New York,"* the very pumped, very dark, very neck-veined Joe Tacopina, Trump's new lawyer. Matt Craig (the man making the string cheese sandwich and not offering an opinion on the Chanel jacket)—as tall and blond and happy and handsome a fellow as anybody has ever seen, a young husband and father with a newborn son named Pablo—gives an Academy Award–grade performance as "Snarlin' Joe." He presents the former president's case and plays clips from Trump's unsealed deposition:

> "I still don't know this woman. I think she's a whack job. I have no idea. I don't know anything about this woman other than what I read in stories and what I hear. I know nothing about her."

And . . .

> "It didn't happen. . . . . It's the most ridiculous, disgusting story. It was just made up."

Each one of the twenty-seven typical New Yorkers has been given an iPad with a sliding scale, 1–9. And each has been judging the credibility of the attorneys and witnesses second by second throughout the day. Shawn and Matt deliver closing arguments, and the twenty-seven New Yorkers are divided into three juries—nine members each. Under the observation of the Carroll Team, they retire to discuss the case and arrive at their verdicts.

---

* The *New York Post,* Slate, NBC News, etc., etc.

*   *   *

And now the Carroll Team is arriving at Lafayette restaurant and climbing the stairs. These are people who take two steps at a time. These are people who get out of bed at 5 a.m. because they *enjoy* a seven-mile run. These are people who "jog" to work during their pregnancies. These are people who prize being "the smartest person in the room," no matter the size of the room, or the number of persons in it. These are people who tell you *as they are entering the courtroom*, "We come back with our shields. Or *on* them."

It seems to me these people are now *crawling* up the stairs. It seems to me two members of the team haul their stunned carcasses up the last couple of steps, and pass by me shaking their heads. But this may be after I see Robbie Kaplan, and part of what I want to tell you about is Robbie.

When Robbie is preparing to appear before the Supreme Court in *United States v. Windsor*—the case to overturn DOMA, the cruel and archaic Defense of Marriage Act—she uses moot court sessions. In a moot court, a lawyer delivers her oral argument to a panel of "judges"—usually other lawyers—to help decide what's working and what is not, and Robbie's first moot for *Windsor* attracts a big crowd at New York University's School of Law, and the whole place—attorneys, panelists, students, academics—tear her arguments to shreds. She recalibrates. She moots again. It goes better. Another moot, and another moot, and at the last moot in Washington, DC, she makes a single, but terrible, mistake. Three days later Robbie delivers the argument that wins *Windsor* and paves the way to gay rights in America.

And now Robbie drags herself to the top step.

She looks like she's been hit with a shovel. She glances at me, and speaks three words:

"Bob your hair."

*   *   *

Reiko Hasuike, the jury consultant, follows Robbie up the steps.

"Reiko! Reiko!" I cry. "How'd the mock juries go?"

Reiko, heading toward a glass of wine, doesn't even stop.

She says:

"Bob your hair."

*   *   *

"And . . . go lighter," says Rachel Tuchman, following Reiko into the dining room.

*   *   *

It takes five, six days to find Lisa Corvelli, the Great Giver of Bobs. When I call NBC—the *Ask E. Jean* show is owned by NBC—Lisa Corvelli is no longer there. I message Lisa Corvelli's sister, Lisa Corvelli's cousin, Lisa Corvelli's daughter, Lisa Corvelli's old coworkers. I search for Lisa Corvelli's husband, Billy Corvelli, a fireman with a side business in the "duct-cleaning" line. Finally, on the fourth or fifth day, I find a restaurant in Mountain Lakes, *New Jersey*, of all places, called Hapgood's. It is owned by a Billy Corvelli. I call. A waitress answers the phone. I ask for Lisa Corvelli—and BOOM! Lisa Corvelli has the "Salon and Spa at Mountain Lakes" in the wine cellar of the restaurant.

If you ever get an appointment (good luck!) with Lisa Corvelli, here is what you do. You stride past the tables of fashionable Mountain Lakes personalities dining outside, you enter Hapgood's, weave through the lunchtime crowd, and poke your head into the kitchen. If the chef waves you in, you enter, turn to the left, and open a door. If you wear glasses, put them on. Because you must descend a stupefying set of back stairs and pass into the museum of canned goods. The glass door that leads to the wine cellar and Lisa Corvelli's salon is straight ahead.

Open it.

*   *   *

After we cling to one another screaming, and after Lisa has a waitress bring me an olive and cheese omelette, and after I tell her about the test trial and the three juries, Lisa says:

"Don't tell me the three juries said Trump's '*not guilty*'?"

"*Wellll*," I say. "That's why I'm here."

"They couldn't've!"

"The weird thing is," I say, "and this is top secret—*all* three juries agreed on three facts."

Lisa, who is tiny and dark, a bantam Lollobrigida, and just chock-full of Italian spark, has also ordered me, besides the olive and cheese omelette, Hapgood's crispy-yet-buttery slices of black bread. I am served with an amusing linen napkin at a little pull-out board in the wine cellar. Across from me sits Lisa on the black ersatz-leather shampoo sink chair, eating a chopped salad and drinking from an unduly, almost preposterously large glass of ice, club soda, and fresh lemons.

"The three juries agree on *what* three facts?" says Lisa. "There're *a lot* of facts."

"Well, they had *no* trouble believing two people could end up in a Bergdorf dressing room in 1996," I say. "All three juries conceded *something* sexual happened in that dressing room. And all three agreed it involved Trump and me. Absolute unanimous agreement on *that*. But! *Because* it's Trump, two out of the three juries think *I wanted it*."

"No!" cries Lisa.

"Yes," I say.

Lisa's large black eyes hold mine for a moment as she turns this over in her mind.

"They think you were *asking* for it?" she says.

"I *had* to be the one to egg Trump on," I say. "Because I'm too old and unattractive to attack."

"Oh my God!" cries Lisa, bending over. For a moment I think she's going to turn and be sick in the shampoo sink.

When she straightens up, she eyes me for another moment and says:

"What were you *wearing* at this mock trial?"

"I wasn't there—the juries saw videos. In the videos I was wearing a silver-and-gold metallic-check Armani blazer."

"I *love* that jacket!"

Actually, Lisa has never seen this jacket. It is a gift from Arleen Sorkin, the real-life Harley Quinn, the inspiration for the DC Comics character—a hilarious woman, plays Calliope Jones on *Days of Our Lives,* marries Christopher Lloyd, the creator of *Frazier* and *Modern Family*—she buys the Armani jacket, gives it to me, saying as only Harley Quinn could say:

"When you meet Donald Trump in court, I want you to look like you have more money than he does."

(And if you are reading this, Arleen, wherever you are, Salute!)

Lisa puts down her giant glass of lemons, and, with the slightest frown, studies me a moment.

She says:

"How was your hair?"

I put down my fork, lift my hands to my head, and remove the two clips holding it up.

*   *   *

"You see, Lisa?" I say, shaking out my shoulder-length, thinning, soot-blond hair. "A jury can't picture me. They simply can't *imag-*

ine me in 1996. So we gotta give them an idea—a hint, a vibe, a shadow of that younger E. Jean in the dressing room so they can connect her to the older E. Jean in the courtroom."

Lisa extends both her hands to me, palms upward, slides them under my scraggly locks and says softly:

"If your hair looked like . . ." and she lifts my hair up from my shoulders like the heroine she is.

*　　*　　*

The whole discussion of plastic surgery follows, naturally. I don't believe in plastic surgery. Also I don't believe I have the money. Lisa cuts my hair into the exact bob I was wearing in 1996, and does the exact makeup she did in 1996, and, after several trials (*trials*!) she blonds me up to the color I was wearing in 1996. And, no, I do not look like I looked in 1996, but I look like somebody who *could* have once looked like I looked in 1996.

*　　*　　*

NOTE 1

A few minutes after the Carroll Team had returned from the test trial and had mounted the stairs at Lafayette, Robbie Kaplan took a glass of wine, dropped into a chair, and said:

"We were idiots! We live in a liberal bubble. We live in a world which believes in equality for women—for *all* women. So we put on a powerful case 'for all women.' But trying a case for all women caused us to lose jury members. E. Jean! I never want to hear you say 'this case is for all women' again! This case is for *you*. The juries don't care about #MeToo. They don't care! They care about one woman and one man in a dressing room. We were so blinded by our own vision, we couldn't even *see* the gender divide in this country. It's much more pronounced than any of us thought. So since we can't fix the gender divide *before* trial, we'll use it, we'll lean into it. This case *now* is about *one* woman, and *one* man. And that man *lied*!"

NOTE 2

Friends, I would like to change my answer on Dr. Edgar P. Nace's Beck Anxiety Inventory. I am no longer "mildly anxious" about my hair. And just so this change does not disturb my stoic score of 8, I tell you that though I am not now anxious about my hair, I am quite mildly anxious about what I am going to wear.

4

YOU'RE NOBODY TIL
SOMEBODY PREPS YOU

You have to stop."
    "OK."
    "Please. Please."
"OK."
"I know it's hard—don't try to be charming."
I nod.
"Don't *try* and have them like you."
I nod.
Robbie Kaplan and the Carroll Team are prepping me for trial.
"Don't use any words you use in your *Elle* column."
"OK."
"Very few three-syllable words."
"OK."
"Try to think about it like this: You're talking to a bunch of kids from Indiana, who you grew up with."
"Go, Hoosiers."
"Be a nobody."
"I *am* a nobody."

"I know you are—" says Robbie. "Uh, I mean you're *not*—but . . . but—"

"I'm an amoeba," I say.

"OK, E. Jean."

"On the hind end of a flea."

*   *   *

Robbie says I don't need to "smile all the time." She says I have to stop saying, "I'm *fabulous*" when people ask me how I am. And "it's not necessary to compliment everybody," says Robbie. Robbie says it is especially not necessary to compliment Alina Habba, Esq. who reminds me of a—well, Friends, never mind what Alina Habba, Esq. reminds me of.

I do not tell Robbie that the constant aim of my life is to spread sweetness and light. Instead I tell her to just bring a mallet to court "and hit me over the head with it."

"I am planning on bringing a mallet to trial every day," says Robbie.

Besides the saying I am fabulous and the complimenting and the smiling, another problem I have is the jurors at the mock trials think I am "part of the elite." How anyone can think a hick raised in sticks so deep the hick is still pulling twigs out of her hair eighty years later is "elite," is beyond me.

"Whether it's true or not," says Robbie, "and obviously, it's not true in terms of money—they *perceive* you as elite and there's a certain amount of hostility to that." One of the solutions to this problem:

"We are going to train you to speak like a normal person."

As for the gender divide problem that so astonishes Robbie, Shawn, and the Carroll Team at jury exercises—if the male jurors like a strong man and believe what happens in the dressing room is "consensual," well . . . we will *give* them a strong man.

To address the jury and lead me through my testimony at trial, Robbie picks Mike Ferrara, partner at Kaplan Hecker, and God's last word in macho perfection.

I love the Duke of Ferrara.

"Mike, can I just say your hair looks really good today?" I say.

It's saying things like this that make Robbie swear she is going to bring a mallet to court.

"My hair?" says Mike, whose short rich brown curls stand straight up like little planes ready to take off on the runway of his forehead. "Thanks," he says. "It's coconut oil."

"Ahhh!" I say.

"My hair smells so delicious," says Mike, "I'm always hungry."

It is Mike's and the Carroll Prep Team's job to help me understand what to expect during trial, and to prepare me to give clear, truthful, effective testimony.

"The key is to not be artificial about it," says Mike. "If you were to look at me in the courtroom and answer every question, that would be absolutely fine. But if you were to turn and look at the jurors and answer them—look at them and answer the questions, that would also be great! You're not going to naturally do it for every question, but at times I am going to encourage you."

When Mike is an assistant United States attorney in the Southern District of New York, he prosecutes some of the world's most violent criminals. I am not a hundred percent certain, but I think Mike sometimes wears a dark-violet suit and heliotrope tie while prosecuting the murderers and terrorists, and Miss Shawn G. Crowley, whose portrait hangs in the Daniel Patrick Monahan United States Courthouse, has a crush on Mike Ferrara.

"I'm going to say things like, 'Ms. Carroll, would you please explain to our jurors what your family was like growing up?'" says Mike. "And you can look at the jury. I'm going to try to make it *natural* for you to speak directly to them. Make sense? But with someone like *you,* that doesn't mean you're performing. Right? That's sort of the line we're getting, right? It's just answering the questions. It just happens that you're explaining it to this group of people—the folks who actually need the information and who are assessing your credit. Now. I'll start. I'll begin by saying, 'Ms. Carroll, would you introduce yourself to the jury and would you spell your name for our court recorder?' All right? That's how we start. Here we go."

He is not wearing the dark-violet suit.

"Ms. Carroll, how old are you?"

"I'm in my eightieth year," I say.

"What do you do for a living?"

"I'm a writer."

"And why are you here today?"

(*Pause*)

I look at Mike.

"I'm here—(*slowly*)—"

Mike nods in encouragement.

My mind jitterbugs.

I ask myself, "What am I doing here?" fifty times a day.

I have never been able to answer it. Am I here because Molly Jong-Fast invites me to a party? Am I here because I meet George Conway at Molly's party? Am I here because when I meet George Conway, he explains the difference between a criminal lawsuit and a civil lawsuit and says, "Jean, you could sue Donald Trump for defamation?" Am I here because George says he can "recommend someone"? Am I here because two days later I find myself riding the Empire State Building elevator a quarter of a mile up and entering an office that looks like the bell towers of Notre Dame de Paris, and meeting the "someone" George recommends: a blond woman, a legend built low to the ground, cute, athletic, talking at about 133 mph, with a smile ready for anything, clasping my hand, and saying, "Hi, I'm Robbie Kaplan"?

"I am here . . ." I say.

*   *   *

I watch myself being watched by Mike as he waits for my answer.

The Carroll Prep Team watches me watching Mike watch me. Robbie Kaplan, Matt Craig, Shawn G. Crowley, Rachel Tuchman, and Helen Andrews are the Carroll Prep Team. Helen Andrews is taking notes on her laptop. Helen and Rachel have read every word I have ever published or said in every magazine, every book, every newspaper interview, every TV show since 1979. They have read my emails. They have read the notes I write to myself in the margins of the notes I write in my notebooks. They have read my legal pads. They have read twenty-seven years' worth of "Ask E. Jean" columns. Rachel Tuchman not only has read my last book, but Rachel has also read *all* 105 versions of my last book that were stored on my Mac computer. Helen Andrews's job is to check every single thing I say *today* in this prep session against every single thing I have *ever* said.

I ask you, Friends, could *you* speak under these circumstances?

Me? I am a pathological people-pleaser. I try to parse what Mike and Robbie and Matt and Shawn and Rachel and Helen would like to hear. And Mike and Robbie and Matt and Shawn and Rachel and Helen do not want to hear about George Conway.

"I'm here . . ." I say.

They want me to tell *why I am here.*

"I'm here," I say, "because Donald Trump sexually assaulted me in a Bergdorf Goodman dressing room—(*long pause*)—then he lied and said it didn't happen—" (Weak! Weak! Weak! Weak! Weak! Mike and Matt and Shawn and Robbie and Rachel and Helen will *never* understand the pain in my heart, because I *want* to be here and I am mad as hell that I have to sit here trying to find the words to explain what I will *never* be able to explain in prep session, at trial, after trial, in this book I am trying to write)—"and ruined my life."

*   *   *

Six lawyers mull.

*   *   *

"Powerful," says Mike Ferrara.
"I'll work on it," I say.

*   *   *

Robbie and Matt Craig have meetings, so it's just Shawn G. Crowley, Mike Ferrara, Rachel Tuchman, and Helen Andrews prepping me this afternoon.
"Should I wear eyelashes in court?" I ask.
I figure if this is prep—let's prep the primp.
"Ummmm," says Mike.
He looks at me, trying to imagine false eyelashes on an old woman who is currently wearing black-framed rectangle glasses from the '90s and staring at him. This is too much even for the inventive mind of the Duke of Ferrara.
"Whattaya think?" I say.
"Let's do a test run and then see how you look," says Shawn.
"Well, you *have* seen me," I say. "I was wearing eyelashes at the first deposition with Alina Habba, Esq."
"You looked great," says Helen.
"They felt heavy," I say.
Helen Andrews is a calm, alabaster-skinned, Scottish blonde, with tremendous style. One day I take her aside and say, "Helen! What eyelashes are you wearing?"

"Oh!" says Helen, smiling and down-lashing—she is the daughter of a minister and has more lashes than the three Brontë sisters put together. "These are my own."

"If you're going to be uncomfortable and *heavy*," says Shawn. "I don't think eyelashes are necessary."

"Would a jury," I say, "*like* seeing a woman really made up?"

"Personally agree," says Rachel Tuchman. Rachel and I drive to Albany and go door to door at the state capitol begging assembly members to pass the "Adult Survivors Act." It passes. I sue Trump for assault. And now we are discussing lashes for court.

"It's going to look a little *done up*," says Rachel. "But let's see what Reiko [the jury consultant] says."

*   *   *

Whenever I am thinking about the trial and worrying that I am too concerned about how I look, I remember that Trump's defense is "She's not my type," and how I look is the very center of the case.

*   *   *

CLOTHES FOR COURT

Brown Bergdorf jacket, cream Oscar skirt
Black Armani jacket, cream Oscar skirt
White Armani jacket, black Piazza Sempione skirt
Metallic Armani blazer, black Piazza Sempione skirt
Aubergine Oscar jacket, cream Oscar skirt
Black sweater with white cuffs/collar, black Piazza Sempione
*   skirt*
Brown silk Oscar dress
Blue LK Bennett dress
Black Bergdorf dress

STILL NEED

Shoes
Cream turtleneck
Black turtleneck
Coin pearl drop earrings

TO DO

Wash white shirts
Wash dickie
Iron

This is the running list that I have taped to a piece of thick cardboard so I can walk around with it and check things off my "clipboard" like I am in charge of the fun activities on a cruise.

Robbie says the trial will be "about two, two and half weeks." Fridays are nontrial days in Judge Lewis Kaplan's federal courtroom. That means ten outfits. The "Brown Bergdorf jacket" is one of the oldest items of clothing that I own. It is a tightly fitted, russet-brown military jacket with a wide belt and gold buckle, designed by ICB, *the* '90s cool girl label. It is the first thing I buy at Bergdorf's with one of my first *Elle* checks in 1993. I will wear it with the Oscar de la Renta pleated cream skirt from his Resort 2014 collection which I buy on the RealReal in March 2023, six weeks before trial, for $148. When it arrives in the mail, I am thrilled to see the skirt is the color of a banana cream pie.

Of all the outfits in my Clipboard Collection, *this* is the outfit that will appear on every front page of every newspaper in America.

The blue LK Bennett dress? It is the kind of elegant, sleek-waisted job Kate Middleton wears, and I get it on the RealReal for $63. I slate it for the first day of trial, but I never feel my waist is *quite* sleek enough to do it justice, and end up never wearing it.

Ditto the "black Bergdorf dress." I look like the Nun of Monza in it. It ends up doing no jury duty. After the trial I give it to John Reddan my handyman/singer/song-writer's wife. She probably sells it on eBay.

I've already told you about the metallic Armani blazer, the gift of Arleen Harley Quinn. Reiko Hasuike, the jury consultant, says it may or may not look "too elite." She wants to wait to give her final verdict "until we have the jury." The black Armani and the white Armani jackets? They fit me so perfectly they are like barnacles clinging to a ship's hull. They have been my old standbys for years. The black Piazza Sempione skirt I will wear with the white Armani. What a beauty! It *moves* when I walk—pleated, of course. I get it three weeks before trial on the Real-Real for $20.

This brings us to the gem of the Clipboard Collection:

The ravishing, dark, chocolate-brown, long-sleeved, pleat-skirted shirtwaist silk dress from Oscar de la Renta's 2009 Resort collection. I wear it with stiff, white, high, *Heaven Knows, Mr. Allison* collar and cuffs.

Oddly, it is the forty-one-year-old belt I wear with it that people comment on. The clasp is a golden hand pulling my waist in and holding me tight.

At 4:20 a.m. the morning of the first day of trial—the day of jury selection—I wake up, well, let me rephrase, I don't wake up, I *am* awake, I slide open the closet door, take Mr. Oscar de la Renta out, hold him up, shake the dark, chocolate-brown silk and say, "You." I also wear it on *Rachel Maddow*. I also wear it to watch Joshua Matz crush Alina Habba, Esq. at the United States Appeals Court, Second Circuit when Trump claims "absolute immunity" just before the second trial. I also wear it two more times in the first trial. I also wear it the first time I face Trump in court the first day of the second trial. I buy it on the RealReal a few weeks before trial for $229.50. This works out to be just a tad over $38.21 per wearing.

*   *   *

I text nine photos of myself wearing the Clipboard Collection to my friend group—Laurie Abraham, features director at *Elle* magazine, 2000–2017; Lisa Chase, features editor at *Elle*, 2005–2017; Rachel Baker, senior features editor at *Elle*, 2012–2017; Maggie Bullock, deputy editor at *Elle*, 2005–2017; and Rachael Combe, managing editor at *Elle*, 2000–2007, and editor-at-large, 2007–2017—in a word: smart women who have worked at magazines like *New York*, *Rolling Stone*, *Outside*, *Atlantic*, *Economist*, etc., etc. their whole lives, and who, having spent a large chunk of their careers thinking seriously about clothes at *Elle*, the planet's largest fashion magazine, are known only to the fashionable world, but in the fashionable world, they are *revered*.

I also text the photos to my *other* friend group—Joyce Vance, former United States attorney, now law professor and MSNBC legal correspondent; Katie Phang, trial attorney and host of *The Katie Phang Show* on MSNBC; Mary Trump, head of Mary Trump Media, Jen Taub, law professor, author, YouTube rabble-rouser; and Kathy Griffin, who has had more TV specials than any comedian in history—in short, Mary, Kathy, and a bunch of brilliant lawyers.

Do the two friend groups agree on what I should wear to court?

The *Elle*s deliver their verdict on each outfit like the outcome of the trial depends on it. And the lawyers? Hahahahahaha! They do not waste a second pondering if the "shiny is too shiny" on the metallic Armani. Or if the black Bergdorf dress is "too Manhattan." After they message one another privately, Jen

Taub simply calls Robbie Kaplan and says, "E. Jean needs new clothes!!"

*   *   *

JOE TACOPINA: Miss Carroll, you hate men, right?

E. JEAN CARROLL: No.

TACOPINA: You've hated men for a long time now, correct?

CARROLL: No.

TACOPINA: In fact, you abominate men!

CARROLL: No.

TACOPINA: Then Miss Carroll please tell us. Do you recognize this?

(*Handing me a full-color printout of a page from* Elle *magazine.*)

Dear E. Jean: I've been suckered, duped, dumped, and wounded so many times by men, I've become a Man Hater. I'm the most cynical, disillusioned 34-year-old you've ever met, plus I've lost the sweetness that makes women attractive to men. The truth is, I'd love to have a boyfriend, but I am so hopeless! Help!—A Big Hug from Miss B.

Miss B.: Why, of course you're a Man Hater. Any woman with half a brain hates men. The dudes have done a surreal job bungling up the whole world since we let them have weapons four million years ago. The trick for disillusioned young ladies is to not abominate *all* the buggers. Pick and choose. (I, for instance, love hundreds of guys, but I hate Dick Cheney.) Withhold your judgment till you know a chap well. Never assume it's only "sweetness" that attracts (honey, the tart can be twice as tempting); a fetching streak of dislike on your part can ignite a man's interest. Remember, in *Pride and Prejudice* it was Elizabeth Bennet's saucy dislike of Mr. Darcy that made him fall in love. So no more of that "I'm so hopeless" twitpiffle. Go out there and give as good as you get!

CARROLL: Yes.

——I do not shout, "Yeeeee gods! How'd you find this ancient Elle *column?" I am trained to give the shortest answer.*

TACOPINA: What is it?"
CARROLL: An advice column.

——Make him work for it.

TACOPINA: Who is the author of this advice column?
CARROLL: Me.
TACOPINA: What is the advice column called?
CARROLL: Ask E. Jean.
TACOPINA: Please read the first two lines of Ask E. Jean's answer.
CARROLL: (*Reading*) "Why, of course you're a Man Hater. Any woman with half a brain hates men."
TACOPINA: Miss Carroll, you hate men, right?
E. JEAN CARROLL: No.

And so on.

This is called "cross practice." Squarely built, straight-on, solid Sean Hecker, name partner at Kaplan Hecker & Fink—Boy! What personality! What grandeur!—plays Joe Tacopina. He is a sensation. A quarter of the firm—partners, counsels, law clerks, staff attorneys, paralegals, case managers, and business directors—crowd into the Ruth Bader Ginsburg Conference Room to watch the slaughter.

I attempt to tell "Tacopina" that I use "humor" and "satire" to get my point across. That's all he needs—*So, Miss Carroll, are we not to take what you say in this court seriously?*—to bury me. It is downhill from there. If I do not learn in the next few days how to handle Joe Tacopina, we will lose to Donald Trump.

And since Robbie believes everybody "should have a voice," I get to benefit from *all* the onlookers' appraisals, comments, critiques, suggestions, slams, and pans of my hideous answers.

*   *   *

Five or six days before trial, Rachel Tuchman calls and says Robbie is buying me new clothes.

I like my old clothes.

"She's hiring Molly's personal stylist!" says Rachel.

I hate personal stylists.

"Robbie says she's great," says Rachel.

Maybe Robbie should receive a call from former deputy editor of *Elle,* Maggie Fucking Bullock, who texts me when she sees the nine photos in the Clipboard Collection:

> This feels like a masterclass. I love how well you know your silhouettes and your signatures, Jean, yet there's a flexibility within the look. Well played.

Shouldn't Robbie be *made aware* that I "know my silhouettes and signatures"?

"Text me your sizes," says Rachel.

Shouldn't Robbie be told that I have major "flexibility within my look"?

On the phone Rachel is laughing and telling me that she (Rachel) is the "last person" who knows "anything about fashion," but that this "great" stylist is getting the clothes and bringing them to the office, and to *pleasssse* text her (Rachel) my sizes.

Rachel put herself through Yale Law School after earning enough money to pay for it by teaching kindergarten and is a milk-and-peony-complexioned, aqua-marine-eyed, natural beach-blonde, could-be-a-*Vogue*-cover young hellion who gave birth to her second daughter two months ago and whose fashion goal in life—Friends, I am not kidding—is to be the "hot mom" in the bike shorts and sun visor when she and her husband, Nick, go to Disneyland with their little girl, Elle, and the new baby, Leila.[*]

I text her:

Rachel! Yo! First I will share that I HATE SHEATHE [sic] dresses. I look best in a dress that shows my waist and hides my neck. Your shopper has probably never shopped for an 80 year old woman. Everything on the human body at 80 is collapsed into the middle of the trunk. . . . .so though I am skinny, though I am tall. . . . .IT IS FUCKING DIFFICULT TO PUT ME IN A DRESS. . . . I want no Dr. Jill Biden. I want no Junior League. Hence I look BRILLIANT in fitted jackets and skirts to the knee. Hint Hint. It's best I go with this "shopper." So. I am 5'8" and weigh—-I have no idea, but somewhere between 110–114.

---

[*] Rachel accomplishes this.

I weigh, as I find out after I send the text, 106. This is Thursday. Trial starts next Tuesday. No matter how much I eat—and I am eating *stacks* and *stacks* of peanut butter and banana sandwiches around the clock—I cannot keep the weight on.

*   *   *

The stylist Jessie Freschl and her assistant arrive on the sixty-third floor of the Empire State Building with many bags. I hate the assistant. I hate the bags. I hate Jessie Freschl.

"This you would wear with one of your belts," says Jessie, as the assistant pulls out a long, hairy—it looks like unborn opossum pup—ankle-length, putty-gray knit—*knit! Dear Gawd!*—sheath, a sheath, Friends! with a high rolled collar.

I yelp.

"We can have it shortened," says Jessie.

"No. No. No. No. *No. No. No,*" I say, trying to back up, but we are all tumbled together with the boxes and bags into a hallway about the size of a bread pan.

"E. Jean," says Rachel, laughing nervously, "always tells us what she thinks!"

"That's good," says Jessie Freschl, without turning a hair.

The assistant removes a double-breasted, dark-charcoal jacket from a garment bag.

I glance at it.

"No." I say.

"E. Jean, you might want to try that on," says Rachel.

"I loathe it."

The assistant, who is on the floor and is in charge of all the boxes and bags, looks a question at Jessie Freschl. Jessie nods at the largest shopping bag.

"Now *this . . .*" says Jessie.

The assistant holds up a short, closely cut, navy-blue jacket, with two small flap pockets cut at the slightest angle over the front of the hip bones.

It looks familiar, *very* familiar.

"And *here's* the skirt," says Jessie, pulling out a dazzling spinner—full, magnificent, cut to a small waist. Audrey Hepburn could dance *Swan Lake* in it.

With a glance at Jessie Freschl who looks like a woodland sylph, dark-haired with the cleanest face I ever saw this side of a Goop newsletter, I take the navy skirt in my hands, and, holding it at the waist, slowly raise it up.

I dare not breathe. I had beheld this skirt and jacket at Saks. It is Dior. The skirt alone costs $6,000.

I feel like doing a Simone Biles floor routine.

"My God!" I whisper.

"Zara!" says Jessie.

"Ah!"

Now I deduce that Robbie and Rachel have probably given Jessie Freschl the guidelines from the jury consultant, Reiko Hasuike:

"What you should wear is a dress that makes you look serious (without being stiff and boring), attractive (without being flirty and girlish), and elegantly dignified."

Later I find out Robbie hired Jessie Freschl because she was worried my own wardrobe collected over decades, appeared "too fashionable," and when I look up "Jessie Freschl," she turns out to be a do-gooder like Robbie, and founded ShopRepurpose, which focuses on sustainable fashion. She is also *Molly Levinson's* stylist, and Molly Levinson is the most powerful communications consultant in the country, handling the US Women's National Soccer Team, Robbie's law firm, the Biden White House, etc., etc., and always looks superb.

While I am still soaring over the navy-blue knockout, the assistant produces, from another bag, a beautiful boxy jacket in cream (*cream*!!) and matching, twirling skirt, and I have to grip Rachel Tuchman's arm I am so off balance ripping off my clothes to get everything in these bags onto my carcass and see how fabulous I look.

*   *   *

Navy-blue Zara suit with ballet skirt
Boxy cream Zara suit with twirl skirt
Paul Smith blazer (Repurposed)
Rag & Bone admiral jacket (Repurposed)
2 cream turtlenecks from Zara
2 black turtlenecks from Zara
Jimmy Choo navy-blue pumps
Porte & Paire dark-butterscotch pumps
Manolo Blahnik crème brûlée pumps
Black Reformation block-heels
8 pairs of Wolford panty hose in navy, bisque, eggshell, nude,
    etc., etc., in Luxe and Satin Touch

This is a list of items that arrive at my hotel two days before trial. If Joyce Vance, Katie Phang, Jen Taub, Mary Trump, and Kathy Griffin had not called Robbie, and if Robbie had not grasped the gravity of the "situation" and had not called Molly Levinson, and if Molly Levinson had not called Jessie Freschl, the body that is the center of this trial—like all survivors of sexual assault who take their cases to court, my body is at the heart of the case—would not have been so beautifully clothed.

I still wear my chocolate-brown silk Oscar dress to court, of course, and the brown Bergdorf jacket that I bought in 1993, and my black tights, and my sunglasses. And when the *New York Times* announces their Most Stylish People of 2023, and *I* am on the list, what am I wearing in the photo?

The dear old white Armani.

5

'TIS THE NIGHT BEFORE TRIAL

The time has come to introduce myself. I am Emma De-Courcy. I am in a suite on the fourth floor of the Sixty LES hotel, 190 Allen Street, New York, New York.

Tomorrow, at 8:15 a.m. former detective of the Manhattan South Homicide Squad, Rick Tirelli, will meet me in the lobby and escort me to an unmarked car so completely unmarked we could drive at 83 miles per hour right through Manhattan traffic and nobody would see us. Robbie Kaplan will be in the back seat. We will clasp hands, and, with two security men, we will proceed down Allen Street, turn right on Division Street, turn left on Bowery, turn right on Worth, and soon arrive at the Daniel Patrick Moynihan United States Courthouse.

The driver will halt between the cement barricades.

Herman Weisberg, former detective, lead investigator for the New York County district attorney and head of Robbie's security, having scouted potential "vulnerabilities," and performed an advanced sweep to identify and eliminate threats, will open the car door. Herman's men will be behind him. If there is a "problem," they will pick Robbie and me up and "throw" us into the car. Or, they will "run" us into the building, if it is "closer."

I wonder. What will happen if Herman's men become confused and run Robbie into the car and throw me into the

building. Anyway, Herman Weisberg gives me the following instructions:

"Put yourself entirely in our care."

And because Herman Weisberg was Robbie's security when
Robbie, who is strong, but small—about the height of an Ol-
sen twin—confronted the White supremacists, the Proud Boys,
the neo-Nazis, the white nationalists, the Loyal White Knights
of the Ku Klux Klan, and far-right extremists every day in federal court for four weeks in the famous Charlottesville trial, and
because Robbie *was not shot once*, and because Robbie was not
thrown into a car or run into a building, I do. I *do* put myself
"entirely" into Herman Weisberg's care.

Also Robbie wins Charlottesville.

*   *   *

You stupid bitch aint nobody gonna believe, fuck u,
yuck u nasty hoe, you just want attention end your
lies you bitch Lying bitch fuck u nobody gonna believe u against trump so shut the fuck up.

Thousands and thousands of people send me "fuck u" messages
before trial. But *this* one says "yuck u." I feel tender toward this
message. Please. Yuck me! Yuck me! This is a beam of benevo-
lence in the fuck u, rape u, hang u world I live in. And it arrives,
thoughtfully, at 7:43 p.m., like a nightingale, like a lullaby, the
night before trial.

*   *   *

The night *before* the night before trial I do not sleep because I
do not sleep the night before that. Or the night before that. The
night before *that,* I do sleep, but now? I am too tired to sleep. I
have too many thoughts. I have too many facts. I have too many

notes to myself: "Keep it short!" "Tell the truth!" "Stop smiling!" "If Mike stands up, that means he's objecting to Tacopina's question so *STOP YAMMERING!!!!*" I have too many "amenities." The snacks are too tangy. The pillows are too velutinous. The bed is too vast. The tub is too sunken. The shower is too torrential. I am like a New Guinea Big Man from Munbil who sleeps on the floor of his hotel when he visits Port Moresby for trade talks. I can't think. My mind is a sieve. My restless leg could qualify for the hundred-meter dash. And, Friends, as for any bowel movements?

"To have a right bowel movement," says Montaigne, "one must have peace, quiet, punctuality and privacy to avoid unruliness of the belly." I have lawyers, I have snacks, I have a shower like a waterfall in Tahiti. But no peace.

*   *   *

The night before trial Mike and Shawn call.

Shawn raced moguls for the United States ski team, and she is the Carroll Team's designated chastiser. Shawn once hauled a dumpster into a federal courtroom—I am not talking about Shawn schlepping a garbage can, I am talking about Shawn dragging into a courtroom a *New York City dumpster*—and convinced a jury to put a terrorist away for life. Shawn is the Jack Palance of trial lawyers. Her long, dark hair, her long, sinewy movements of a lynx, her sudden ferocity of a bear—one time in the Ruth Bader Ginsburg Conference Room, Shawn sees me texting before a prep session.

"E. Jean, who are you texting?" she says.

I look up.

"Oh! Just Mary," I say.

"Mary—Trump?" says Shawn.

"Yeah, just Mary, and uh, Kathy—(*pause*)—Griffin."

"*Give me your phone.*"

It is impossible to refuse Shawn anything. I hand her my phone. She reads a couple of the messages and *removes* me from the group conversation.

When Shawn calls, it means I have done something dumb which will lose us the case.

"E. Jean," says Shawn on the phone, the night before trial. "Mike and I are sending you your 2019 *Elle* contract so you can refresh your memory. It may come up in cross."

"Good!" I say.

We talk about the *Elle* contract and then Shawn says:

"E. Jean! Don't hang up! Mike and I have something to say!"

"Oh!" I say.

I lower my head like a donkey and wait for the blows.

"E. Jean," she says, "this is Mike's and my first *civil* trial. We're used to prosecuting criminals. And we've both done some very good work. We've made a difference. But representing you? Presenting your case against the former president? I have never been prouder."

"We love you and it's an honor to represent you," says Mike. "Now get some sleep, E. Jean!"

6

JANE AUSTEN'S BREAKFAST

I n the novel *The Great Gatsby,* when Gatsby is shot and dies in
the pool, his father comes to West Egg for the funeral. With
him he brings a "ragged old copy" of a book called *Hopalong
Cassidy.*

"Look here," says the father, to Nick Carraway, "this is a book
he had when he was a boy." On the fly leaf of the back cover is the
word "Schedule."

Rise from bed: 6:00 a.m.
Dumbell exercise and wall-scaling: 6:15–6:30 a.m.
Study electricity, etc.: 7:15–8:15 a.m.
Work: 8:30 a.m.–4:30 p.m.
Baseball and sports: 4:30–5:00 p.m.
Practice elocution, poise and how to attain it: 5:00–6:00 p.m.
Study needed inventions: 7:00–9:00 p.m.

This schedule—almost as famous as Joan Didion's Packing
List—is one of my favorite passages in all Scott Fitzgerald. Routines, especially morning routines fascinate me. Fitzgerald himself? Rises at 11 a.m. and starts work in the afternoon. Darwin?
Rises, takes a short walk, eats a solitary breakfast, begins work at
8 a.m. Catherine the Great? Rises at 6 a.m., drinks coffee, works

alone till she calls lovers and friends to join her for breakfast. Harry Truman? Rises at 5 a.m., dons suit and tie, walks two miles, returns for a shot of bourbon, starts the day. Salvador Dalí? Wakes and "experiences the supreme pleasure of being Salvador Dalí."

Writers' routines *really* get me: Hemingway? Rises with the sun, and writes standing "in a pair of his oversized loafers on the worn skin of a lesser kudu—the typewriter and the reading board chest-high opposite him."* Toni Morrison? Rises, writes three hours, sends her son off to school, and goes to her job as an editor at Random House, wins the Nobel. Hunter S. Thompson?

3:00 p.m. rise

3:05 Chivas Regal with the morning papers, Dunhills

3:45 cocaine

3:50 another glass of Chivas, Dunhill

4:05 first cup of coffee, Dunhill

4:15 cocaine

4:16 orange juice, Dunhill

4:30 cocaine

4:54 cocaine

5:05 cocaine

5:11 coffee, Dunhills

5:30 more ice in the Chivas

5:45 cocaine, etc., etc.

6:00 grass to take the edge off the day

7:05 Woody Creek Tavern for lunch—Heineken, two margaritas, two cheeseburgers, two orders of fries, a plate of tomatoes, coleslaw, a taco salad, a double order of fried onion

---

* George Plimpton, "Ernest Hemingway, The Art of Fiction No. 21," *Paris Review* 18, spring 1958.

rings, carrot cake, ice cream, a bean fritter, Dunhills, another Heineken, cocaine, and for the ride home, a snow cone (a glass of shredded ice over which are poured three or four jiggers of Chivas)

9:00 starts snorting cocaine seriously

10:00 drops acid

11:00 Chartreuse, cocaine, grass

11:30 cocaine, etc., etc.

12:00 midnight, Hunter S. Thompson is ready to write

12:05–6:00 a.m. Chartreuse, cocaine, grass, Chivas, coffee, Heineken, clove cigarettes, grapefruit, Dunhills, orange juice, gin, continuous pornographic movies

6:00 the hot tub—champagne, Dove bars, fettuccine Alfredo

8:00 Halcyon

8:20 sleep

*   *   *

I am not in Saint Petersburg to meet the empress of Russia or at Down House in Kent to meet the author of *On the Origin of the Species*. But I do stay a while at Owl Farm, Hunter S. Thompson's spread outside of Woody Creek, Colorado, and I can tell you, Friends, I personally clock Hunter's routine when I am writing his biography.* And, yes, routines captivate me. So, I am thrilled to tell you that the morning routine on the first day of trial turns out to be exactly like the morning routine on the second day of trial, and the third day, and every morning of trial throughout April and May 2023.

---

* *Hunter: The Strange and Savage Life of Hunter S. Thompson* (Dutton, 1993).

*   *   *

4:30–5:30 a.m. rise, coffee, wash
5:30 breakfast
6:00–7:30 hair and makeup
7:30–7:50 read notes
7:50–8:10 dress
8:10–8:15 meet Carroll Team in lobby
8:15 escort to vehicle
8:30 arrive Daniel Patrick Moynihan United States
Courthouse

"Coffee" I make in a large glass jar. Balzac drinks fifty cups of black Turkish a day and writes eighty-five novels. I once personally witness Kathy Griffin calling room service at the old Rihga Royal, ordering coffee "for one" and the bill coming to $58.

"Breakfast" is Good Culture cottage cheese on two slices of Dave's 21-grain bread, walnuts, almonds, orange juice, and a banana—not from room service. The swimmer Michael Phelps eats three fried egg sandwiches, three chocolate-chip pancakes, a five-egg omelette, three slices of French toast, and a bowl of grits for breakfast and wins twenty-three Olympic gold medals. Jane Austen breakfasts on pound cake and dies at forty-one.

"Hair and Makeup" begins with Lisa Corvelli shoving my head under the tap and ends with a touch of lipstick. Robbie's final decision:

"No lashes. Little makeup."

"Good," says Lisa. She has done Trump's hair and grooming in the past. "*You* will look natural, and *he'll* arrive looking like . . . like, what's her name?"

"Marie Antoinette?" I say.

Some "notes" made by Leonardo da Vinci are on loose sheets

of paper, bound in leather, and are owned by Bill Gates. He paid $30.8 million for them. My notes are on my phone, on Post-its, on scratch pads, on backs of paper plates, and in the margins of the April 24 and May 1, 2023, *New Yorker* I am reading trying to follow Montaigne's advice.

The "dress" on the first day is the previously mentioned chocolate-brown silk Oscar de la Renta. The shoes are my ancient black-and-white Vivienne Westwoods with toes so pointed I can pierce Alina Habba, Esq.'s ears with them. It is coldish on April 25 and I wear a long gray Adam Lippes coat, soft as the "skin of a lesser kudu." On a cold morning in 1536, Anne Boleyn wears a long gray robe over a crimson dress when she is beheaded.

Carroll Team members from DC and LA are staying at the Sixty LES. They are Joshua Matz, "the Man with the 583 IQ"; Matt Craig, the chap of such strong arguments and movie star looks, I name him "an honorary woman"; and young baseball phenom, Kate Harris, the next clerk for Supreme Court justice Sonia Sotomayor. Not since Three Dog Night debuted at Whisky a Go Go has there been such a sensational gathering, though Potsdam comes close.

The "vehicle" is so unmarked, as I mentioned, I cannot see it until I am in it with Robbie. LeBron James leaves for *his* office in his Rolls-Royce Phantom (a present from Shaq for his twenty-fifth birthday), or his Mercedes-Benz Maybach, or his Bentley Continental GT, or his Range Rover HSE, or one of his three Porsches or three Ferraris, or his custom jungle-green-and-gold-flowered Lamborghini Aventador Roadster, in which he can go from 0 to 62 mph in three seconds.

We "arrive" at the courthouse and heave into the crush of news photographers waiting with semicontrolled hysteria. Taylor Swift—wakes, frisks with cats, works out, eats buckwheat crepes—has replaced Her Majesty Queen Elizabeth II—wakes, tea, bath, hair, makeup, toast and marmalade—as the most photographed person in the world.

*   *   *

My routine a year *before* trial: rise at noon, throw the ball for the dog, work, throw the ball for the dog, Good Culture cottage cheese on Dave's bread, throw the ball for the dog, etc., etc. (I throw the ball for the dog an average of nineteen to twenty times a day, and when George Stephanopoulos asks me after trial, "What are you going to do now, E. Jean?" I answer, "I'm going home and throw the ball for the dog.")

It takes four months, getting up earlier and earlier each week, to get me half-ass ready to exit the vehicle in front of the Daniel Patrick Moynihan United States Courthouse, lock arms with Robbie, make our way through the gauntlet of shouted questions and flashing cameras, and enter the building where I can tell the world: "No, Donald Trump. *You* are the liar, and I am here to prove it."

7

"E. JEAN CARROLL IS AN AFFRONT TO JUSTICE"

W hat jury do we want?
A blue, New York Times–*reading Manhattan jury.*
What jury do we fear?
A jury of nine men.
What jury do we get?
A reddish, Facebook-news-reading upstate jury of six men and three women.

*   *   *

Nine is a hexagon, a nonagon, and my age now if you multiply 9 x 9. Joe DiMaggio wore No. 9. Nikola Tesla said, "If you understand the numbers of 3, 6, 9, you understand the universe. There are nine muses and nine anonymous members of my jury. An anonymous jury is unusual. Mafia trials have anonymous juries, not former presidents. The jury is anonymous to protect them from being menaced, mauled, punched, slapped, shot, bludgeoned, bribed, and killed.

After they are selected* and a sleepy, chunky young man who will become known as the "Tim Pool Guy" slips onto the jury because when we ask where prospective members "get their news," we think he answers, "Temple," when, in fact, as is immediately reported by the press, he says "Tim Pool," and Tim Pool is a peppy, podcasting, beanie-wearing, far-right combination of Laura Loomer and JD Vance. After the Tim Pool Guy settles in, the Honorable Lewis A. Kaplan, senior judge of the United States District Court for the Southern District of New York, presiding, delivers such a terrifying and uplifting speech about maintaining their anonymity, I suspect that several of them go home to their wives and husbands and refuse to tell them where they have been all day.

*   *   *

---

* Forty-eight dazed-and-numbered human souls, who live in the most elaborately intrusive, snooping, spying, watching, social-media-oriented society in history, are led into the courtroom. Fifty or so additional souls are corralled in a holding room listening on speakers. Judge Kaplan bids them a stately good morning, describes the case to them, and then asks questions such as, "Is there anything about the nature of this case or the parties that would make it difficult for you to be entirely fair to both parties and to come to a just and impartial verdict?" Anybody who answers yes to any of the questions is excused. The Carroll Team wants to know what everybody does for a living and where they get their news. The Trump team wants to know if anyone thinks the 2020 election was stolen and do they believe all women. Each side gets three strikes. The first nine people who both teams agree upon—with our illustrious jury consultant Reiko Hasuike delivering a quick nod or shake on each—gets us nine anonymous jurors by lunch.

United States District Court, Southern District of New York

Jury Trial, April 25, 2023

COURT TRANSCRIPT

OPENING ARGUMENTS

THE COURT: Who is opening for the plaintiff?

MS. SHAWN CROWLEY: (*Rising*) I am, your Honor.

THE COURT: Ms. Crowley.

MS. CROWLEY: (*Addressing members of the jury*) I'd like to take you back to the evening in the spring of 1996. E. Jean Carroll, the plaintiff in this case, was leaving the Bergdorf Goodman department store in Manhattan. But as she was exiting through the revolving doors, she saw Donald Trump coming in the other way. They recognized each other. Trump was famous in New York City. His name was on a bunch of buildings and his face was often in the tabloids. And Ms. Carroll was a well-known writer. She had her own advice column and a daily TV show. They'd even met each other once at a party.

So they started chatting. Trump asked Ms. Carroll to help him pick out a gift for a woman. She agreed, thinking it would make for a funny story. They moved through the store joking and laughing and eventually made their way up to the lingerie department on the sixth floor. As usual, it was empty that time of night.

Trump walked over to the counter and picked up a lacy body suit. He tossed it to Ms. Carroll and told her to try it on for him. She laughed and told him to try it on himself. "Wouldn't it be hilarious," she thought, "if he put this thing on over his clothes?"

Still laughing, they moved to the dressing room, Ms. Carroll thinking: "He might actually try on this lingerie!"

But the moment they went inside, everything changed. Suddenly, nothing was funny. Donald Trump slammed Ms. Carroll against the wall—

*   *   *

The jury sits in their oaken box amazed, awed, stunned, unable to believe their luck. They are notified to appear for jury duty—dreadful. They travel seventy, eighty miles to Lower Manhattan—hideous. They answer questions posed by a majestic, gray-haired judge who looks like he belongs on the ceiling of the Sistine Chapel—unnerving, but not terrible. They are picked for the "Trump Rape Trial"—omg!

Shawn G. Crowley, US moguls champion, wearing a conservative tan suit cut to show her splendid figure—I use the word "tan," but on Shawn it looks like the color of a Thompson's gazelle on the Kalahari. Shawn tells the jury the same story three ways and, saying, "Members of the jury, we will present overwhelming evidence that Ms. Carroll is telling the truth," lays out the evidence. The first time she tells the story, the jury is too excited to listen to her. The second time, she is too good-looking to concentrate on what she is saying. The third time, they get it.

She tells them that by the end of the trial, when they "consider the evidence," it will be clear that "Donald Trump sexually assaulted Ms. Carroll. And it will be clear that years later, after Ms. Carroll came forward and spoke the truth, Donald Trump lied and defamed her." There will be "only one conclusion here," she says: Donald Trump is liable on *both* counts: assault and defamation.

THE COURT: Thank you. We will take a ten-minute break.
——I spend the ten minutes eating a peanut butter and jelly sandwich in the witness room and hugging Shawn G. Crowley.

THE COURT: (*After everyone has returned*) Okay. Mr. Tacopina.

MR. JOE TACOPINA: (*Rising*) Thank you, your Honor. Counsel, ladies and gentlemen of the jury. . . . The evidence will show you what E. Jean Carroll is doing is an affront to justice. The evidence will show you that she is abusing the system by advancing a FALSE claim of rape for money. For political reasons. And for status. And in doing so, in doing so, she is really minimizing *true* rape victims. REAL rape victims! She is exploiting their PAIN and their suffering. She is capitalizing on *their* stories. The evidence is going to show you this loud and clear. After you hear the evidence in this case, you *cannot* let her profit from her abuse of this process and her attempts to deceive you!

Ladies and gentlemen, my name is Joe Tacopina.

And I want to talk to you about the EVIDENCE, ladies and gentlemen, right now. I want to talk to you about E. Jean Carroll's story. It all comes down to: Do you believe the unbelievable? That's what this case is going to come down to: *Do you believe the unbelievable?*"

*　　　*　　　*

Excuse me. I am here. Over here, Friends. At the plaintiff's table. I am looking straight ahead. My back is to Tacopina. His voice is deep, very deep. Like cello in a stone quarry.

I take a quick look at the jury.

I look away.

The whole box of them: petrified with delight.

So let me take this opportunity to tell you—advise you, I *am* an advice columnist, ya know—if you ever get into trouble, if, for instance, you bludgeon a college girl with a cinder block and don't know who to call—Tacopina is your man.

Why call Tacopina? Because when Rihanna is thirty feet in the air on that giant, suspended flame-lit platform announcing the coming of her second child at the Super Bowl and the father of that coming child is soon to go to trial for assault with a deadly weapon, who do Rihanna and A$AP Rocky call? *Tacopina.* When Joran van der Sloot is jailed as the prime suspect in the murder of the beautiful Alabama college girl, Natalee Holloway, who does his father call? *Tacopina.* When Michael Jackson is accused of molesting little boys, who does he call? *Tacopina.* When that *Sopranos* actor is accused of killing a cop, who's he gonna call? *Tacopina.* When that police officer is accused of raping a drunk woman, who's he gonna call? *Tacopina.* When Donald Trump is on trial for sexually assaulting and defaming a person, who's Trump gonna call? *Tacopina.*[*]

Let us skip forward a bit and let the man proceed:

MR. TACOPINA: Evidence will show you that E. Jean Carroll was in fact *lying* because she was *never* raped by Donald Trump in a Bergdorf Goodman shopping store in the woman's lingerie changing room in the middle of the day!

And you are going to learn that while she was at a party, E. Jean Carroll—she is now on the party circuit! She was invited to every party!—while at a party, E. Jean Carroll met an attorney named George—

MS. CROWLEY: Objection, your Honor.

THE COURT: Sustained.

---

[*] Tacopina gets the *Sopranos* actor off. Gets the rape cop off. Gets Michael Jackson acquitted. Keeps Joran van der Sloot out of jail for years. And, on February 19, 2025, gets A$AP Rocky off.

MR. TACOPINA: The evidence will show you that after that conversation, Ms. Carroll went and hired Ms. Kaplan.

MS. CROWLEY: Objection, your Honor.

THE COURT: Sustained. The jury will disregard that.

MR. TACOPINA: "IT'S ALL A LIE! Because Donald Trump never raped E. Jean Carroll! Even calling her a liar was the truth! He never raped her, and he never defamed her!"

*　　*　　*

Friends, maybe you've been in a big federal courtroom and can imagine Tacopina's gun-shot voice vibrating off the oak-timbered walls, or maybe you have never been in a courtroom. The ceilings are quite high. The carpet is navy-blue with a gold laurel wreath pattern. To our right is the jury. In front of us, elevated on his vast oaken perch, leaning back in his chair, listening to Tacopina, the tips of the fingers of one hand touching the other, is the tall, dark, and frightening Judge Lewis A. Kaplan. Beside me are my attorneys, Robbie Kaplan, Shawn G. Crowley, Mike Ferrara, and Matt Craig, all of them sucking on Hall's sugar-free menthols, passing Post-its, gazing straight in front of themselves—no four human beings on earth look like they could give *less* of a big flying fig what Joe Tacopina is saying. Scattered about are the US Marshals, the press, the courtroom artists, the spectators.

Behind me is Joe Tacopina.

Now here is the problem: I am supposed to appear composed, contained, unruffled, and unconcerned. I am supposed to be looking casually in front of me. At all costs, the jury must not see me upset. The last thing I should do is turn around and look at Tacopina—No. *I must not look.* I must not turn! I must not turn and look! I am unimpressed. I am unperturbed. I am undisturbed.

I turn around and look at him.

MR. TACOPINA: As soon as she stepped into the dresser room (sic), the locker room where you try on women's lingerie, Donald Trump, without locking the door—according to her, he didn't lock the door—he lunged at her, immediately shoving her up against the wall twice.

It was so hard that E. Jean Carroll banged her head, causing it to hurt. She claims the noise was so loud that someone in the next dressing room could have easily heard it. She claims the noise was so loud that, had a sales attendant been on the floor, they would have heard it.

E. Jean Carroll will tell you that Donald Trump put his mouth on hers. She understood at that point that this was a battle, that this was a fight. And so how did she supposedly respond to this battle-fight-combat? Well, in her own words she will tell you how she responded.

She laughed! She *laughed*! Normal thing to do, you just got hurt, some guy who is 100 pounds more than you weighs— you know, 6' 2", pounding her head against the wall, and she realized she is in a battle and her reaction is to laugh. LAUGH!

*　　*　　*

I do not know how long I turn and look at Tacopina. I *do* know my neck and back feel the strain from holding my head turned backward from my body like a figure in the Egyptian Book of the Dead. I *do* know I have waited years to be in this courtroom. I *do* know I have been nuts for days imagining what Tacopina will say. And now I am hearing it. And now I know it is worse than I could imagine. Now I know—for the first time—that every single time Joe Tacopina stands up to address the court, every witness he cross-examines, every objection he makes, he will be telling a completely wrong story to the jury. So, though I do not know how long I look at him, I *do* know that Joe Tacopina doesn't know jack shit.

Lisa Rubin, MSNBC's legal correspondent, is in the courtroom, and puts it more elegantly:

Lisa Rubin
@lawofruby

A final thought for tonight, friends: Witnessing @ejeancarroll turn around in her seat at plaintiff's table to watch Trump lawyer Joe Tacopina attack her character was searing. However this case turns out, I don't think I'll ever forget that sight.

9:46 PM · Apr 25, 2023 · **567.8K** Views

136   1.2K   8.9K   41

8

PROUST'S CORKED BEDROOM

There is a lot of insomnia in the universe. Some of that insomnia has been lying in wait for me. Napoleon was an insomniac. Margaret Thatcher was an insomniac. Michael Jackson paid $150,000 a month to die a little every night in order to dance in the day. Marcel Proust corked his bedroom walls and tossed on his narrow boyhood bed. Abe Lincoln actually never slept in the Lincoln bed ... Van Gogh, Kafka, Plath, Nabokov, Monroe, Dickens, Groucho, and God only knows about Balzac with his eighty-five novels and fifty cups of coffee a day, all suffered.

Tomorrow I will begin giving my testimony in court. What do you think the chances are I sleep tonight, eh?

*   *   *

All my life I have been a good sleeper and a *brilliant* sleepwalker. Boy, do I walk! Across bridges, down roads, through bushes, over neighbors' yards. My parents tie hangers to my bedroom door, and still they find me across the street at the McArdles. I fetter myself to my cot in Montana, and wake up in Ralph Paugh's barn. I put glass jars in front of the door in Nyack and wake up on my way to the Grand Union grocery store. Up here in the mountains, the dogs wake me if I open the cabin door. Also the alarms. Also the police come if I don't enter, within sixty seconds, the alarm code. The threats, of course, have given me a bout or two of insomnia—and I endured a few rounds in the 1990s, etc. The doctor prescribed Ambien. It kept me awake. Ativan? Made me jumpy.

Normally (*normally!*) two bananas cut up in a bowl of Siggi's vanilla yogurt knocks me out for a nine count. But on trial? The only way two bananas will work is if they are laced with cyanide.

I look up Benadryl on the internet.

Benadryl can sometimes cause decreased memory, confusion and troubled thinking. These side effects are more common in older adults.

I look up Benadryl because it is supposed to make you sleep. Friends are worried about my not sleeping. Several of them have given me Benadryl. I am like Gussie Fink-Nottle in P. G. Wodehouse's *Right Ho, Jeeves* with everybody lacing Gussie's orange juice with whiskey to give him courage to present the prizes at the Market Snodsbury Grammar School.

*   *   *

I run into Joshua Matz in the lobby of the Sixty LES. He is returning from a local Italian restaurant with his dinner. I am returning from Whole Foods with a bunch of bananas. I tell him I am afraid of the Benadryl.

"Try," says Joshua, pushing his glasses up on his nose, "halving the dose."

His dinner is chicken parmesan and spaghetti.

"But, Joshua!" I say. "Benadryl decreases memory in older adults!"

"That's long-term use," says Joshua.

Joshua was counsel for the United States House of Representatives in *both* impeachments of Trump. This is why I call him the Man with the 583 IQ.

I smile, doubtfully.

"You need to sleep, E. Jean," he says. "If you don't sleep, you can't think. If you can't think, you can't give effective testimony. And if you can't give effective testimony, the jury will believe Trump."

I take the Benadryl.

9

THE RUNWAY

Reporters call Judge Kaplan's courtroom a battlefield. It *is* a battlefield. Soon Joe Tacopina will say, "Good Morning, Ms. Carroll," walk right over, and knock me down. But Judge Kaplan presided over *Virginia Giuffre v. Prince Andrew* in this courtroom, and *Anthony Rapp v. Kevin Spacey* and *United States v. Samuel Bankman-Fried* and fourteen cases of the Gambino family, and the trial of John Gotti, "the Teflon Don," and, Friends, His Honor's federal courtroom is also one of New York's *great* runways.

From the wide oak doors of the entrance, the runway rolls between the heavy, squared-off oak spectator pews, through the swing gate, past the giant oak-and-leather tables full of Trump's horrible male lawyers, past our giant plaintiff's table, past the oaken jury corral, past Andy the Deputy Clerk's command post of oak, past the witness box and its bulky, overweight oak-and-leather chair, and halts at Judge Kaplan's sovereign seat elevated upon an oaken dais. A lot of oak, yes. The walls are oak too. And through this oak forest sweeps the navy-blue runway.

If I were in charge of this runway? I would have the US Women's Olympic Track and Field Team dishing out ice cream sundaes, and dogs chasing balls. I would have Sofia Coppola shooting the

Sacagawea story. I would have Anita Hill and Christine Blasey Ford and Stormy Daniels and a marching band of small girls playing cymbals led by a majorette from Trump University.

Almost as good as a majorette on the runway is Trump himself on the runway. On his good days, in his majestic blue suit, he looks like a finely aged Troy Donahue. And his supporters declare he has never looked better. On his bad days, with his red tie lunging out in front of him, he looks like an elderly gigolo, and his detractors (my sister Barbie—classic dark-burgundy tunic dress, Proenza Schouler bag—and my niece Lauren—Chloé trousers, Khaite top) just sit and stare at him in shock.

Judge Kaplan's wife, Lesley Oelsner, the journalist and publishing lawyer, always wonderfully dressed, usually arrives early, gives a genial nod to the courtroom artists, and takes her seat in the front row. Alina Habba, Esq. never fails to be a bright light—the Ritz diamond alone is worth whatever you have to pay to fly to New York to see. And I am fascinated by Habba's hair. Some days it is long. Other days short. She is not here today, so I cannot tell you if it waves down in streams like a mermaid's or bobs up like Uma Thurman's in *Pulp Fiction*. As for the other Trump lawyers? With the exception of a short, fierce little fellow with a black beard and a young suit by the name of Chad D. Seigel, they all look like Uriah Heep. They sit together at the two testosteronic tables.

*   *   *

On this particular Wednesday morning, the second day of trial, April 26, before court begins, Robbie Kaplan, more alive in a courtroom than any place on earth, her blond hair blown to perfection, her bespoke trouser suit a far-off white, crystals in her ears, pearls on her neck, Ferragamos on her feet, walks up and down the runway in front of the empty jury box. Joe Tacopina, brilliantined to a fare-thee-well, his tight curls glittering under the big bowl lights of the ceiling, excited like Robbie, juiced up, flexing and unflexing his biceps, joins Robbie, and they fall into a friendly, jousting conversation. Shawn G. Crowley saunters down the runway and simply yawns in Tacopina's face.

This makes me yawn.

I *did* get two hours of sleep last night, maybe three, thanks to Joshua Matz's timely advice—but I am not a person who can resist the precedent of a yawn. From the vast plains of the plaintiff's table where I sit, my jaws fly open like a root cellar door in an Indiana tornado.

And now Andy the Deputy Clerk is signaling. Everyone returns to their corners. We rise for the entrance of Judge Kaplan.

THE COURT: Good morning, folks. The plaintiff will call her first witness.

MS. KAPLAN: Your Honor, plaintiff calls to the stand Cheryl Beall.

And down the runway comes a cool, trim, stylish blonde.

THE SCENE OF THE CRIME

United States District Court, Southern District of New York

Jury Trial, Wednesday, April 26, 2023

COURT TRANSCRIPT

Witnesses Give Evidence for the Plaintiff

**CHERYL L. BEALL called as a witness by the Plaintiff,
having been duly sworn, testifies as follows:**

DIRECT EXAMINATION

BY MS. KAPLAN:
——*After pleasant "Good Mornings," Robbie establishes the
following facts: Ms. Beall is a respected retail executive who has
worked for Prada, Hermès, David Yurman, Louis Vuitton,
Ermenegildo Zegna; and in the spring of 1996, when the attack
happens, she is store manager of Bergdorf Goodman.*

Q. What is Bergdorf Goodman?
A. Bergdorf Goodman is a luxury retail specialty store.

Q. Where is it located?

A. 57th and Fifth Avenue.

Q. Did you like your job as store manager at Bergdorf Goodman?

A. I *loved* my job.

Q. Where was your office located?

A. It was on the sixth floor behind the client service department.

Q. Based on your experience, do you have familiarity with other department stores in New York City?

A. Of course.

Q. Which ones?

A. Nordstrom's, Neiman Marcus, Saks Fifth Avenue, Bloomingdale's, Macy's, formerly Barneys.

Q. Can you explain to the jury what would be the difference for a shopper in their experience of walking into Bergdorf's, on the one hand, versus a store like Bloomingdale's on the other?

A. I think the primary difference is that the other stores that we were referring to are *department stores*. Bergdorf's is a multi-brand luxury specialty store. The Goodman family owned the building originally. They had an apartment at the top of the store, so the rest of the store was designed to look like that.

*   *   *

We all have favorite periods in our lives.

I cannot pick my absolute favorite, but around the time I first walk into Bergdorf's is one of them. It is 1985. My first book is coming out and the reviews are ravishing. Here is the poster. It hangs with its crumbling folds, battered border, and spiderweb (see lower left) in my bedroom.

So Bantam is sending me on a book tour, and I need something to wear. I need something to wear because my wardrobe

THE AMERICAN WOMAN LIKE YOU'VE NEVER SEEN HER BEFORE!

FEMALE DIFFICULTIES: SORORITY SISTERS, RODEO QUEENS, FRIGID WOMEN, SMUT STARS, AND OTHER MODERN GIRLS

E. JEAN CARROLL

BANTAM BOOKS

consists almost entirely of cowgirl boots, jeans, a cheerleading sweater, a corduroy shirt, a buckskin jacket with fringe, the red silk V-neck a photo assistant ran out in the rain to buy during the book cover photo shoot, a gentleman's white dress shirt I find on the street, etc., etc. These are the dry goods I have been wearing the last twelve years—ten years in Montana and the last two in New York, and they *are*, I grant you, superb. They work for a working journalist. But not for a woman on book tour.

THE PERFECT BOOK TOUR OUTFIT

Must not wrinkle
Must dry quickly after washing in the sink
Must pack easily into carry-on
Must look dynamite on television

My most fashionable friend tells me to go to Bergdorf Goodman.

I go. I stagger about the place like the thrilled guest of a rich madcap who invites me to a party in his seven-floor mansion. On the third or fourth floor, a gentle, knowledgeable, quiet, self-effacing, and excessively forgetful sales associate asks if she can help.

"My Gawd, yes," I say.

I tell her TV, carry-on, sink, non-wrinkle.

She mulls.

"I have *just* the thing," she says at last, and leads me into what looks like Edith Wharton's coziest guest room in Newport and presents a selection of sleek jersey knits in Hoo-Rah colors. She cuts two skirts and two tops out of the herd—all sink-washable, air-dryable, non-wrinkling wonders which in combination make *four* outfits.

I loathe knits.

She begs my pardon softly and says, *of course* I loathe knits, but I *must* try them on. She shows me to the dressing room. The dressing room lights would make Norma Desmond look thirty-five years younger. After a gracious ten minutes, the sales associate knocks gently on the door. She says in the lowest possible voice that she does not wish to disturb, and asks, through the door, how the skirts fit.

I open the door.

She crosses her arms and clasps herself. What can she say? I look *fabulous!*

*   *   *

Later, after I write a check for something like $2,100 ($3,247 in current dollars), the most I have ever spent on duds up to that point in my life, the sales associate lovingly wraps each garment in tissue paper, then wraps the tissue-wrapped collection into one beautifully swaddled presentation and places the whole array into a large Bergdorf bag, and after she wishes me a melodious adieux and I descend to the ground floor, I am prevented from *leaving* Bergdorf's because she has forgotten to remove the antitheft tags. A nice vice president comes and apologizes profusely, making me love the store twice as much as I do before.

Q. You testified, Ms. Beall, that you had an office on the sixth floor of Bergdorf Goodman at this point in time?
A. Yes.
Q. What merchandise was sold on the sixth floor?
A. The sixth floor was a more contemporary floor, so it had lingerie . . . designer sportswear.
Q. In terms of busy-ness, Ms. Beall, how would the sixth floor compare to the other floors?
A. Probably less so because lingerie wasn't a huge focus for us . . . It was a popular floor, but it wasn't our busiest floor.
Q. For the store as a whole, how busy would it get on Thursday evenings?
A. Thursday nights could be rather quiet.
Q. What about the sixth floor on Thursday nights during this time period?
A. Same thing. It wasn't one of our busiest floors.
Q. Based on your recollection and experience, Ms. Beall, on a Thursday night in the spring of 1996, would there always be an attendant in the lingerie department?
A. Unfortunately, no. I wish there were.
Q. You said unfortunately. What do you mean by that?

A. They might go to a break; they might have to step away with a client to look at another part of the store.

Q. I want to direct you to the fitting rooms. What is your recollection of what was inside the fitting rooms, their designs?

A. On the sixth floor specifically, the fitting rooms were rather small. They have a mirror. They have either a hook or they would have a bar, and either a bench or a chair.

Q. The doors of the fitting rooms, Ms. Beall, what were they made out of?

A. Wood.

Q. Would the doors of the fitting room sometimes be open?

A. Unfortunately, yes.

Q. You say unfortunately. Why?

A. Because we would have liked for them to be kept closed, but many of the sales associates would either prop them open, tie a ribbon to keep it open, or would just not close it. They weren't necessarily on springs.

Q. Once the doors are closed, did they lock automatically?

A. Yes.

Q. In terms of the size of the fitting room, you said it was smaller than other fitting rooms at Bergdorf. Could two people still fit inside?

A. Oh, sure, yes! People shop together.

Q. In the period of the mid 1990's, Ms. Beall, was it common for famous people to shop at Bergdorf Goodman?

A. Yes. Absolutely.

Q. When famous people or celebrities came into shop at Bergdorf Goodman, did Bergdorf Goodman have a policy about how they were supposed to be treated?

A. Yes. Basically, we were trained and my expectation with my team was that we were to be *very* discreet.

*   *   *

Kathy Griffin is in town, and we decide to take a walk. The place we decide to take a walk to is Bergdorf's to have lunch. It is cold and sunny and Kathy is just wearing her old navy-blue Dolce & Gabbana coat* with the gold buttons which she has had twenty years, and her old Nike shirt which is so old she says she "actually got it in the late '90s when she was on a show called *Suddenly Susan* starring Brooke Shields, who was then married to Andre Agassi who had such a big deal at Nike that Nike actually came

---

* I fact-check the old "Dolce & Gabbana coat" with Kathy. She confirms, and the next day she sends me this text: "I've been thinking about this all day, and I'm so pissed because I know I wore many more fancy designer outfits than that. Feel free to write 'typically I like to wear Mrs. Herrera.' 'Jason Wu has become very important to me.' Shit like that."

I happen to snap this in Kathy's hotel room just before we leave for our walk. That's little Maggie on the sofa.

to the set of *Susan* and let us all go to the Nike warehouse and get like, four bags of stuff."

And I can also tell you that as we walk, Kathy's red hair is blazing all over in the sun and several citizens are *not* "discreet" between Fifty-third and Fifty-seventh Streets and are happily screaming, "We love you, Kathy!!!" and "Yo, Griffin!" and a whole family from Milwaukee (or possibly Detroit) runs up at a stop light and hugs her, crying, with stars in their eyes: "We can't *believe* it! We're going to (or possibly they cry they had "gone to") your show tonight!" (Or last night.)

But when we reach Bergdorf's?

America may love her comedians because we are a nation that adores a good laugh, but as Kathy walks through the door, as she beams and gleams under the chandeliers, as she moves through jewelry toward the escalator, there are no shouts, no waves, no "I love you, KGs"—no, no, just smiles of recognition blooming from behind counter after counter after counter, and, of course, we get a *very* good table at BG, the restaurant on the seventh floor.

Q. During the time that you worked at Bergdorf Goodman, were you ever alerted to the fact that Donald Trump was in the store?

A. No.

Q. Why not?

A. Because if Donald Trump were the president, I would be alerted because there would be secret service. But at that particular time he was a regular person. He is a real estate guy. There would be no need to let me know that he was coming.

MS. KAPLAN: No further questions, your Honor.

THE COURT: Cross-examination. Thank you.

MR. BRANDT: Thank you, your Honor.

THE COURT: Mr. Brandt, right?

MR. BRANDT: Yes, your Honor.

THE COURT: Thank you.

CROSS-EXAMINATION

BY MR. BRANDT:

Q. Ms. Beall, Perry Brandt. Nice to see you.

A. Nice to meet you as well.

Q. I have just a few questions for you.

*   *   *

Here is all I can tell you about Trump's new lawyer, W. Perry Brandt, a "business litigator" from Kansas City: He is a Plains-spoken, mild, balding, slim version of the Pillsbury dough fellow who has a nice wife who I run into in the ladies' room, and we talk about the excellence of Lumify.

And if the jury is unclear if W. Perry Brandt is *defending* Trump or *prosecuting* him, they will not find out by listening to his questions for Ms. Beall. After he chisels away everything superfluous, he leaves the jury with three naked facts:

(**1**) There is no attendant in the lingerie department. (**2**) The doors of the dressing rooms are open. And (**3**) the sixth floor of Bergdorf Goodman is empty on Thursday nights.

II

THE BEAUTY QUEEN

MIKE FERRARA: The plaintiff's next witness is E. Jean Carroll. May I inquire, your Honor?

THE COURT: Let's get her sworn first.

E. JEAN CARROLL, the plaintiff herein, having been duly sworn, testifies as follows:

MR. FERRARA: Now may I inquire?

THE COURT: Counselor.

DIRECT EXAMINATION

BY MR. FERRARA:

Q. Good morning, Ms. Carroll.

A. Good morning, Mr. Ferrara.

Q. How old are you?

A. 79.

Q. What do you do for a living?

A. I am a writer.

Q. Where do you live?

A. I live in a tiny cabin in the mountains in upstate New York.

Q. How long have you lived there?
A. Since the mid 1980s.
Q. Where did you grow up?

* * *

My nerves are making a fizzing sound, a hideous sensation.

I am sitting on a chair the size of a John Deere tractor seat. Standing about 1,880 yards away is Mike in a blue suit asking me questions, but the adrenaline pouring out my ears is making it difficult to hear.

"Where did you grow up?"

I look *waaayyyy* down the runway at Mike.

Friends, do you have any idea what it takes to answer this question?

* * *

"Ya know what the jury is asking themselves?" says Mike to me, in the very first session with the Carroll Prep Team.

I say I do not know what the jury is asking themselves.

"'Is E. Jean authentic?'" says Mike. "'Is she the real deal? Or is she putting on an act?' The jury will see through an act, I promise you. The groupthink of nine people is very powerful. Are you putting on an act? Or"—he looks at me through his glasses with the square, light flint-gray frames—"are you trying not to *waste* their time? So, okay. All right. Let's try it again. Where did you grow up?"

"I grew up in the heart of the heart of the country."

Bad looks from the Carroll Prep Team.

I try again.

"I grew up in the sticks."

Very bad looks from the Carroll Prep Team.

"Can't I just fucking say I grew up in the fucking sticks?"

Really awful bad looks from the Carroll Prep Team.

"We are trying to get you to talk like a *normal person*," says Shawn G. Crowley.

"OK. OK."

"Try it again," says Mike.

"I grew up in the country. (*Hesitation*) In Indiana."

Silence.

"I grew up in a redbrick schoolhouse. The redbrick schoolhouse is now in the National Register of Historic Places. In Indiana." (*Ruminating*) "In the sticks."

Mike and Shawn exchange a look that kind-hearted visitors give one another when they meet a patient in the public lunatic asylum.

"Just go for the factual answer," says Mike.

"Those *are* the facts," I say, and so on, and so on.

*   *   *

My ears, which have been standing out on stalks, snap back on my head. I am beginning to feel myself inside myself again. I see the US Marshal with his shirt tightly buttoned on his bulletproof vest. I see the six men and the three women of the jury looking at me. I see Mike. I see his suit is not just "blue"; it is true, star-spangled blue. His shirt is blazing white. His tie, a rose. He is standing behind a heavy, oak-paneled lectern fourteen or fifteen paces away. I see that I just need to remember where I am from to know where I am.

Q. Where did you grow up?

——*The big, wet, dirty wad of white noise in my skull fades. I can almost hear myself think.*

A. Rural Indiana.

And so begins my three days of testimony.

MR. FERRARA CONTINUES:

Q. Why are you here today?

A. I am here because Donald Trump raped me, and when I wrote about it, he said it didn't happen. He lied and shattered my reputation, and I am here to try to get my life back.*

Q. We are going to talk at length about that in a few minutes, but let's first cover a little bit more of your background. Okay?

——*Friends, you can slice my life into three parts: Bucolic childhood. Trying to be a journalist. Being a journalist.*

Q. Where did you go to college?

A. Indiana University.

Q. Can you give us a sense of what sorts of activities you were involved in?

A. I was in a sorority, and I was a cheerleader.

Q. How about beauty pageants?

A. My sorority would nominate me to be in beauty pageants.

Q. I want to show you what's been marked for identification as Plaintiff Exhibit 13. Do you recognize this?

A. Yes. That's Miss America on the right. And that is my sorority sister, Linda Lou Mugg who was the previous Miss Indiana University. And that's me in the middle.

---

* This answer will later be performed brilliantly syllable by syllable by three actresses: Ellen Burstyn, Kathryn Hahn, and Lexi Underwood in an eighteen-minute documentary, *E. Jean Carroll V. Donald J. Trump,* by Robert Greenwald. Regina King plays Robbie Kaplan. You can see it on YouTube.

The former Miss Indiana University, Linda Lou Mugg, crowning the Plaintiff with Miss America Jacquelyn Mayer presenting the roses. Photo by the illustrious Elinor Hendrix.

——*I get crowned quite a bit, Miss Cheerleader USA, Indianapolis 500 Princess, Miss Beach Ball, etc., etc., but Mike does not dawdle on an aspect of my life where people stare at me on a runway.*

Q. What year did you graduate?
A. My class graduated in 1965, but because I did not return a library book, I didn't get my diploma until 1967.

——*A sorority sister, pulling an all-nighter, finds the book in the bowels of the Pi Beta Phi library, returns it, and the university sends me my diploma.*

Q. What did you hope to do professionally after graduating?
A. I wanted to be a writer.

——And we whirl through my jobs. Founding a cheerleading camp, working for Procter & Gamble as a market researcher, running off to South Africa, being a gym teacher in the inner city of Chicago, working at a reform school in Idaho—and this whole time I am congesting the US mails with pitches to magazines trying to get published.

Q. Did you get married?

——We spin through Steve Byers and going off to Montana together to be young and married and live an adventurous life.

Q. Did you divorce?
A. Steve and I split up in 1980 or 1981 after a very successful companionship. Just because a marriage ends, doesn't mean it fails.

Steve and I at St. John the Baptist church, Fort Wayne. I wore a straw hat (by Halston!) cocked on the side of my head for our first wedding at City Hall in Chicago.

Q. Let's talk about your professional career in the 80's and 90's. Okay? Can you list the magazines you worked for?

*   *   *

Mike is skipping the Fran Lebowitz story here. Robbie Kaplan, who grows up in Ohio wanting to *be* Fran Lebowitz, is crazy about the Fran Lebowitz story. "It's such a Manhattan story!" says Robbie. "It explains how you get from Montana to New York. If we get a *Manhattan* jury, we will definitely ask you about it."

But we do not get a Manhattan jury. We get an *upstate* jury. And we also get Joe Tacopina who is not backward when it comes to pouring over transcripts of depositions, particularly depositions in which I talk about George Butler photographing Fran Lebowitz on the camping trip and being number four on my List of Eight Lovers.

And what is the Fran Lebowitz story?

You have heard a bit about it when the ravishing Alina Habba, Esq. is questioning me in the opening of this memoir. In 1981, I am in the shed behind our house on O'Dell Spring Creek, outside Ennis, Montana, reading stacks of magazines, eating enormous bowls of popcorn, and writing pitch letters to New York magazine editors. I see a photo of Fran Lebowitz in *Vogue*. She is talking on the phone. It is a big old black dial phone. I get a magnifying glass. I study the phone in the picture and read Fran Lebowitz's phone number.

I drive to the laundromat (Steve and I do not have a phone), call Fran Lebowitz, introduce myself, and ask to take her camping for *Outside* magazine. She says yes. I go to New York, haul Fran Lebowitz out to the Shawangunk Mountains, cook her dinner over a fire, zip her into a tent, etc., etc., drop her back at her flat in the Village, take a look around at Manhattan, and BOOM!—so long, Montana.

"Fran Lebowitz, Tenderfoot" lands on the cover. (Take another look at page 17.) *Outside* wins the National Magazine Award.

Q. Let's talk about your professional career in the 80's and 90's, OK? Can you list the magazines you worked for?
A. *Esquire*, *Playboy*, *Outside*, *Rolling Stone*, *New York* and later I write for *Vanity Fair* and the *Atlantic*.
Q. What did you write for *Elle* magazine?
A. *Elle* magazine is the world's largest fashion magazine. American *Elle* is thought of as "the thinking woman's fashion magazine," and I wrote the advice column.
Q. What was the name of the column?
A. Ask E. Jean.
Q. What year—around what year did you start writing that column?
A. 1993.

Adam Klasfeld @KlasfeldReports · May 5, 2023
A window into E. Jean Carroll's career from the 1990s:
These are two promotional images for her Elle column "Ask E. Jean," released among the exhibits today. She guessed on the witness stand that they were taken in '97 or '98, judging from her hairstyle.
EAN
26
115
599
63K

Q. How long did you write it for?

A. 27 years at *Elle*. I'm still writing it on Substack.

Q. Let me show you what have been marked for identification as Plaintiff's Exhibits 15 and 16. Do you recognize this?

A. Yes.

Q. What is it?

A. This is a picture of me from the Ask E. Jean column.

*   *   *

Mike has a seventy-nine-year-old woman here whose four grand-parents were born in the 1800s. *The 1800s!* Mike has to pull the jury through ten years of the old woman's childhood, ten years of her girlhood, thirty-two years of her career and marriages, and land her in front of Bergdorf's on a Thursday night in 1996 when she bumps into a future president of the United States. How does Mike do this without boring the jury out of their skulls?

First, as you notice, he asks what magazines I write for. *Esquire, Rolling Stone, Outside, New York, Vanity Fair* and the *Atlantic* lead to the "Ask E. Jean" column. The "Ask E. Jean" column leads to the *Ask E. Jean* TV show. The *Ask E. Jean* TV show runs live at four in the afternoon and reruns at eleven p.m. every week-day, and is nominated for best cable talk show along with Bill Maher's *Politically Incorrect,* which leads to my boss, Roger Ailes (the future founder of Fox News), and *his* TV show, which runs live at eight p.m. every night and reruns at midnight, which leads to Donald Trump coming to our studios and being *on* Roger's show, and our shows rerunning together every night, the whole line of TV show questions implying that it is totally *impossible* that Donald Trump does not "know" me, which leads to my be-ing a writer at *Saturday Night Live,* and how I am nominated for an Emmy, and how I marry John Johnson, the respected New York anchorman.

Second, he asks how John and I run into Trump and his wife Ivana at an NBC party.

Mike's questions are straight as a cattle prod and my answers are as factual as a box score, but running under my answers is the *other* fact:

I start pitching story ideas to magazines when I am twelve. I continue pitching story ideas to magazines until my first story is accepted by *Esquire* when I am thirty-seven years old. Can you imagine the relentless, insane, glorious, hot, blistering beat-your-self-up, plow-ahead, never-say-die enthusiasm that drives a woman to go on and on and on through a blizzard of blunt editors' numbing "Nos" for *twenty-five years*?

And once I get my foot in the door, once I am snapping that seat belt across my lap on a plane and that plane is taking off and flying me somewhere marvelous I have never been, where I am going to write a story about fascinating people I have never met, I never stop. Never. It is how I live now, how I lived then. And though it is the mistake of my life, there is no way, after bumping into Trump, and he asks me to advise him about a gift and the hilarious "shopping with Trump" is underway, there is no way I am *not* going into that dressing room.

12

THE DRESSING ROOM

DIRECT EXAMINATION CONTINUES

BY MR. FERRARA:

Q. Ms. Carroll let's turn to the reason you are here. I would like to ask you some questions about what happened with Donald Trump. Okay?

A. Um-hmm.

Q. Let's just start with when you first recall meeting Mr. Trump.

A. It was in 1987 at one of two places. It was either at a *Saturday Night Live* party, an NBC party; or John was working at ABC at the time, so it could have been an ABC party.

Q. Let me show you what's been marked for identification as Plaintiff's Exhibit 12. Do you recognize this?

———*This will not be the only time we all see this photo.*

A. Yes.

Q. What is it?

A. This is a picture of myself, John Johnson, Ivana Trump, and Donald Trump.

Q. Do you recall when it was taken?

A. I believe it is 1987 because I have always thought it was an NBC *Saturday Night Live* party.

Q. Where did this photo come from?

A. I always had it in my possession.

Q. You appear to be speaking in this photo, do you recall what, if any, conversation you had with the Trumps? Do you recall what's being discussed?

A. No.

Q. Do you recall approximately how long the conversation lasted?

A. Yes, it was at least five or six minutes.

Q. What was your general opinion of Mr. Trump at that time?

A. I thought he was a raconteur. A man-about-town, well-liked.

Q. What's a raconteur. Is it a nice word or a mean word?

A. A raconteur is a sophisticated man who is entertaining to be around.

Q. Did you find him attractive.

A. Yes.

Q. Why?

A. He was very personable.

Q. When was the next time you saw Donald Trump?

——*We briefly talk about Trump waving to me on the street, and now Mike asks when the next time is I see Trump.*

A. At Bergdorf's.

Q. Okay. So sitting here now, *when* do you believe Donald Trump assaulted you?

*   *   *

I have always believed it is a Thursday night and have placed the date in the fall of 1995 or the spring of 1996 based on three facts: (**A**) the temperature: cold, but not freezing; (**B**) the light: the entr'acte between twilight and dark; and (**C**) what I am wearing. And there the date has hung suspended from the time I file my lawsuit until my friend Lisa Birnbach, several months before trial, is cleaning out her files and is astonished to come across a twenty-eight-year-old *New York* magazine piece she wrote about Donald Trump. Maybe you remember the photo of young Ivanka sitting on Trump's thigh?

Lisa's piece causes *quite* a ruckus.

The date of the issue? February 1996. Who do I call just minutes after the attack in the dressing room? Lisa Birnbach. Lisa says she "never" would have gone to Mar-a-Lago to write the piece if she had known about what he did to me in Bergdorf's. This eliminates the fall of 1995 and moves the date to the spring of 1996.

BY MR. FERRARA:

Q. I think you started to mention this, but just give us the *specifics* of what you were wearing when you encountered Mr. Trump for the—during that period?

*   *   *

ANSWER: The most expensive dress I own. My black wool Donna Karan dress, thick black tights, black patent-leather heels. *New York* magazine puts it on the cover. The far-right conspiracy theory that the dress did not exist in 1996 is

bullshit. We have the dress. We have the date of manufacture of the dress. I speak to Donna Karan herself *during* the *New York* photo shoot and verify it.

The most consequential fact of the photo shoot is not the dress. Not the fact that the dress actually exists. Not the fact that I talk with Donna Karan herself during the photo shoot. It is the fact that I am wearing no makeup. The photographer, Amanda Demme, sees me arriving bare-faced for the shoot in my old jumpsuit tied at the waist with my ex-husband's brown-and-gold-stripped Gigli tie and says, "That's it! We are going for the *whole truth!* No makeup!"

At the time, I think it is a glorious step forward for women. Bold! Revolutionary! Clean face! Truth! Nothing to hide! A writer telling her story! Ha! Boy, was I wrong! Within a minute of the cover hitting the internet, you know *who* people see on the cover? Not the writer telling the truth. Not the clean face. No. Who they see on the cover is an old woman not hot enough to be believed.

For the next four years it is a roadblock in bringing our case.

*   *   *

And what am I wearing when I testify about what I was wearing?

Friends, I am armored. I am borinoxed. If a bomb goes off in the Daniel Patrick Moynihan United States Courthouse, I will flick the dust from my immaculate Mechlin lace cuffs, check if Judge Kaplan is still upright, perform first aid upon all members of the jury who require it, bandage up Robbie, resuscitate Mike, and go on testifying.

*   *   *

Because Trump calls me a "whack job."

I will look calm.

Because Trump calls me "mentally ill."

I will look smart.

Because Trump calls me "deranged?" "Crazy?" A "sick woman."

I will look rational.

My dark-navy jacket encases me like a bullet. The gorgeous, stiffly billowing skirt fences my area, protects my perimeter. It is the navy-blue Dior-inspired Zara suit. It may as well be cut from steel.

Mike will soon ask how "long" my dress is when I meet Trump. He will ask how "long" my dress is, to head off Tacopina asking how "short" my dress is. He will ask what underwear I have under my tights, to head of Tacopina continually using the word "panties," and because this is so common a question, and because like every woman who has ever testified about a sexual assault in a courtroom, my body and what I clothe that body in is so important, I wonder:

"Why does nobody ask what Trump is wearing?"

DIRECT EXAMINATION CONTINUES

BY MR. FERRARA:

Q. I'm going to show you what's been marked for identification as Plaintiff Exhibit 14. Do you recognize this?

A. Yes.

Q. What is it?

A. That's a picture of myself taken in 1995 or 1996.

Q. How old are you—about how old were you in this photograph?

A. 52.

Q. So turning to this period of time—1995, 1996—just give

*Photo by the great
Antoine Verglas.*

us very briefly, what a typical day would look like, a typical weekday would look like for you?

A. I lived in a little cottage outside Nyack. I would feed the dogs, I would feed the cats, I would feed the wild birds, and then I would write the television show, the intros, the introductions, I would read the research, and I would get ready to do the show, drive to Fort Lee, go into hair and makeup, and then go live at 4:00.

Q. What was in Fort Lee?

A. Fort Lee was where the NBC cable channel was.

——And here Mike asks about taping the live show, driving from the studio to New York, going to Bergdorf's, how long the drive is, the route I would take.

Q. Do you recall specifically on that day *why* you were going to Bergdorf's?

A. I'm guessing that it was a sale.

Q. Do you recall sitting here today?

A. No.

Q. Did you buy anything that day?

A. I don't think I did because I didn't have carrier bags with me. I didn't have shopping bags.

Q. Do you recall how long you were in the store?

A. No.

Q. When did you first see Mr. Trump that day?

A. I was leaving the store, I was exiting the 58th Street entrance, and I was just about to go out the door. He was standing on the other side of it and put up his hand.

Q. You're putting up your hand to indicate what, Ms. Carroll, so it's clear?

A. It's the universal signal for stop.

Q. What did you do?

A. I stopped.

Q. What happened next?

A. And he came through the door, and he said, "Hey, you're that advice lady."

Q. How did you respond?

A. I said, "Hey, you're that real estate tycoon."

Q. What was your impression of Donald Trump at that time when you saw him at Bergdorf's?

A. Very personable, engaging.

Q. What happened after you said, "Hey, you're that real estate tycoon"?

A. He said, "I need to buy a gift, come help me. Come advise me."

Q. Did you agree?

A. I was delighted.

Q. Why?

A. Well, it was such a funny New York scene. I'm a born advice columnist. I love to give advice, and here was Donald Trump asking me for advice about buying a present. It was a wonderful prospect for me.

Q. Who was he shopping for, if you know?

A. I asked him. I said: "Who's it for?" He said: "A girl." And then I asked him, trying to figure out who it could be: "How old is she?" And he replied with: "How old are you?"

Q. What did you say?

A. I said 52.

Q. How did he respond?

A. He said: "You're so *old.*"

Q. Was that in a fresh way or in a sort of teasing way?

A. No. It was humorous the way he said it.

Q. What did the two of you do next?

A. At the time, in 1996, the little circular alcove we were standing in had displayed three or four handbags, which were so beautiful and such works of art I thought, Wow, any girl would love one of these handbags. But he didn't like the idea of a handbag. So we went—we turn to the left, and walk through the first floor to the hats. I'm thinking a hat would be great. She is going to love a hat.

Q. As far as you were able to tell—what floor of Bergdorf were you on at this point?

A. First floor.

Q. As far as you were able to tell, did anyone recognize you or Mr. Trump?

A. There was a shopper. She was tiny. I remember her staring up at him in awe. She recognized him. He was very pleasant.

Q. Anyone else?

A. There was a sales attendant, and she was also very pleased to see him. He was pleased to see her.

Q. What, if any, words did they exchange?

A. I think he said "hello, how are you doing, how are you."

Q. What happened after hats?

A. He was holding—he picked up a hat that was a fur hat and he was petting it like a little cat or a dog. And as he was petting it he said, "I know! Lingerie!"

Q. Lingerie meaning underwear?

A. Yes.

Q. Where was the lingerie section in the store? Where was that located?

A. I didn't know where it was. I do now know where it is. But he led the way to the escalator, and we started to go up the escalator.

Q. What floor do you recall lingerie being on at that time?

A. Six.

Q. Was there anything sort of discomforting to you about the fact that Mr. Trump had proposed the lingerie?

A. No. By this time—first of all, he was *very* talkative. In the escalator he talked about how great Bergdorf's was. At one time he said he was thinking of buying Bergdorf's. I was absolutely enchanted. I could only think of it as a scene. Such a great story! I was delighted to go to lingerie with him.

Q. Were you chatting?

A. Yes. He was very funny.

Q. Do you recall what the two of you were discussing as you made your way to the lingerie area?

A. He was talking about Bergdorf's. I don't remember precisely.

Q. What was the tone of the conversation?

A. Very joshing and light.

Q. Who, if anyone else, in the store did you see as you rode up to the lingerie area?

A. I wasn't looking. I was watching him and watching that I didn't fall when I boarded the escalator and when the escalator hit the top.

Q. When you arrived at the sixth floor on the escalator, do you recall how you walked to the area where the lingerie was?

A. Yes. We walked—

Q. Sort of walk us through how you remember moving through the floor, which way you would turn, etc.

A. Do you mind if I stand up? Because I cannot—I'm very, *very* bad on direction.

MR. FERRARA: Your Honor, may the witness stand up to orient herself?

THE COURT: Yes.

A. We go to the top. We turn to the left.

Q. Then what? Is the lingerie, like right there?

A. No. No. If you just keep going, you will see lingerie a little bit to the right, just slightly off in a little section.

Q. What happened when the two of you arrived at that section?

A. There is a glass-covered cabinet, very elegant piece of furniture. And on the top of this glass was a lovely piece of see-through grayish blue bodysuit. And he snatched it up. He held it up and he said: "Go put this on."

Q. Is a body suit a type of lingerie?

A. Yes. It was quite a lovely piece. It looks like a swimsuit, except this was see-through. They used to be called teddies.

Q. Who else was in the—in that area with you and Mr. Trump?

A. I didn't see anybody.

Q. Was that surprising?

A. It didn't surprise me, no.

Q. What about sales attendants?

A. Didn't see any.

Q. Why didn't that surprise you?

A. Bergdorf's was not busy in the evenings.

Q. Have you written before that you were surprised by the lack of people on the floor?

A. Well I was not surprised, and yet I was surprised.

Q. How is that?

A. The whole thing about going up in the escalators with Donald Trump was surprising. The fact that we didn't see any salespeople, I think I noticed it. I may have described it before as being surprising. I may have been surprised. I really can't say. *Now* I find it surprising.

Q. What happened after Mr. Trump picked up the piece of lingerie?

A. He said: "Go put this on."

Q. Did you?

A. No. I had no intention of putting it on.

Q. What was his demeanor when he said go put this on?

A. Jesting, joshing.

Q. How did you respond?

A. I said: "*You* put it on! It's *your* color."

Q. What did he say?

A. He held it up—he held it against me. He said: "You're in shape. Go put this on." I said: "No. It goes with *your* eyes. It's *your* size. *You* put it on."

Q. Why in the world would you think that Mr. Trump would put on that piece of lingerie?

A. Because his tone was—he was having a very good time and so was I. The idea was funny. I could just picture it in my mind: Donald Trump putting on this filmy see-through bit of lingerie over his pants! That's how I pictured it.

Q. So what happened next?

A. He said: "*Let's* try this on." And he motioned towards the dressing room.

Q. What did you do?

A. Well, I thought, hmm, he had me by the arm—he motioned with his arm, he had me by the arm with his hand, and the door was open, and he went like this. (*Making an "after you" gesture*) And I said "OK." I saw it as a *Saturday Night Live* sketch. I had written a sketch that was similar to this very scene I was entering. And Donald Trump was being very light, and it was very joshy and pleasant and *very* funny.

Q. Just to be clear, was he dragging you into the dressing room?

A. No. He went like this. (*Again, demonstrating the "after you" gesture*)

Q. In your mind, at the time, Ms. Carroll, had things—withdrawn. Had you been flirting sort of much this time with Mr. Trump?

A. I was flirting the *whole* time, probably.

Q. At this point now, when Mr. Trump has proposed going to the dressing room, have things escalated in your mind?

A. The comedy was escalating, and I thought it was getting funnier and funnier.

Q. Did you ever think about saying, no, "I'm not going in?"

A. No. It didn't occur to me. I didn't really think about going "into a dressing room." I thought of it as sort of an open area. The door was open, we walked in. I didn't picture anything about what was about to happen. Didn't picture it.

——I did picture him trying to put the small, see-through filmy little thing over his pants, and the vision was making me chuckle to myself.

Q. What happened once you—first off, was the dressing room open or closed?

A. The door was open. That open door has plagued me for years because I just walked into it. Just walked in!

Q. Let's take it one step at a time. What happened once you entered the dressing room?

A. He immediately shut the door and shoved me up against the wall. He shoved me so hard my head banged.

Q. What were you thinking at that moment?

A. I was extremely confused, suddenly realizing that what I thought was happening was *not* happening.

Q. How did you react in that moment?

A. I was laughing as we walked in, and I continued to laugh because I thought—I wasn't sure. For a minute I thought maybe it was a mistake, that he didn't mean to do that. He didn't mean to shut the door. And just to make sure—I continued to laugh just in case he was thinking of something intimate. And so I'm very rapidly trying to figure out, what's going on and trying to get out of it at the same time.

Q. What did he do next?

A. I pushed him back, and he thrust me back against the wall again, banging my head again.

Q. Were you still laughing at this point?

A. I think I may have been. I really—Here's the thing. I didn't— just in case—this is going to sound odd. I didn't want to make a scene. I know that sounds strange. I didn't want to—I didn't want to make him angry at me. I didn't want to stop what started out as something light and fun and comedic and a great story to tell people I am having dinner with, and it suddenly turned absolutely dark.

Q. What did he do after he pushed you up against the wall the second time?

A. He put his shoulder against me to hold me against the wall.

Q. Then what happened?

A. I remember him being—he was very large, and his whole weight came against my chest and held me up there, and he leaned down and pulled down my tights.

Q. What, if anything, were you doing while that was happening?

A. I was pushing him back. It was quite clear that I was not going—I didn't want anything else to happen. It was quite clear. I pushed him back. This arm was pinned down. This arm had my purse. Trying to get him back.

Q. At any point during this encounter, do you recall saying "no?"

A. No, I don't recall saying it. I may have said it.

Q. At any point during this encounter did you scream?

A. I don't remember screaming. I'm not a screamer. I'm a fighter. I'm much more physical than I am vocal.

Q. What about his head? What is happening?

A. His head was beside me, breathing. First, he put his mouth against me.

Q. Do you mean he kissed you?

A. Yes.

Q. Did you kiss him back?

A. No. I didn't consider it a kiss. It was such—it was a shocking thing for him to suddenly put his mouth against mine. I thought what? What? What? No.

Q. Do you think—based on what you were experiencing, do you believe that if someone had been nearby, they would have been able to hear what was happening in the dressing room?

A. They would have heard my head hitting and definitely would have heard me laughing.

Q. You described Mr. Trump as a—you described Mr. Trump as sort of, I think, larger than you?

A. Yes.

Q. Do you recall approximately what the difference—or how tall are you?

A. At the time I was five-nine. Because I'm 79, I have sort of all compacted down due to gravity, but at the time I was five-nine. I was wearing four-inch heels. So it put me about level with Donald Trump, who I think is six-two. I was six-one. And I weighed at the time about 120, and I believe he weighed about 100 more pounds.

Q. Were you afraid while this was happening?

A. I was in—this is going to sound strange. I was too frightened to think if I was afraid or not. I was stamping. My whole reason for being alive in that moment was to get out of that room.

Q. How were you trying to accomplish that?

A. Stamping and trying to wiggle out from under him. But he had pulled down my tights and his hand went—his fingers went into my vagina, which was extremely painful, extremely painful. It was a horrible feeling because he curved, he put his hand inside of me and curved his finger. As I'm sitting here today, I can still feel it. It was—

Q. Then what happened?

A. Then he inserted his penis.

Q. What did you do in that moment?

A. I tried—

———*Trying to find words to describe the indescribable.*

Q. Do you need a moment, Ms. Carroll?

———*I did not need a moment. I have had enough moments.*

A. You asked me what I did in *that* moment? I always think back to why I walked in there to get myself in that situation, but I'm proud to say I got out. I got my knee up. I got my knee up and pushed him back.

Q. Was anything in your hands?

A. My handbag.

Q. Why were you holding your handbag?

A. I have no idea.

Q. I want to be—I want to make sure I understand it. How were you able to—? How were you able to see what Mr. Trump was doing with his hand, or are you telling us what you experienced sort of physically by feeling it?

A. He was against me, his whole shoulder—I couldn't see anything. I couldn't see anything that was happening. But I could certainly feel it. I could certainly feel that pain in the finger jamming up.

Q. How long was your dress?

A. Mid knee.

———*Well, now, that I'm looking again at the New York cover, I see it is slightly above the knee.*

Q. Do you recall how far down he pushed your tights?

A. Yes. A little bit below mid thighs.

Q. Are you wearing underwear?

A. No. To me, tights *are* underwear. I wouldn't wear two pair of underwear, no.

Q. Do you recall either of you saying anything as this was happening?

A. I can't say if I said—I can't say. I had so much adrenaline pouring through me at this time, I can't tell you if I said anything.

Q. Do you know if he ejaculated?

A. I don't think so.

Q. You said you got your knee up. What happened next?

A. Once I could get my knee up, I could get him to back off. I could actually move his body. I was quite strong. I was an athlete. I could push him back by putting that knee up.

Q. What did you do after you were able to push him off?

A. I exited the room, and I got out of the store as quickly as I could.

Q. How long do you believe the encounter, the assault in the dressing room, do you recall how long that assault lasted?

A. From walking in, from walking in?

Q. Just in the dressing room.

A. A very few minutes, very few. That was another thing that surprised me.

Q. What surprised you?

A. To go from a very funny story, light, joshing, and me thinking this is just going to be the most terrific scene. I can't wait to tell everyone—to having his hand jammed up me. Not a lot of time lapsed.

Q. How did you get out of the store?

A. I walked out.

Q. Do you recall whether you took the escalators? Did you take the elevator? What do you recall?

A. I have never been able to find the elevators in Bergdorf's. I am never sure where they are. So I headed back the way I came, the escalator.

Q. Were you running? Were you walking?

A. I am going to guess—I'm guessing I walked swiftly.

Q. Did you tell anyone in the store what had happened?

A. I didn't see anybody. I am not saying they weren't there. I just didn't see anybody.

Q. Did Mr. Trump, do you know—? Were you able to tell whether he came after you?

A. I was never sure if he was behind me. I got out as quickly as I could.

Q. How did you leave the store?

A. On Fifth Avenue, one of the Fifth Avenue doors.

Q. Do you recall what time of day it was when—

A. It was pretty dark when I was outside.

Q. Did Mr. Trump follow you out of the store?

A. No. Not that I know.

Q. I think you were touching on this Ms. Carroll, but sitting here today, how do you feel about your decision to go into that dressing room?

A. It was stupid. I know people have been through a lot worse than this, but it—it left me. It left me unable to ever have a romantic life again.

13

THE MINIBAR

"In the heart of New York City's Lower East Side lies luxury amid haute minimalism. Sixty LES carries the artful spirit of the city through its every suite, space and dining venue, from an Andy Warhol filmstrip pool to Lee Friedlander–made glowing headboards to bespoke Jim Walrod interior design elements."

—DESCRIPTION ON WEBSITE

I return to my hotel room "in the heart of New York City's Lower East Side."

I cut across the "haute minimalism" of the shiny black tiled floor, enter the bedroom with the "Lee Friedlander–made glowing headboard," unbolt the tight navy-blue jacket, and hang it up. I remove the formerly fresh, now withering, alabaster blouse. I *pas* out of the *Swan Lake* skirt. Do I don the bikini and visit the "Andy Warhol filmstrip pool"? The last time I pack a bikini, *Home Alone 2: Lost in New York* is being shot in Manhattan.

No. I put on my ancient set of Uniqlo long underwear and visit the "artful spirit" of the minibar. I rip open a bag, eat the contents, rip open another bag, eat the contents, and continue ripping open bags and eating the contents until I have eaten every chip, crisp, cookie, cracker, biscuit, bar, nut, Cheeto, Frito, Dorito, Goldfish, M&M, Snicker, Oreo, Ruffle, and Pringle right down to picking the crumbs off the complimentary pack of playing cards.

Limp, loose, relaxed, serene, I sit down with a glass of white wine, open my computer, and look at images from my day in court.

*   *   *

Photos are not allowed to be snapped in Judge Kaplan's federal courtroom, so I look at the day's drawings done by the immortal historian of the bench, Jane Rosenberg. I look at Getty photos of myself entering the Daniel Patrick Moynihan United States Courthouse and I look at Google photos of myself leaving the Daniel Patrick Moynihan United States Courthouse. Most of the pictures have Robbie, whose blond hair waves up in front like Gene Tunney and who can pull a thirty-pound trout out of the Bering Strait with a *fly rod,* hauling me along through the roiling sea of photographers.

I

can

not

get

enough

of

the

photos.

I look and look and look and look at them. They remind me who I am. It is important to remind myself who I am because Tacopina keeps telling the jury I am somebody else. I read the reports in the newspapers. The reports tell me what I am doing.

It is important to know what I am doing because Trump is telling everyone what I am doing is a crime.

> ## In Searing Detail, Trump's Accuser Tells Her Story
>
> E. Jean Carroll, who says Donald Trump raped her, told a chilling story on the stand. The former president harangued her from outside the courtroom.

The very instant I see the word "Searing" in the headline and the photo of Robbie holding my arm, I put down my glass of wine, the Sixty LES and its "Jim Walrod interior design elements" cease to exist, and the whole day wafts, rises, and the very late afternoon of today's trial comes back to me. I see myself testifying about the death threats, the buying bullets for my gun, the attack flashbacks, the losing my job at *Elle*, the loss of my eight million readers, the death of my mother, and the power of the presidency bearing down upon me, and I have, I'm afraid, what is known in courtroom circles as "a meltdown on the stand."

*   *   *

Mike Ferrara, tall, strong, powerless to conceal his buoyant hope that he is about to bring us *both* through a full day of testimony without my going off on a crazed "E. Jean tangent," asks one of the last questions of the day:

"Sitting here today, Ms. Carroll," says Mike, "are you happy you have spoken publicly about what Mr. Trump did to you? Or do you regret it?"

"I have regretted it about a hundred times," I say, and abruptly lose my breath. "But in the end—" Without breath I sound like a balloon being squeaked. Worse, I feel like I am going to cry. I would rather die than cry. "In the end—" I feel it coming—"being able to get my day in court finally is—"

I jab away two fat tears. But no. Two more follow, hotter, fatter, heavier, and BOOM! My anger at Donald Trump comes pouring down my face. I finish: "Is *everything* to me. So. I am happy."

I square my shoulders, but they start to shake anyway.

"Are you okay to keep going?" says Mike, stepping out from behind the lectern. "Do you—"

He looks like Sugar Ray Robinson standing in the fight ring after knocking out the wrong person.

"I'm *happy*!" I say, swatting the tears away. "I'm *glad* I get to tell my story in court!"

Mike, addresses Judge Kaplan: "Your Honor—I don't want to . . ."

And a box of Kleenex appears in front of me.

I grab a wad. And even in my height of anger, with the tears rolling so fast they are about to wet the front of my suit jacket, I have enough self-control to press the tissue to my nose—*not* my eyes and smear my mascara. I even take a split second to wonder if it is Mike who has stepped down the runway and put the tissue in front of me.

"Ms. Carroll," he says. "Do you want to take a moment?"

I am not a philosopher. I am not Artie Schopenhauer. I never ask the universe, "Why am I here?" I know I am *not* in this courtroom to blubber like the Walrus in *Alice in Wonderland*.

"I am going to get myself together!" I say, raising my voice. "This is my moment. I'm not going to sit here and cry and waste everybody's time."

"So shall I keep going?" says Mike.

Yes!!

*   *   *

Friends, I notice the *Times* headline mentions "the former president harangued her from outside the courtroom." I will tell you about that at another time. It's an evil story. You will love it. But this is my book. Not Trump's. And I am going to bed.

14

THE HARANGUE

n 1954 in the great Rocky Marciano era, a ragged old pair of red leather boxing gloves mysteriously appear in the city of Fort Wayne, Indiana, and take up residence on various kids' fists on Illsley Place, our street. Mike Simmons hit Bobby Simmons. Bobby Simmons hit Mary Jane Miller. Mary Jane Miller hit me, and I have been a big fight fan ever since.

In 1964, in an Indianapolis theater, on a closed-circuit screen, I see Cassius Clay, the handsome Olympic champion and the 8:1 underdog, beat the undisputed champion of the world, the scariest man in the history of combat sports, Sonny Liston, and take the World Heavyweight Championship in seven rounds. After this fight, Cassius Clay changes his name to Muhammad Ali.

In 1987, I meet Mike Tyson, undisputed heavyweight champion, 1987–1990, at a *Saturday Night Live* party, and later I am wearing a "waist eliminator" when I meet Joe Frasier, undisputed heavyweight champion 1970–1973, at the Tyson-Bruno Heavyweight Championship in Las Vegas. I am ringside with Jack, Tupak, Eddie, and Denzel, and the "waist eliminator" nearly causes me to pass out in the third round when Mr. Tyson hits Mr. Bruno with an uppercut, sending Mr. Bruno into the air, and when he crash-lands in the ropes, Mills Lane, the tiny referee, removes Mr. Bruno's mouthpiece, and with Jennifer Tilly jumping up and down beside me with her hands clamped over her face, he stops the fight.

And so it is fitting that every morning going to court, all day in court, and every evening coming back from court, Robbie and I are protected by Herman—Herman is the one who gets Robbie out of Charlottesville (alive!)—and Herman's guys, the giant redhead, Rick Tirelli, former New York homicide detective and current podcaster ("Life's Tough, but Rick Tirelli is TOUGHER, solving nearly 600 homicide cases as one of the NYPD's greatest detectives,")* and the fabled MMA fighter, Joe Monahan, also a former NYPD detective, and now cofounder of Maxum BJJ & MMA, a Brazilian Jiu-Jitsu and MMA training academy.

There are metal detectors. There are armed US Marshals. There are triple security checks. But if you want to feel safe, Friends, just glance down the runway and see Joe the boxing Brazilian Jiu-Jitsu Irishman standing in the back of the courtroom, his chest broad as a card table, and his ears like two gobs of well-mashed potatoes sticking out on either side of his head.

Friends, I am sorry if you don't like boxing. I am telling you about it because Trump's "harangue" is his attempt to control the fight. "If Donald Trump," says the Reverend Al Sharpton, "had been born Black, he would have been Don King."†

By the second day of *Carroll v. Trump,* three slug fests have taken place when the jury is not present, and Judge Kaplan has

---

* The log line from Rick Tirelli's podcast "Life's Tough: You Can Be Tougher."

† Matt Flegenheimer, "What Donald Trump Learned from Don King," *New York Times,* June 18, 2024.

made three rulings against Trump: the famous DNA decision,[*] the Reid Hoffman decision,[†] and the knockout Natasha Stoynoff decision.[‡] Three decisions. Three rounds for Carroll.

*   *   *

It is a clear-cut case. Trump is losing. Do you think he is going to let an old woman beat him? You better think again. If Trump cannot win in court *with* Tacopina, Trump will win outside of court *without* Tacopina.

How?

By not staying in his corner. Viz: by talking to the jury. But how does somebody speak to an anonymous jury? Their names are unknown, their spouses a riddle, their workplaces unheard of, their home addresses hidden, their phone numbers a secret.

---

[*] After defying court orders for *three years* to provide his DNA to me so I can match it against genetic material found on the Donna Karan dress, in February 2023, Trump hires Tacopina, does an about-face and suddenly *demands* to give his DNA. This would delay the trial another year. Judge Kaplan rules that as the genetic material found on the dress is from handprints and not sperm, it will not provide proof of rape either way and that Tacopina may not mention "DNA" before the jury.

[†] *Carroll v. Trump* is well into its second year when Reid Hoffman, the founder of LinkedIn, steps up and provides some funding for the costs of *Carroll I* and *Carroll II*. Judge Kaplan rules that Tacopina may not mention "Reid Hoffman" before the jury.

[‡] Natasha Stoynoff and Jessica Leeds both accused Trump of sexual assault. Tacopina argues they should not be allowed to give evidence at my trial. We argue that in *federal* court, in cases of sexual assault, witnesses may be called to give evidence that supports the case against the defendant. Judge Kaplan is a federal judge of a federal court and Judge Kaplan rules Jessica and Natasha—a boxer!—may appear.

But Trump does not need names, addresses, workplaces, or phone numbers. He's the world's champion. He simply starts trash-talking me on Truth Social.

> The E. Jean Carroll case, Ms. Bergdorf Goodman is a made-up SCAM. Her lawyer is a political operative financed by a big political donor that they said didn't exist, only to get caught lying about that. Just look at her CNN interview before and after the commercial break, like a different person. She said there was a dress, using the old "Monica Lewinsky" stuff that she didn't want to produce. The dress should be allowed to be part of the case. This is a fraudulent and false story—witch hunt! April 26, 8:51

He will begin posting forty times *an hour* about me, Robbie, Judge Kaplan, the dress, "the Andy Cooper" video on CNN, Reid Hoffman, and my cat; but for now let us consider this one, simple, April 26, 8:51 message and see how it goes from his lips to the jury's ears.

His team will take it from Truth [Truth Social] and then they'll put it out as a press release and it will repeat in newspapers, podcasts, campaign speeches, on TV, Twitter, Facebook, TikTok, Instagram, texts, alerts, notifications, and thousands of platforms across the country.

Publicity for Henry David Thoreau's first book, to put this in perspective, reaches three hundred people.

Everything Judge Kaplan rules the jury may not hear, Donald Trump is telling them. All they need do is turn on their phones. It takes only one juror to hang the jury and cause a mistrial.

From the Ben Weiser, Lola Fadulu, Kate Christobek, and Karen Zraick story in the *New York Times*:

On Wednesday morning, Mr. Trump used Truth Social to call Ms. Carroll's case a "made up SCAM" and a "fraudulent & false story," which led the judge, Lewis A. Kaplan of Federal District Court, to suggest that the former president was trying to influence the jury.

Speaking without the jury present, Judge Kaplan told Mr. Trump's lawyer Joseph Tacopina:

"Your client is basically endeavoring certainly to speak to his 'public,'" Judge Kaplan said, "but, more troublesome, to the jury in this case . . ."

Now, Friends, you know, and I know, and Tacopina knows that his boss is the soul of indiscretion. But Tacopina tells Judge Kaplan he will "speak with his client and ask him to refrain." It is a speech full of respect for the judge, but I notice Tacopina's eyes are bloodshot. I attribute this to his constant worry about what will happen if his client tweets the offer of his plane to fly the upstate jury back to their homes each night.

As for *my* bloodshot eyes? After Tacopina gets done cross-examining me tomorrow, I will no doubt be happy to *have* eyes. His boss has lost three rounds. The only way Tacopina can put him back in the fight is by beating me to a bloody pulp on the stand.

15

THE SCREAM

United States District Court, Southern District of New York

Jury Trial, Thursday, April 27, 2023

COURT TRANSCRIPT

CROSS-EXAMINATION OF MS. CARROLL

BY MR. TACOPINA:

Big-necked, big-shouldered, hair-oiled, and handsome, with a voice like a load of river rock being delivered and rolled on my driveway, Joe Tacopina, in a dark-blue suit cut right down to his corpuscles and a shimmering white shirt, commences the beating.

I do pretty well. I listen to his questions. I tell him the truth. He ripples his muscles under his jacket. He rolls his shoulders. And soon we find ourselves at the door of Bergdorf Goodman's.

The door, Friends. *The door.*

Now. You would think a door is not a big deal. You open a door. You close a door. But not Tacopina. Tacopina is so wound up this morning, so zesty, so bouncy, so blitzed on knocking me to the floor right off the bat, he says:

"When you were leaving Bergdorf Goodman that day, you supposedly saw Donald Trump coming in?"

"Yes."

"In your book, which you published in 2019, you don't recall whether it was a revolving door or just a regular hinge door, correct?"

I take a moment to remember what I wrote, and Tacopina, superbly conditioned, bounces up and down on his toes to keep his calves from tying up.

"*Is that correct?*" he repeats.

"Yes."

"Now, as you sit here today, are you *definitive* that it was a revolving door?"

"As I sit here today, I *know* it's a revolving door."

"As you sit here today, you *know* it's a revolving door? Okay."

Tacopina, hardly able to contain himself, rippling and rocking, hair gleaming, puts a couple of lines from my book up on the screens for the jury to stare at, and every one of them does something with their eyes, squinting, rubbing, rolling, blinking.

"You just testified that you are *certain* it is a revolving door as you sit here today. In your book, on page 245, you write, 'I am going out the revolving door and one of New York's most famous men is coming in the revolving door, or it could have been a regular door at the time. I can't recall.' This is from your book back in 2019, right?"

"Yes."

"Correct. And today, *despite what you wrote in your book*, today it is your testimony that—*not* that you can't recall, but that you are *sure* it was a revolving door?"

"Yes."

"What cleared up your memory on that?"

"I went to Bergdorf's."

"So!!" he shouts with a burst of boyish glee. "*After* you publish the book where you say you *can't* recall if it is a revolving door, you went to Bergdorf's to check it out?"

"Yes."

"You agree that 2019 is more than twenty-plus years from 1995 or 1996, right?"

"Yes."

"And you are certain that Bergdorf would never have changed their doors?"

"No. I am not certain. I was never sure about the door when I wrote the book. Not sure about the door. I could see him. I couldn't remember whether it was a revolving door, or a push-in-and-out door."

And so on.

If he gets this excited about a door, Friends, can you imagine what is coming? But it shows you how Tacopina works. He dances around, he sees a small cut, a tiny cut above my eye, and jab, jab, jab, jab, jab, jab, jab, jab, jab, he hits the cut till it opens and I bleed to death in the witness box. That's the Tacopina Program.

Now, ladies and gentlemen of the jury, let us see if it works.

*　　*　　*

CROSS-EXAMINATION

BY MR. TACOPINA:

Q. According to you, Donald Trump picked up that piece of lingerie and said to you: "Go put this on"?

A. He said: "Go *try* this on."

Q. And the lingerie is that see-through, very pretty, lilac, grayish-blue, one-piece bodysuit with lace?

A. Yes.

Q. And Donald Trump is about six-foot-three inches?

A. I think so.

Q. You say he weighed 100 pounds more than you, so approximately 225 pounds back in 1995 or '96?

A. That's what makes it so comical. If Donald Trump weighed 130 and was five-foot-eight, there would be no humor in it. But Donald Trump being a large, tall, very manly man, it made it twice as funny, the idea of Donald Trump putting this lingerie on over his pants.

Q. It's your claim that that was your plan, to get this large man to put on a not-so-large, see-through lace bodysuit over his *suit pants?*

A. It struck me as very funny. If a man tells me to go put on some lingerie, my natural instinct is to tell *him* to go put on the lingerie. I was just turning everything around.

———*This is standard advice from "Ask E. Jean."*

Q. In order to get Donald Trump to try on this lingerie over his clothes, it's your story that you tossed it at him and told him it goes with his eyes?

A. Yes.

Q. Obviously, it wasn't his size. You were just kidding.

A. I didn't think *any* of it was serious. I had written a similar scene on *Saturday Night Live* and got nominated for an Emmy for this very thing of a man getting dressed in front of a mirror. The idea was, to me, hilarious.

Q. You wrote a scene for *Saturday Night Live* about a man putting on lingerie over a suit?

A. About a man getting dressed in the bathroom, and he was wearing his underwear.

Q. Over his suit?

A. No. It was just a man in his bathroom falling in love with himself in front of the mirror.

Q. To you that's a similar scene as Donald Trump, in the middle of Bergdorf Goodman, with his suit on, trying on a piece of women's lingerie?

A. That's how my mind works. That's how comedy is born. You take two opposite things, you put them together, and it makes a new scene. That's where comedy comes from.

Q. Did that ever air on *Saturday Night Live*?

A. Yes.

Q. When was that?

A. 1987, William Shatner played the role.

Q. According to you—by the way, there was no woman involved in that skit. It was just one person alone in a bathroom?

A. No, no. Nora Dunn was playing his wife and was making very unflattering comments as he was falling in love with himself in front of the mirror.

Q. Are you done?

*   *   *

I am the worst writer in the history of *Saturday Night Live.* After one of my sketches receives not a single laugh at the Wednesday table read, and after most of the cast has left the room, Al Franken, future senator, picks my sketch up from the table, and, not knowing I am standing behind him, says in a low, scorny voice to Phil Hartman: "Why was this *allowed* in?"

Lorne Michaels hires me because I write funny profiles about famous men in *Playboy* and a book called *Female Difficulties,* but he does not think what I write for the show is funny. I try, and I try, and I try. I cannot get my sketches on the air. Thirty-seven years later, Lorne opens the show with *Carroll v. Trump.*

Q. And your testimony is the dressing room door was opened and unlocked.

A. Yes.

Q. And your plan, again, was, once inside, to get Donald Trump to try this lingerie on over his clothes, not under it?

A. The *last* thing I wanted to see is Donald Trump taking off his clothes. I wanted him to put it on over his clothes and, frankly, I didn't really expect that to happen. I just expected the sort of joshing to continue. We would walk in the dressing room, turn around and walk out.

Q. So you walked into the dressing room not really expecting him to try on the lingerie—

A. I pictured in my mind the most hilarious image of him putting it on over his pants. I didn't have a minute to think any further because he slammed the door and thrust me up against the wall. So my thinking about what was going to happen was overcome with what actually did happen.

Q. But the plan was at least to enter that dressing room, to have him try that lingerie on over his suit, not under it, yes?

A. That's what I was picturing. I didn't have a plan. I didn't want the scene to stop. It was, you know, very funny. I didn't want to be the one to call the end to it.

Q. At that time you still saw no one on that floor, correct?

A. No. I saw no one.

Q. Why did you have to go in a dressing room for this? If there was no one on this floor, he wasn't taking off these clothes, he was just putting this lingerie over his clothes, why did you have to go to a dressing room for him to do that?

A. I don't know. Making it all funnier.

Q. All the funnier?

A. There are mirrors in dressing rooms. That's why you go into a dressing room. There are mirrors.

Q. It's your story that once you stepped into the dressing room, the door banged closed, and Donald Trump pushed you up against the wall?

A. Yes.

Q. Is it correct that he didn't lock the door behind you?

A. He did not lock the door.

Q. And, instead, he immediately pushed you up against the wall so hard that you banged your head?

A. Yes.

Q. According to you, it was so hard that it hurt?

A. Yes.

Q. It's your story that he pushed you a second time?

A. Yes. Because I pushed back. After he pushed me the first time, I pushed back.

Q. And that caused you to hit your head again.

A. Yes.

Q. It is also your testimony you didn't feel like Donald Trump was trying to hurt you, you said, correct? I'm sorry. Withdrawn. It's also your testimony that you said that you don't feel that Donald Trump was trying to hurt you?

A. I didn't think so. I was very confused. I thought maybe it was a mistake. The first push, I thought, he *couldn't* have meant that. I thought he had made a mistake. I thought that's *very* strange. I thought it was a mistake.

Q. In any event, with regard to the noise from the alleged

assault, it is your story that you heard a bang when you hit your head?

A. Yes.

Q. According to you, the bang was so loud that if someone was in the dressing room next door they would have heard it?

A. Yes.

Q. According to you, the bang was so loud, if there were a sales attendant outside the dressing rooms they would have heard it?

A. Yes.

Q. So, based on your own account, Donald Trump was trying to attack you quietly so others couldn't hear.

A. I don't think he was thinking about what noise was being made.

Q. It's only after that second push into the wall it's your story that you realized at this point the situation was serious?

A. Yes.

Q. It's your testimony that when Donald Trump, this big and heavy man, lunged at you and banged your head against the wall so hard it hurt, you still didn't think it was serious at that point?

A. I was trying to figure out what the hell was going on. This is a man—this is Donald Trump. I thought I knew him. We had just been laughing 12, 15 seconds before. And here I am being pushed up against the wall. I had no idea. It took me several seconds to process what the heck was going on. It didn't make any sense. It didn't make any sense at all. Then he put his mouth against mine. Then I understood. OK.

Q. In fact, you viewed what went on in that dressing room as a fight.

A. Yes.

Q. In fact, in response to this supposedly serious situation that you viewed as a fight, where you got physically hurt, it's your story that you not only didn't scream out, but you started *laughing*?

* * *

I laugh when I am nervous. I laugh in awkward social situations. I laugh to get other people to laugh. I laugh with babies. I laugh when I am talking to myself. I laugh to make my dogs leap and spin in the air. I laugh when I try to poach an egg. I laugh when I'm afraid to be afraid. I laugh at my friend Lisa Birnbach. I laugh when I open my bills. I laugh when I see the first robin in spring. I laugh with my sister Barbie in the last minutes of my mother's life to keep Ma's spirits up. I laugh when I want people to like me. I laugh to give myself courage. I laugh when I am mad. I laugh when I drink champagne and there is a period in my life when I drink champagne every night at 12 a.m. no matter what. I laugh to turn a guy off. I laugh sledding down the hill behind my cabin.

I do not laugh when the plane ride gets bumpy. I do not laugh when the cat suddenly drops down from the mantle onto my keyboard and causes me to jump out of my skin. I do not laugh when I buy a box of hair color "just to try it" and my hair turns orange.

A. I don't think I *started* laughing. I think I was laughing going into the dressing room, and I think I laughed pretty consistently after the kiss to absolutely throw cold water on anything he thought was about to happen. Laughing is a very good—I use the word weapon—to calm a man down if he has any erotic intention.

Q. According to you, after Donald Trump had you against the wall, he pulled your tights down?

A. Yes.

Q. It's your story that at some point you felt his penis inside you?

A. Yes.

Q. But before that, it's your sworn testimony that you felt his fingers, what you said was "rummaging around your vagina"?

A. It's an unforgettable feeling.

Q. Now, when you say, "rummaging around your vagina," that's different than inserting a finger inside your vagina?

A. At first he rummaged around and *then* he put his finger inside me.

Q. In your book you wrote that he was forcing his fingers around my private area and then thrusts his penis halfway completely, I'm not certain, inside me. Is that accurate?

A. Yes.

Q. And this attack or this fight, based on your word, this *fight* that you were in, could have taken as long as three minutes?

A. From entering the dressing room to my leaving it, I don't think it could be any more than three minutes. I may be wrong. I didn't have a stopwatch, but it was about three minutes.

Q. Even though you understood you were in the middle of this *supposed* battle, you never screamed at Donald Trump or screamed for help?

A. I'm not a screamer.

*   *   *

Don't make a scene. Don't frighten him. This is just a mistake. This is just a joke. He's just playing. This is stupid. This is nuts.

Get it over with. Get him off. Don't freak him out. Hahahaha!
Don't make a scene. Stay quiet. He'll stop. If you scream, he'll
kill you.

Q. You said that yesterday, I'm not a screamer, right?
A. I'm not a screamer. Here's the thing. I was too much in a
panic to scream. I was fighting.
Q. When you're fighting and being sexually assaulted and raped,
because you are not a screamer, as you describe it, you wouldn't
scream?
A. I'm not a screamer. You can't beat up on me for not
screaming.

———*It is a surreal feeling being beat up by a man who is asking
me to describe being beat up and assaulted by the man he is
beating me up to defend.*

Q. I'm not beating up on you. I'm asking you questions, Ms.
Carroll.
A. *No!* Women who come forward, one of the reasons they
don't come forward is because they're always asked: "*Why didn't
you scream?*" Some women scream. Some women don't. It keeps
women silent.
Q. And, according to you, this attack wasn't taking place in
some secluded place in the middle of nowhere in a forest. That
was in a crowded department store in New York City.
A. Yes. Not crowded, though.
Q. Right. The inconceivable part, right?

MR. FERRARA: Objection your Honor.
THE COURT: Sustained.

Q. When you spoke with Dr. Lebowitz after filing your lawsuit, you were still trying to come up with an explanation for your story as why you did not scream.

A. I wasn't coming up with a story. It's usually—I would say more than usually under discussion when a woman is raped and she doesn't scream. It's usually discussed: Why didn't she scream? "Why didn't you scream, E. Jean? Why didn't you scream?" It's what a woman—you better have a good excuse why you didn't scream. Because if you didn't scream, you weren't raped. I'm telling you: he raped me! Whether I screamed or not.

——*My voice turns to tapioca.*

Q. You need a minute, Ms. Carroll?

——*I look at Tacopina rippling and rolling, his eyes jittering, and think, "You'll need a minute before I do, buster!"*

A. No. You go right on.

——*Adding to myself, "And I hope you choke!"*

Q. Aside from you not being a screamer, another reason you gave for possibly not screaming was because you were wondering if the pressure Donald Trump's shoulder placed against your chest interfered with your ability to scream, correct?

A. It could be. I don't *need* an excuse for not screaming.

Q. Okay. Despite that, you certainly wish your story included you having screamed?

———At about this point, I am guessing that Joe Tacopina, former assistant Brooklyn DA, winner of thirty-nine out of forty trials, many as a homicide prosecutor, former criminal defense attorney for mobsters like "Mickey the Dunce," famous trial attorney, is going in for the finish. Swinging wildly now, he is probably thinking I will go down if he hits me just right. He confidently waits for my answer so he can go in and slug me again.

A. Of course I do. More people would have believed me if I had screamed . . . if I was going to make up a lie, I would have lied when I was writing this and say I screamed my head off. I didn't. When I came forward, I told the truth. I said I didn't scream. We could probably come up with more reasons I didn't scream, but I did not scream. *I did not scream.*

Q. Well, Ms. Carroll, the reason why you wrote that you wish you had screamed was why? Why did you write you wish you had screamed?

A. Because more people would have believed me.

Q. How about more people may have heard you and helped you? Is that a possibility?

A. No. I didn't want to make a scene.

Q. Oh. So you didn't scream while you were getting violently raped because you didn't want to make a scene?

MR. FERRARA: Objection your Honor.
THE COURT: Overruled.

Q. You could answer.

A. Repeat your question.

Q. You didn't scream while you were getting violently raped because you didn't want to make a scene.

A. That's right. That's probably why I didn't scream.

Q. Okay. Now, with the specifics to the rape allegation, Donald Trump, you said, had his penis inside of you while your tights were obviously still down?

A. Yes.

Q. And to be clear, it's your story that Donald Trump did not take off your tights?

*　　*　　*

I get my first pair of tights in eighth grade. I wear them with my short, white corduroy ice-skating skirt with the red satin lining. Nobody else in the great metropolis of Fort Wayne even *has* tights. I skate on frozen ponds in 16 degree weather with my tights and my white corduroy skirt. The red lining flashes above the ice when I twirl. My mother says I can't wear the tights and I gotta put on my wool pants if it is below 30. This is like telling Coco Chanel to put on a corset.

I wear black tights in college with kilts, white tights in the Swinging Sixties with short, crocheted dresses, and, in fact, never stop wearing tights, even when I go hiking because tights tick-proof better than EPA-registered tick repellant. Soon Joe Tacopina will start snapping questions at me about tights, so I should tell you what I am wearing now. I am wearing two pairs of Wolford tights: Nude 8 and Luxe 9—a combination which makes a beautiful crème brûlée color with my boxy, cream Zara suit with twirl skirt.

A. No, no, just pulled down. They were still above the knees.

Q. They were above the knees.

A. Um-hmm.

Q. And because your tights were above the knees, you couldn't get your knee up?

A. I couldn't get it all the way up. I finally got it up, though.

Q. Okay. And it's your story that you tried to stomp on his foot?

A. Yes. That didn't work.

Q. According to you, Donald Trump had his hands on your arms.

A. Briefly, but mainly he was holding me against the wall with the weight of his shoulder.

Q. And it's your story you tried to get your arms up to push him back.

A. Yes, this hand had to be—I was a little pinned because his shoulder was right here, so this arm was pretty much inert, but I could move it a little bit and (*here I make little hunting nudges, the movements of looking for an armhole when trying on a very small jacket*) go like this. *This* arm was almost completely free.

Q. And according to you, you did push him back.

A. I hit him back with my knee up.

Q. Okay. And while all this was happening, your purse was still in one of your hands.

A. Yeah, I know. Yes. I never let go of my purse.

Q. What kind of purse was it?

A. It was a Coach—a square bag with stand-up handles.

*   *   *

It was ugly. It was a present from my mother-in-law, Leah Byers, a sweet and stylish woman. I brought it with me to New York from Montana when I came to take Fran Lebowitz camping. I had it when I lived at the Allerton Hotel for Women on Fifty-seventh Street. ("No men allowed above the first floor, or below the waist" as Bob Datilla, Number Four on the list in the first chapter, says). The bag looked even uglier in Manhattan than it did in Montana, and I threw it out. One of the women on my floor at the Allerton found it in the trash and brought it back to me. She said, "I found your pretty bag!" After that, it grew on me.

Q. It had stand-up handles on it?
A. Um-hmm.
Q. Okay, so stand-up handles are the solid fixtures, the hard handles?
A. Yes, and they are leather stand-up. The leather stood up, too.
Q. Leather stand-up handles. Okay . . . . You did hit him with your purse.
A. I believe I did.
Q. Okay. When did you recall that fact, Ms. Carroll, hitting him with your purse?
A. I've always recalled that fact.
Q. And you mentioned that when you were giving your television interviews about this case or your video deposition?
A. I'm not sure if I did.
Q. Okay. You describe what was going on in there as a colossal—being in the locker room, changing room, a colossal struggle.
A. To me it was a colossal struggle.
Q. And despite this colossal struggle while you were being violently raped, you—for as long as three minutes, you never let go of your purse.
A. No, I never did.
Q. And at one point it's your testimony you managed to get your knee up and push Donald Trump off of you by yourself.
A. Yes.
Q. And even though the tights or your panties were above your knees?

A. Yeah. I could—they are called "tights" because they are stretchy. Tights are amazingly—I wasn't wearing control top hose. I was wearing tights, which are extremely stretchy.

Q. And what portion of your knee came in contact with what portion of his body? Or let me withdraw and rephrase. Your knee came in contact with what portion of his body?

A. Can I stand up?

Q. If that would help?

MR. TACOPINA: Your Honor, is that okay?

THE COURT: Yes. Go, ahead.

A. Right about here.

Q. So it went to his—just for the record, you are indicating your right hip?

A. About hip level. We were basically the same height, because I was wearing four-inch heels and I was 5' 9" at the time—so I was 6' 1."

Q. So you are saying that you got your knee up to his—it would be waist, as high as his waist?

A. No, below his waist.

Q. Below his waist. And you just said something. Four-inch heels. It's your story you did this while you were balancing on four-inch heels, you said?

A. I can dance backwards and forwards in four-inch heels. I can raise one leg in heels.

——*Being a man, Tacopina does not seem to get the Ginger Rogers reference. When she talked about dancing with Fred Astaire, she said: "I did everything Fred did, except backward and in high heels."*

Q. Well, you are not dancing here, you are—

A. No, it was—*fighting,* and as you know, it required—well, (*Pause. I throw him a look.*) *you* work out all the time. We have read about it. . . .

*   *   *

And when I say, *"We* have read about" Tacopina's workouts, I mean *I* have read *New York* magazine which says Tacopina's workout is an "intense resistance-training workout," and a most enlightening 2023 *Washington Post* profile of Tacopina by Kara Voght, appearing a week before trial, which says Tacopina's workout is five days a week:

> As a Manhattan attorney, he cultivated a taste for the lavish—nice watches, luxury cars, a 49-foot yacht. He says he's ditched most of those trappings in recent years, though his casual look includes a Patek Philippe wristwatch so rare it last sold for $3.2 million at auction. He works out five days a week—including the morning before Trump's arraignment. ("I can't *not* do that," he says. "When I don't do that, I get into a low-energy spot.") He has several tattoos, including one of a Roman eagle on his right hip.
>
> His overall aesthetic answers the question: What if Billy Flynn, the tap-dancing attorney from the musical "Chicago," was swallowed whole by Lou Ferrigno?

Q. All right.

——*He draws his head back, tilting it, considering my remark about his "workout"—was it a crack? A compliment? He pushes his lips together, but his eyes are asking, "Can this be what I think it is?"*

Q. Let me ask a question.

——I can see he is deciding whether to jump on it.

Q. That will get me in trouble if I do.

——I smile.

Q. I won't respond to that. So, I'm just going to move on. But the fact is the entire time you were wearing four-inch heels?
A. The entire time, yes.
Q. So just to make sure I understand the story and then we will move on, this man was almost twice as large as you, weighed 100 pounds more than you, right?
A. Not twice as large. He weighed probably over a hundred more pounds than I.
Q. How tall are you?
A. I was at the time 5′ 9″.
Q. 5′ 9″. Are you talking about with your heels or—
A. No. With my heels I was 6′1″.
Q. Okay. And this man who was, as you said, probably more than a hundred pounds. Just so I understand the story correctly, as your tights were pulled down, you were able to get one knee up, after fighting for as much as three minutes against a man who was much heavier than you, while being sexually penetrated without ever letting go of your purse?
A. Yes.

*   *   *

When Tacopina was a senior at Poly Prep in Brooklyn, he won the state championship in wrestling. When he was at Skidmore, he was captain of the hockey team and held the record, according to NBC news, for most minutes in the penalty box. (Some magazines report that Tacopina's astounding number of minutes in the penalty box—three or four times what an entire college team whacks up in a year—has never been broken, but I do not credit it. I believe Tacopina was never *out* of the penalty box.)

I do not know in what weight class Tacopina wrestled. The male sex is so crazed about weight it invented the deranged "flyweight," "bantamweight," "featherweight," and "welterweight" for boxing, I dare not hazard a guess for Tacopina's wrestling championship.

I am talking about weight here because Tacopina is dubious as to the truth of my testimony that I fought a man who weighs a hundred pounds more than I weigh. At the time, I reply with a simple, "Yes." But now I have a better answer. I wish I had asked Tacopina:

"Have you ever tried to give a pill to a cat?"

I weigh one hundred pounds more than my cat. And yet my cat can tear me to shreds before I can get a pill down her.

Q. After that occurred, you pulled your tights back up and walked out of Bergdorf Goodman wearing those tights?
A. I wore the tights. They did not come off.
Q. Okay. And you pulled them back up, right, Ms. Carroll?
A. I pulled them up, yes.
Q. And those tights never ripped during this colossal struggle, correct? I'm sorry, your Honor. Those tights never ripped during this colossal struggle.

A. I don't believe they did.

Q. And it's your testimony that you don't know if Mr. Trump ejaculated?

A. I couldn't see what was going on.

Q. After you claimed to have pushed Donald Trump off of you, you turned and got out of the dressing room?

A. Yes.

Q. You didn't say anything to him?

A. No.

Q. And in fact, even at that point, you still didn't scream?

A. I did not scream.

——A few minutes later . . .

MR. TACOPINA: One second your Honor.

THE COURT: How much longer do you expect to be?

MR. TACOPINA: Oh, a bit, a bit.

THE COURT: We will take a—

MR. TACOPINA: You want to take a break? I don't even know what time it is.

THE COURT: It's a quarter after three.

MR. TACOPINA: You want to take a break now?

THE COURT: 15 minutes.

And with that we all stand up, and the members of the jury— if they had not been clear what happened in the dressing room before, now have every detail seared into their brains thanks to Tacopina's virile cross-examination—file out of the courtroom.

16

"YOU DIDN'T BURN IT!"

The jury departs. I step down from the witness chair, walk up the runway, and exit the courtroom. In the *Iliad's* famous boxing match, Epeius, the Rocky Balboa of his day, receives a "stately mule" from Achilles. In the *Aeneid,* Entellus is given a "bullock with golden horns" from Aeneas. In the Daniel Patrick Moynihan United States Courthouse, the prize ass has not even shown up for his trial, and I get a peanut butter and jelly sandwich.

I eat the sandwich. I check my teeth. I apply Revlon's no. 325, Toast of New York. I walk back down the runway, past the tables of Trump attorneys, past the dark, fierce chap with the beard, past the Pillsbury Doughboy from Kansas, past Alina Habba, Esq. looking sensational in a sky-blue suit. I step up to my seat in the witness chair. I sit. The peanut butter and jelly sandwich has made me thirsty. I am about to take a drink of water from my plastic glass which I left in the witness box and *whooooooooosh!* Mike Ferrara appears, lean and swift as a wolf-hound. *Swaaaaaaaaaaaaaaak!* He sweeps the glass out of my reach. Holding it out in front of himself as if he is using tongs, he walks it back to the Carroll table, puts it down, picks up a new bottle of water, opens it, pours the fresh water into a new plastic glass, returns to the witness box, and hands the glass to me.

This irks every single Trump lawyer no end.

*   *   *

Judge Kaplan arrives. He mounts his oaken throne. He calls for the jury. All nine turn their eyes away from me as they enter the courtroom, all clutching their pens and notebooks like first-year residents making rounds in the nut ward at Bellevue. The Tim Pool Guy, the blank, pasty, but not unhandsome, young man with slitting eyes like a lizard, who "gets his news" from the right-wing podcaster Tim Pool, takes his seat on the far right in the oaken corral.

His acolyte, a young, innocent-looking out-of-work mainte-nance man straight out of Guido Reni's *Adoration of the Shep-herds*, sits down beside him and immediately falls into a doze. And for the next hour Tacopina, knowing a three-day weekend is a mere sixty-some minutes away, and wanting to leave the eight jurors who are still awake with the impression that I am a filthy, money-grabbing, conniving liar, asks me why I do not "seek help" from the Bergdorf security, why I do not call 911, why I cannot stop laughing when I call Lisa Birnbach, why I do not go to the police when Lisa Birnbach suggests I go to the police, why I think rape is so "hilarious," why I do not "sit down or do any-thing to take care of myself" after I leave Bergdorf's, why I do not tell any "family members," why I do not "check my head" for in-juries, why I do not go to a hospital, why I do not go to a doctor, why I do not show Carol Martin the bump on my head, why I wait to tell my story till after Donald Trump becomes president, why I do not see a psychiatrist, why I do not see a psychologist, why I have no medical records "showing physical injuries from this colossal battle," why I have no photographs of "any physical injuries," why I do not report the death threats to the police, why I do not go back to Bergdorf's the day after the attack and ask for the security videos, why I do not bring criminal charges against Donald Trump, and why I do not burn the dress.

*   *   *

I do not "seek help" from Bergdorf security, or call 911, or go to the police because I do not want to end up on a witness stand being attacked by an attorney asking me why I do not "bring criminal charges against Donald Trump"—this is just one of the reasons that do not seem to occur to Joe Tacopina.

As the three-day break arrives, the press takes two different angles on the day, as reflected by two *New York Times* headlines:

Trump's Lawyer Spars With E. Jean Carroll Over Rape Accusation

Joseph Tacopina asked Ms. Carroll to retell her story in minute detail, probing for inconsistencies. His aggressive questioning irritated the judge.

In Trump Trial, a Lawyer Pushes, and E. Jean Carroll Pushes Right Back

The writer E. Jean Carroll and Donald Trump's lawyer, Joseph Tacopina, clashed repeatedly over her account of how she reacted after she was attacked.

17

HOW *DID* I GET HERE?

O. K.

So...

Donald Trump is president of the United States. The first time. At around 6:30 p.m. on July 15, 2019, clad in a pair of old riding breeches and an ugly vest, I enter a baronial building on East Eighty-sixth just off Central Park, and ride up in an elevator so fancy I imagine myself in Casanova's water closet.

The building is very tall, and the lift is very slow, and I hear sonic waves of excited shouts before I come to a thumping stop. The elevator door slides open on a little vestibule, and I step into a roaring hive of editors, writers, anchors, Twitter stars, reporters, crooks, critics, money men, beautiful women—every one of them eating, drinking, laughing, shouting, schmoozing, sucking up, snubbing, and scooping one another. I say scoop, not "scope" because this is a Molly Jong-Fast party. And, yes, Molly Jong-Fast parties *are* wild if you think of a bunch of bum writers like Margaret Sullivan as saucy hussies and old journos like Nobel-winner Paul Krugman as dashing hotheads.

Molly, brick-red hair, ivory-doily bangs, giant glasses, Missoni frock, MSNBC commentator, *Fast Politics* podcaster, *Vanity Fair* journalist, liberal media's croak-voiced ecstatic hugger, is making everyone feel so friendly, with such a glow of being alive, I walk over to a total stranger.

(Later, he will be the one hiding behind Soledad O'Brien when a photo catches him.)

We are squeezed into the alcove here: Kathy Griffin is on the floor, I am standing above Kathy on the far left, Molly is next to me, and the chap scowling next, to Molly is Nobel winner, Paul Krugman. George is peeping out from behind Soledad O'Brien on the right. Photo courtesy of Molly Jong-Fast.

*   *   *

"Hello," I say.

Dark-haired, with a boyish, open face, merry brown eyes, and a stinging, nipping wit, George Conway, the only conservative in a sea of babbling liberal media stars, free of social duties because he doesn't need to pay his respects to anybody, is standing in the quietest—but still clamorous—corner of the party just inside a little alcove.

I force my voice into cheerleader mode so George can hear me.

"Hello, I'm E. Jean," I say. "Thank you for your *Washington Post* piece.* For a Republican—" "I'm an Independent now," says George—"for an *Independent,*" I say, "you're a swashbuckler!"

Now, Friends, I possess a sterling memory. George (magna cum laude Harvard, Yale Law, cofounder of the Lincoln Project, and instrumental in Paula Jones winning her $850,000 defamation settlement against President Clinton) also has a sterling memory. After we discuss his *Post* piece, *I* recall that George says, "Listen, you could sue Trump," and *George* recalls that I ask, "Listen, could I sue Trump?"

Either way, George tells me there are two kinds of lawsuits—criminal and civil. He explains the difference and the procedure of each. He also says because Trump called me a liar countless times, and, because the statements Trump made are false, George believes I can bring a defamation suit against Trump, and the next day at 8:47 a.m. he sends an email with the subject line: "Introductory email," and presents me to the Nazi-slaying civil rights attorney Robbie Kaplan.

And *that* is how I come to be here.

---

* George Conway, "Republicans Believed Juanita Broaddrick. The new rape allegation against Trump is more credible." *Washington Post*, June 22, 2019.

18

THE SUPERSTITION

United States District Court, Southern District of New York

Jury Trial, Monday, May 1, 2023

COURT TRANSCRIPT

t is my third day of testimony, my second day of "cross." In boxing, which you are sick of hearing about, a *cross* is the power punch thrown with the rear hand into the dental work of one's opponent. A "cross" in federal court is Joe Tacopina with his big arms and big calves whaling away at me trying to shake my story—the kind of interrogation, which in any other place: a dinner party, a neighborhood bar, would produce a near riot; the kind of interrogation that irritates a conservative, by-the-book, no-nonsense judge like Lewis Kaplan and causes the protective Duke of Ferrara to jump to his feet and object to; the kind of interrogation that gets Tacopina himself so carried away that at one point he may have given away Trump's motive for attacking me in the dressing room.*

---

* Amanda Marcotte, "Donald Trump's defense attorney in rape trial may

It is now just after lunch on Monday. The judge and the jury have not yet arrived back in the courtroom.

Tacopina, too resplendent to stay seated, pushes his chair back from the Trump table and stands up. With a burst of vivacity, he throws off his suit jacket and walks about the room. His figure is ripped, and he walks well—but Mike Ferrara, at whom it is aimed, is steadfastly looking at his notes.

From the witness chair, where I am already seated, I can see two reasons Tacopina, so famous for his suits, is running around in his blazing white shirt with spread collar:

1. He has spent the three-day break in the gym and thinks he looks sensational without his jacket.
2. His *deltoids* and *latissimi dorsi* are so swollen from trying to knock me down all morning, he fears a *split* in the jacket's gorgeous lining.

It is seeing things like this that show you what a state I am in. Nearly two days of being interrogated by Joe Tacopina, and I am like Joseph K in *The Trial* seeing the "two gentlemen's faces pressed cheek-to-cheek" as they turn the knife in his heart twice.

*   *   *

The Duke of Ferrara, sleeker, smarter, smoother than Tacopina, takes over in the late afternoon and conducts the "redirect." The purpose of Mike's redirect is to "clarify issues" that Tacopina has raised in the jury's mind during his "cross-examination."

---

have accidentally revealed the motive." Joe Tacopina showed E. Jean Carroll embarrassed Trump at Bergdorf Goodman. Humiliation famously triggers his rage," *Salon*, May 1, 2023.

Some of the issues Tacopina has raised in the jury's mind are: why don't I remember the exact date . . . why I didn't come forward sooner . . . what have I bought at Bergdorf's since 1996 . . . why I said I liked *The Apprentice* . . . why certain men did not make my Most Hideous Men List . . . why I advised my "Ask E. Jean" readers to go to the police when *I* did not go to the police . . . what George Conway told me about suing Donald Trump . . . when exactly did George Conway recommend Robbie Kaplan . . . why I said to Anderson Cooper, "Most people think of rape as being sexy" . . . how much money I make a year on my Substack . . . how much money I was paid for writing the article in *New York* magazine . . . why I didn't sue Les Moonves . . . why I led a walking tour called "The Most Hideous Men in New York" . . . why I am always saying I'm fabulous when I am suing Trump for emotional and reputational damages . . . what about all those party invitations I'm continually being sent . . . why I steal a plot from *Law & Order*. . . why I think I was fired by *Elle* . . . when was the last time I had sex . . . why I haven't been diagnosed with depression . . . why I haven't been diagnosed with anxiety . . . would I have sued Trump if he *didn't* call me a liar . . . would I have sued Trump if he had said it was "consensual". . . and would we all be in this courtroom today if it weren't for a silly disagreement over whether or not I "consented."

Mike, tall, calm, cool in a blue-gray suit the color of a sled dog's eyes, cleans up every bit of Tacopina's barf by the simple expedient of asking me clear, brisk, questions—so straight and blunt he makes Tacopina look like, as the *New York Times* described him, "a rookie." Nearing the end, Mike clears up the "consensual issue":

Q. Was there ever any doubt in your mind that Mr. Trump had penetrated you with his fingers and penis?

A. Never a doubt.

Q. Was there a doubt in your mind that you tried to shove him away?

A. Oh, no. There was never a doubt about that.

Q. Was there ever a doubt in your mind regarding whether you had consented to this, to what he had done to you?

A. Never.

Q. Was there ever a doubt in your mind that you tried to fight him off?

A. No. Never. That's how I got out.

Q. Before you spoke to Ms. Birnbach how, if at all, had you processed all of that information?

A. I had *not* processed it. I was just happy to somehow find myself alive when I thought I had been killed. It was just—it seemed like the whole front of my head had been wiped out. I couldn't think. But *whatever* I did, I did the right thing because I got out. So, it was going to take my brain a few minutes to catch up with my body. My body did the right thing, my body got out, so it took—I was a little behind on putting it together.

*   *   *

And then—incredibly!—despite Twitter's blazing for the last three days with women telling their own "I did not scream" stories,[*] despite news sites reporting that Tacopina's cross could be

---

[*] Friends, the Twitter stories hashtagged #IDidntScreamEither and #IDidntScream present a completely different reality than what the Trump team is trying to paint in court, viz:

"I was 17, a waitress in the summer. Had no ride home. In a car with my 35 year old married boss with 2 kids I trusted. He offered to "take me home." I felt stupid for getting into his car. Who would believe me? Who would I scream to? #IDidntScreamEither" "the most tone-deaf cross-examination in a rape trial since *To Kill a Mockingbird*,* despite the networks' amazement that Tacopina is "yelling" and "berating" a "victim of sexual assault,"† I kid you not, Friends, Tacopina stands up for his "recross," and, happily strangling with rage, spends five minutes asking me why I did not scream.

And then, *this:*

MR. TACOPINA: Thank you, Ms. Carroll.
THE COURT: Mr. Ferrara, anything else?
MR. FERRARA: Nothing further, your Honor.
THE COURT: Ms. Carroll, you are excused. Thank you. (*To the jury*) Ladies and Gentlemen, tomorrow morning, 10:00 a.m. And thank you, all.

And I am done! I am finished! I step down from the witness chair. And, without remembering one single death threat, night-

---

"Never ask a woman who has been attacked why she didn't scream. I was attacked at 19 in my own Toronto apartment and was totally unable to squeak out a syllable. Grow up and respect our experience. #IDidntScream"

"I was raped, beaten and sodomized in 1998. I still remember biting my lip until it bled to keep from yelling out. It would have been worse if I did. #BelieveWomen #IDidntScream"

"Well #IDidntScream when I was molested by a church leader on a bus full of my friends and his wife 20 rows up. I froze. I counted electricity poles along the highway. I disassociated and cracked my brain into pieces. And then we went to Dairy Queen. We don't scream. #WeSurvive"

* Mitchell Epner, *Daily Beast.* April 27th, 2023.

† "*Cross-examination Heats Up in Trump Rape Trial*," April 28th, 2023, MSNBC's Morning Joe.

mare, or tear, without a thought for the months of prep, the fits of insomnia, the fear I would fail, fuck up, and forget, I smile up at Judge Kaplan who, looking down at something on his desk, doesn't see me—with the liquid blue runway rising up with a chirping farewell, I walk out of the courtroom.

NOTE 1

The Ruth Bader Ginsburg Conference Room never saw such hugging and screaming. Mike Ferrara? I estimate he hugs me about fifteen times. From the ecstatic look on Shawn G. Crowley's face, I suspect she is amazed I made it through two minutes of Tacopina, let alone two days.

And the woman who thought "we might have a case"? The woman whose energy keeps us going through New York Superior Court, federal court, the United States Court of Appeals, the DC Court of Appeals, and the eighty-fifth (Bill Barr) and eighty-sixth (Merrick Garland) United States attorneys general defense of Donald Trump? What is Ms. Robbie Kaplan doing? Why, Friends, Ms. Robbie is sittin' at the head of the conference table smiling to herself and making notes for her summation!

NOTE 2

Dinner from Shun Lee Palace and many bottles of cold Veuve Clicquot are arrayed in the Ruth Bader Ginsburg Conference Room. Matt Craig, the handsome Honorary Woman, seizes the first bottle, and pops the cork.

"You can go ahead," says Mike. "*I'm* not touching it."

"*I* pass," says Robbie.

"Nope," says Shawn.

Not one attorney, partner, associate, law school dean, witness, or paralegal in the Ruth Bader Ginsburg Conference Room will go within ten feet of the stuff.

"Superstition," says Joshua, the Man with the 583 IQ, to me, while he backs away from Matt. "We have *nine* more witnesses to put on the stand. No champagne unless we *win*."

Now, it so happens that Matt Craig is the man most responsible for dragging me—kicking and screaming, unruly and dumb—through the weeks and weeks of preparation for depositions and trial.

"Well," says Matt, as he and the bottle emit happy shock waves. "E. Jean is done. And I'm *drinkin'*!"

19

GEORGIA O'KEEFFE VISITS
THE COURTROOM

I remember to rise, make coffee, wash, eat breakfast, have hair and makeup, read notes, dress, meet the Carroll Team in the lobby of the Sixty LES, and travel with Robbie Kaplan to the Daniel Patrick Moynihan United States Courthouse, but I cannot remember what happened in the courthouse yesterday. I remember Matt opening the champagne and everyone refusing to drink it. I remember the Shun Lee noodles—and, really, who could *forget* Shun Lee noodles—but I cannot, for the life of me, remember a single word I said on the stand yesterday. Or any other day, for that matter.

Do I go to the ladies' room and splash water on my face like people do in movies when they cannot remember? Let me ask you, Friends: Would *you* splash water on *your* face if *you* were spending over $600 a day for hair and makeup? Why would I *want* to remember "Now, when you say, 'rummaging around your vagina,' that's different than inserting a finger inside your vagina?" People who study this kind of thing would say my forgetting is a "survival strategy," or "stress chemicals." I would say my brain is just fed up.

*   *   *

Robbie, Mike, Matt, and I are in the courtroom sitting at the Carroll table. It is May 2, 2023, the fifth day of trial. At 9:50 a.m. Judge Kaplan bids everyone a bracing "good morning," and says, "Ms. Crowley, call your next witness," and Shawn G. Crowley replies, "Thank you, your Honor. The plaintiff calls Lisa Birnbach."

*　　*　　*

I look around. Lisa Birnbach is my best friend, and so let me tell you at once: Lisa Birnbach is *dazzling*. Lisa Birnbach is *hilarious*. And here she comes, walking briskly down the runway looking pale and severe as Georgia O'Keeffe in the New Mexico desert out to listen to the coyotes howl. When she takes the stand, this sparkling wit of a thousand New York dinner parties, this Gracie Award winner for most humorous radio show, is so somber, so stark, and so serious, I half expect Alfred Stieglitz to materialize and take her picture.

I will tell you one story about Lisa Birnbach. My house floods. Lisa gives me half her wardrobe. Wait. I will tell you another story. I collapse in front of the Minetta Tavern in the Village. I fall to the pavement on East Fifty-second Street. I pee my pants in Central Park. This is how uncontrollably Lisa makes me laugh.

Born into one of Manhattan's prominent families, raised on East Ninety-third Street in Manhattan and in Greenwich, Connecticut, she is the mother of Sam Haft the musician, Boco Haft the writer, and Maisie Haft the director, and is married to Michael Porte, the advertising mensch. Her dog is Sheila. Her dog before that was Henry. Her dog before that was Archie. In other words, I have known Lisa Birnbach for thirty-four years. She is an admirable journalist, writes for *Vanity Fair*, *New York*, the *New Yorker*, the *Washington Post*, etc., was a TV writer and commentator, and one of the twenty-two books she writes is *The*

Preppy Handbook. You probably went to school with her. She is tall, dark, and striking. She makes an apricot pandowdy for my breakfast, puts a pinch of salt in my coffee, and I place myself in her heart. Lisa Birnbach is the person I call right after Trump attacks me, and when I say "right after," I mean minutes.

*   *   *

United States District Court, Southern District of New York

Jury Trial, Tuesday, May 2, 2023

COURT TRANSCRIPT

DIRECT EXAMINATION OF LISA BIRNBACH

BY MS. CROWLEY:
——*After establishing who Lisa is, her journalism, our friendship . . .*

Q. Okay. So, you have testified that at some point Ms. Carroll called you and told you that Donald Trump had assaulted her. Where were you when you received this call?
A. I was giving my children dinner in our kitchen at home.
Q. Do you recall what date you received the call?
A. No.
Q. What year was it?
A. It was 1996.
Q. How do you know that?
A. I know that because I believe E. Jean called me, of all her friends and acquaintances, because she knew I had just been at Mar-a-Lago.

*   *   *

Oddly, I actually do not recall reading Lisa's famous *New York* magazine piece at the time. Dr. Leslie Lebowitz, the psychologist who interviewed me for three days, believes I call Lisa because "she is the funniest person E. Jean knows, and that if E. Jean calls Lisa and tells her what happened, and if Lisa laughs, then the terrible thing that just happened to E. Jean wouldn't be so terrible."

My opinion? It is 1996, and our cell phones are creaky. I think I call Lisa because I know she asked the phone company for an easy number so her little kids can remember it, and because it is a number so easy a three-year-old kid can remember it, I can dial it when I can't even think.

Q. What time of day was it when Ms. Carroll called you?

A. It was sometime between, I would say, 6:00 and 7:00.

Q. How do you know that?

A. Well, I had two kids at the time, and one was 6 and one was 3, and that's when they ate.

Q. What was the first thing that Ms. Carroll said when you picked up the phone?

A. She said, "Lisa, you are not going to believe what happened to me."

Q. How did she sound?

A. Breathless. Hyperventilating. Emotional. Her voice was doing all kinds of things.

Q. Was she laughing?

A. She may have been a little bit laughing. It sounded like she had just this surge of adrenaline.

Q. What did she say after she said, "Lisa, you are not going to believe what just happened?"

——Lisa says she hears how I run into Trump, the "Hey, you're that advice lady," the looking for a gift, the flirty badinage, the ending up in the lingerie department.

Q. Ms. Birnbach, I'm going to stop you here. What did you think when Ms. Carroll told you that she went with Donald Trump to the lingerie department?
A. I was surprised that she did that. I thought it was kind of nutty. I didn't think it was dangerous because, you know, I had just spent a few days with him. He didn't strike me as dangerous.

*   *   *

To spend those "few days with him," and do the *New York* piece, Lisa flies to Florida on Trump's private plane. To appear as a witness in court today? Lisa pays her own airfare from California, pays her own New York accommodations, her transportation, her food, gets no sleep, goes through "prep" with Shawn and Mike, and because she bravely takes the stand, she is plagued with threats and harassed with antisemitic messages, and is, in fact, because she is Jewish, being hounded with hatred on social sites as I write this very sentence.

*   *   *

"What did Ms. Carroll tell you happened after they got to the lingerie department?" asks Shawn, and Lisa tells Shawn: "He said, 'Why don't you try this on?' and E. Jean, continuing sort of the jokey banter that they had, she said to him, 'Why don't *you* try it on?' And then the next thing that happened is they were both in the dressing room and he slammed her against the wall . . . And E. Jean said to me many times, 'He pulled down my tights! He pulled down my tights!' Almost like she couldn't believe it. She was still processing what had just happened to her. It had *just* happened to her. 'He pulled down my tights!' And then he penetrated her."

"Did she say *how* he penetrated her?" asks Shawn.

And Lisa says, "Yes. She said with his penis."

And Shawn says, "What did you say after Ms. Carroll described this to you?"

And Lisa says to Shawn: "As soon as she said that, even though I knew my children didn't know the word, I ducked out of the room—my phone was wireless—and I said, I whispered, 'E. Jean, he raped you. You should—'"

"What? I'm sorry?" says Shawn.

And Lisa says, "I said to E. Jean: 'You should go to the police.' *'No, no, no, I don't want to go to the police.'*"

And Shawn says, "That's what E. Jean said in response?"

And Lisa says, "That's what she said."

*   *   *

What is it like watching Lisa Birnbach on the stand? If you have ever been at a cocktail party and a misogynistic oaf tells everyone in the room that you are a conniving liar, and your best friend walks up to him and slugs him in the jaw—*that* is what it is like watching Lisa Birnbach on the stand.

*   *   *

"What did you say to that?" says Shawn.

And Lisa says, "I said, 'He raped you. I will take you to the police.' And she said, 'I don't want to go to the police. We had a fight.'" And Shawn says, "Did Ms. Carroll use the word 'rape' to describe what had happened?" And Lisa says, "No." And Shawn says, "How did she describe it?" And Lisa says, "'We fought.' You know, it sounded like a physical fight. She tried to get free from him. She did not like that word. She did not want me to say that word." And Shawn says, "What did Ms. Carroll say after you said, 'I'll take you to the police,' or 'I'll go to the police with you?'" And Lisa says, "She said, 'Promise me you will never speak of this again. Promise me you will tell no one.' And I promised her both those things."

"How did the call end?" says Shawn.

And Lisa says:

"I said, 'Please, come here. I will give you dinner. You can stay here.' Because she lived out of town. She said, 'No, I just want to go home.'"

"How long, approximately how long did the call last?"

And Lisa says:

"Three minutes. Four minutes."

"What did you do after you hung up the phone?" says Shawn.

And Lisa says:

"I think I reheated my kids' nuggets."

NOTE 1

Poor old W. Perry Brandt, the fluffy and ferocious Pillsbury Doughboy from Kansas, muffs his cross-examination of Lisa Birnbach. Like Tacopina, he never grasps that Lisa's testimony is *personal*. Not political—"My friend wasn't raped by a president," Lisa tells the court. "She was assaulted by a guy, a real estate guy, who liked women and harassed a lot of women." Therefore, Perry's continually repeating things Lisa says about Trump on her podcast such as "He's like herpes. We got him, and we can't get rid of him" end up entertaining the jury, instead of convincing them.

20

"SO LET'S GRAB A LITTLE PUSSY"

Oct 1, 2024

"Donald Trump views women as for his entertainment. He is a serial predator."

Jessica Leeds' story will air on NewsNation's post-debate coverage tonight.

0:00 / 1:00

These are some photographs of the next witness.

I am showing you her picture before she gets here so you can imagine what she looks like in 1979 or 1980, when a handsome blond man sitting in first class on a Braniff flight to New York notices her sitting in coach, and sends a flight attendant to invite her to sit with him.

THE COURT: Next witness.

MR. FERRARA: The plaintiff calls Jessica Leeds.

And may old bats like Jessica Leeds never lose their oomph! It's what keeps us alive! Walking down the runway, using her cane as a fashion accessory, her silvery hair cut in a great-looking Audrey Hepburn boyish crop, she arrives at the court reporter's station, swears to tell the truth, and takes the witness chair.

DIRECT EXAMINATION

BY MR. FERRARA:
——*After some preliminary questions about where she lives (Ashville), her age (eighty-one), her career (stockbroker) . . .*

Q. So when you boarded the plane, where were you sitting?
A. I was sitting in the back part of coach.
Q. Did you change your seat?
A. Yes.
Q. What happened?
A. The stewardess came down the aisle, one of the stewardesses came down the aisle and asked me if I would like to come up to first class.
Q. What did you say?
A. Yes, of course.

*   *   *

This event occurs in 1979, 1980—a year or two before Jessica becomes a stockbroker and moves into a great little apartment in a brownstone on East Eighty-third and runs into fellow broker Buddy Leeds in the Eighty-sixth Street subway station (Friends, she marries him). 1979 is when she is a top salesperson for a paper company and flies three weeks out of four. I recall these glamorous days of airline travel in my profile of Jessica in the

Atlantic.[*] You may remember Braniff's turquoise, scarlet, emerald, and orange planes and sipping the cold martini brought to you by a Braniff attendant dressed in head-to-toe Halston.

> This is the era when buying an airline ticket means putting on our best clothes and boarding a cocktail party heading for New York or Chicago or Miami or any jazzy city, USA. The party lacks zip unless somebody very rich or very pretty is present—because to fly fifteen hundred miles without a beautiful woman next to you is like sitting in a restaurant without being served an entrée.
>
> Men in first class will size up the female passengers before boarding and hold a brief conference with the check-in crew. Or, alternatively, a helpful flight attendant on a jumbo jet to LA will simply stand in the aisle next to me waving people away and rearranging the seating chart so that an extremely tall chap with hair like greased felt can have the spot by me. And, after the plane takes off, following the meal, the chap can show me a photo of his private plane and then show me a photo of his Rolls-Royce, and then show me his erection.

Q. So where did you—where were you seated at that point?
A. So I came up and it was the first seat on the right side of the bulkhead.
Q. Did you know who Mr. Trump was?
A. No. I was working out of Connecticut, living in Connecticut,

---

* "Donald Trump Is Waiting for You in First Class," *Atlantic*, September 11, 2020.

and so I wasn't aware of the social scene or the real estate scene in New York City.

Q. What, if any, conversation did the two of you have?

A. I don't remember anything substantial. It was just chat.

——*She tells me, "We talk about him. He doesn't ask me any personal questions."*

*　　*　　*

You might like to know what Jessica is wearing on that plane.

"I have my best suit," Jessica tells me. "A brown tweed. I have a blouse that is a satiny fabric, shiny, and paisley print. Oh, I love that suit! And my hair is dark, *dark* brown. I think I look terrific. It's a *fabulous* outfit. It really is. I hang on to it for quite a while, but—I never . . . wear . . . it . . . again."*

Q. Did there come a time when that (*chatting*) changed?

A. Well, they served a meal, and it was a very nice meal, as it was Braniff's reputation to do, and it was cleared, and we were sitting there when all of a sudden Trump decided to kiss me and grope me.

Q. What led to that? Was there conversation?

A. There was no conversation. It was like out of the blue.

Q. Do you recall saying anything that would have suggested to Mr. Trump that that was an invited advance?

A. Not at all.

Q. What did you—please describe, if you would, what he did exactly.

A. Well, it was like a tussle. He was—his hands—he was trying

---

* *Atlantic* article.

to kiss me, he was trying to pull me towards him. He was grabbing my breasts, he was—it's like he had 40 zillion hands, and it was a tussling match between the two of us. And it was when he started putting his hand up my skirt that kind of gave me a jolt of strength, and I managed to wiggle out of the seat, and I went storming back to my seat in coach.

Q. Were you saying anything as this was happening?

A. I don't think there was a word, or a sound made by either one of us.

Q. What about—did you scream or yell?

A. No.

Q. What about the other people, were you able to see whether other people were reacting in the cabin?

A. I can remember thinking that the people behind us must have thought something was going on because the chair was wiggling around, and I can remember the guy sitting across the aisle from me, his eyes were like saucers. And I can remember thinking "where is the stewardess?" Why doesn't someone come and help me? And then I realized nobody was going to help me, I had to do it myself, and that's when I got the strength to get up and get out.

Q. Why didn't you yell or shout or sort of exclaim something to draw attention to what was happening?

A. Well, in my head, I think I called him a name, but, no, not—it never occurred to me to yell out.

Jessica and I are from the Silent Generation. Of course she does not "yell out." I ask Jessica *why* she thinks Trump grabs women, and Jessica, her face falling in disgust, says resignedly:

"I think he's bored. Nothing is happening, you know, so let's grab a little pussy."

21

THE NEMESIS OF DR. EDGAR P. NACE

Judge Kaplan thanks Jessica Leeds, excuses her, she swashbuckles herself off the stand with her cane, and Judge Kaplan says:

"Next witness."

Mike Ferraro sits down.

Shawn G. Crowley stands up.

She says:

"The plaintiff calls Robert Salerno."

And Mr. Salerno, senior vice president of Bergdorf Goodman at the time of the assault, walks down the runway, a self-possessed, confident chap in a dark sports coat and gray slacks, takes the oath, and establishes the following facts:

1. Bergdorf Goodman's sixth-floor lingerie department is not busy.
2. Bergdorf Goodman's sixth-floor lingerie department in spring is particularly not busy.
3. Bergdorf Goodman's sixth-floor lingerie department on Thursday nights in spring is not busy at all.
4. In fact, Bergdorf Goodman's sixth-floor lingerie department's sales account for less than one percent of Bergdorf Goodman's revenue.

5. Bergdorf Goodman had no security cameras on the sixth floor.

6. Bergdorf Goodman's sales associates sometimes are not to be found in the lingerie department because they are prospecting about the store with clients choosing new handbags or shoes.

7. Bergdorf Goodman's dressing room doors being left open drives V.P. Robert Salerno crazy, and he walks around closing them because, as he says, "I am anal."

8. Bergdorf Goodman's culture is to respectfully "ignore and not give attention to celebrities," because celebrities don't want "people oohing and aahing."

9. V.P. Robert Salerno saw Donald Trump in Bergdorf Goodman.

10. The Bergdorf Goodman dressing rooms are unlike any other dressing rooms in New York—so large and comfortable that Jackie Kennedy, when she worked as a book editor at Doubleday, would come to Bergdorf Goodman to have lunch and then she would spend the afternoon editing books in one of the fourth-floor dressing rooms.

*   *   *

Judge Kaplan thanks V.P. Robert Salerno, excuses him, and says, "Next witness."

Shawn G. Crowley sits down.

Robbie Kaplan stands up.

And who does Robbie Kaplan call as the next witness? Nobody but the temptress, the bane, the rival, the siren, the scourge of Dr. Edgar P. Nace—the very woman who causes him several times to cry out in agony: "I just can't imagine what she finds to talk about that takes three *days*!"

*   *   *

Earrings flashing, hair fulgurating like the tail of a comet, she takes the runway. She takes the oath. She takes the chair. She takes the jury. And when I say she "takes" the jury, I am referring to the thing Dr. Leslie Lebowitz does that Dr. Edgar P. Nace "just can't imagine."

She doesn't talk shop.

Instead, she tells the jury a story about a loving and understanding father who suddenly starts nagging and scolding his fifteen-year-old son and cannot understand why he can't stop yelling at him. . . . She tells another story about a married couple hearing screeching tires and their little child nearly getting hit by a car, the most searing event in their marriage, and fifteen years later the couple is amazed to find themselves arguing whether it happened in Brooklyn or Manhattan. . . . She tells another story about a Vietnam war veteran who suddenly suffers a panic attack in the middle of the street thirty years after the war, and it turns out the tang of Vietnamese cooking is coming from a corner restaurant. . . . And another tale about a friend of her mother who was a child in Finland during World War II and she was holding her mother's hand on a beautiful spring day when the bombs began to fall, and the "force of the bombs blew her mother's hat off, and rather than doing the obvious, rational thing that we all imagine we would do, which is scoop her daughter up and run for safety, she dropped her daughter's hand and ran for her hat."

Now, Friends, you and I know that Dr. Leslie Lebowitz with her doctorate from Duke, her creation of the trauma protocol for the United States Air Force, her work with the Victims of Violence Program at Harvard, her formation of the sexual trauma protocol for the National Center for PTSD run by the US Department of Veterans Affairs—we *know* Dr. Leslie Lebowitz could shock the jury with violent, bloody, stabbing, sickening "psychological" testimony. Hell, just hearing her credentials could turn a juror's stomach.

Instead, she tells a story about a hat—a story so human, so descriptive of what happens to a person experiencing a traumatic event, that by the time Robbie asks Dr. Lebowitz if I am harmed by Trump's attack, the jury understands better than Sigmund Freud why I have flashbacks and never have sex again.

*　　*　　*

What devastation Dr. Edgar P. Nace will rain down upon Dr. Leslie Lebowitz! What terror he will strike into the heart of Dr. Leslie Lebowitz as he strides down the runway in his calm dark tie and brown tweed jacket! How massively Tacopina will reward him with the $750 an hour! What a rousing defense of Donald Trump Dr. Edgar P. Nace will deliver with his Michigan Alcoholism Screening Test! His Beck Anxiety Inventory! His Beck Depression Inventory! His Adverse Childhood Experiences from ACE study! And his Posttraumatic Stress Disorder Symptom Scale!

But, alas, Tacopina reports that Dr. Nace has fallen ill. Robbie offers—and is sincere in her offer—to fly members of the Carroll Team to Texas and take his testimony on video to show to the jury. But Tacopina, who calls Dr. Nace again during the lunch break, returns with the sad report that, no, Dr. Nace is not well enough to give testimony. "I *am* sorry," says Robbie. And, indeed, Dr. Nace dies on September 23, 2023.

22

THE GIRL CALLED "BOOM BOOM"

This is my sister Cande and me with Sergeant Preston, the star of the absolutely sensational radio show *Sergeant Preston and the Yukon.* Cande is the adorable one holding the ice cream bar. I am the one who looks like she is on the fundraising committee of the Junior League.

You see that smile on Cande's face? She drives from Cocoa Beach to New York and smiles like that when Matt Craig calls her as the next witness. She smiles like that when she walks down the runway in her black Piazza Sempione suit. She smiles like that when she raises her hand and swears she will tell the truth, and she smiles like that when she tells the jury that "the Carrolls" smile all the time.

She smiles all the time when W. Perry Brandt asks if she is surprised that "E. Jean had not told you about the sexual assault," and she smiles all the time when she says, "No," because "we didn't talk about those things"; and she smiles up at Judge Kaplan when he thanks her, and she smiles when he says she is dismissed.

My sister Barbie Carroll is in court.

She smiles at Cande as she walks back up the runway, and Cande smiles at her, and Barbie smiles at me after Cande exits and drives back to Cocoa Beach, and, indeed, Barbie has, like Cande, smiled at me without letup through my entire three days of testimony.

*   *   *

Matt Craig sits down.

Mike Ferrara stands up.

Judge Kaplan says:

"Call your next witness, Mr. Ferrara."

And Mike says:

"Plaintiff calls Natasha Stoynoff to the stand."

Natasha—holding dual citizenship in Canada and the United States, with a mother from Macedonia and a father the descendant of a 6-foot-7-inch Macedonian revolutionary who had his head whacked off and carried through town by the Greeks in 1913, appears at the top of the runway—tall, jolly, raspberry-cheeked, piles of champagne-colored hair, and with as magnificent a bosom as ever seen on Judge Lewis A. Kaplan's runway, or as Natasha describes herself: "One hundred percent Eastern Bloc, honey!"

I write a series for the *Atlantic* about some of Trump's accusers—Jessica Leeds, Jill Harth, Karina Virginia, Kristin Anderson, Alva Johnson, and, naturally, I begin the series with Natasha. Natasha is a fellow magazine journalist, currently working on two TV pilots, and is the author of sixteen books. She was one of *People*'s star reporters, her beat was Trump, and, of course, she flies to Mar-a-Lago to do the "first wedding anniversary" with Trump and a very pregnant Melania.

> This is during the heyday of *People*'s "Sexiest Man Alive" and "Most Beautiful People," and by heyday, I mean just *after* Nora Ephron says she could get on a plane with her *People* magazine, buckle her seat belt, and read it start to finish before her flight took off—and just *before* Ephron says she is no longer able to identify a single celebrity in it. It is one of America's most-read magazines, and by 2004, Natasha (who would eventually be named one of the Most Intriguing People of 2016) is *the* Trump reporter.[*]

Natasha interviews the happy couple outdoors at Mar-a-Lago. ("Trump is frustrating to interview," says Natasha. "If all you need are sound bites, he's easy. He's got his one sentence ready for

---

[*] My piece, "I Moved on Her Very Heavily," *Atlantic*, August 26, 2020.

you. If you want something deeper, that's a challenge. Because he doesn't do deep.") Melania goes upstairs to change wardrobe and prepare for the next photo. Natasha and Trump are left alone in a shady area near the pool, during the break.

DIRECT EXAMINATION

BY MR. FERRARA:

Q. What happened during that break?

A. Donald said, "I'd like to have you see this really *great* room—this painting in this really *great* room. There's this really *great* room we've got. Have you seen it?" I can't remember his exact words, something like that. And I said, "No, I haven't." And so, he led the way to show me this room.

Q. So let me ask you a question just to back up really quickly. So where were you conducting the interview, this sort of one-on-one interview of Mr. Trump?

A. So while Melania was doing the photo shoot by the pool, we were all in the backyard. We are sitting in a little area closer to the back doors that has couches and tables and that's where I was talking to him.

Q. How many people were around at that point?

A. Well, all the people in that photo you showed. (*A hideous photo, Friends. Trust me.*) And probably lots of staff going in and out, so I guess—in total—maybe 20 people were sort of back and forth.

Q. So where did you go with Mr. Trump after he said, "I want to show you this room?"

A. So we—I followed him, and we went in through these back doors and down a hall and turned right into a room.

Q. Who was with you at that point?

A. Just he and I.

Q. So what happened next?

A. So we—we walked into a room, and I'm looking in this room, and I went in first, and I'm looking around, I'm thinking, "wow, really nice room, wonder what he wants to show me," and he—I hear the door shut behind me. And by the time I turn around, he has his hands on my shoulders, and he pushes me against the wall and starts kissing me, holding me against the wall.

Q. Was anyone else in the room at this time?

A. Nobody else.

Q. What did you—how did you react?

A. I started—I tried to push him away.

Q. Had you—had anything been said up until that point when you walked into the room? Did he say anything? Or did you say anything?

A. No, not that I recall.

Q. Did you say anything to invite that conduct?

A. No.

Q. So what—I think you said you tried to shove him away. What happened?

A. He came toward me again, and I tried to shove him again.

Q. What was he doing with—let's say the rest of his face and body?

A. Well, he was kissing me, and, you know, he was against me and just holding my shoulders back.

——*Natasha and I talk about him "shoving his tongue."*

Q. Did you—what, if anything, did you say while this was happening?

A. I didn't say words. I couldn't. I tried. I mean, I was just flustered and sort of shocked and I—no words came out of me. I tried, though. I remember just sort of mumbling.

Q. Did you tell him to stop?

A. I couldn't say the words.

Q. Did you scream?

A. No.

Q. How long—do you recall how long that went on for?

A. A few minutes.

Q. How did it end?

A. A butler came into the room.

Q. Sorry? You said the butler? Was that the person's actual title?

A. That was his title. The butler or head butler was my contact for the day.

Q. What did the butler do?

A. Came to tell us that Melania was finished changing, it was time to go back to the couch area and resume the interviews.

Q. How did Mr. Trump react when the butler came in?

A. He stopped doing what he was doing.

Q. Were you able to perceive whether the butler saw what had been happening?

A. I don't know if he saw, but to my mind, I gave him a kind of "get me out of here" look, and I felt like he understood.

Q. So, what happened? What happened next?

A. The butler led us back to the couch area, and Melania was on her way, and Trump said a few things to me.

Q. What did he say to you?

A. He said, "Oh, you know we are going to have an affair, don't you? You know, don't forget what—don't forget what Marla said, 'best sex she ever had.' We are going to go for steak, we are going to go to Peter Luger's. We're going to have an affair."

Q. What was the reference to Marla? What was that?

A. Marla Maples, his second wife, was quoted on the cover of the *Daily News* or the *New York Post*, I think, as saying that Donald Trump was "the best sex she ever had."

Q. What did you say in response to any of this?

A. I had trouble speaking. I was so shocked and flustered at what had just transpired and what was transpiring that, like, I couldn't get words out. I was just choked up. I couldn't answer him.

Q. At some point did Marla return—sorry, pardon me, at some point did Melania return?

A. Yes.

Q. And what happened at that point?

A. So, she sat down next to him and then he suddenly was very doting on her, and I was to continue the interview, which I did.

Q. How were you able to continue the interview after what had just happened?

A. Well, it was not easy. But I had my questions with me. I sort of went on autopilot, and I just knew I had to go back with my work done. So, I really went on kind of an autopilot thing.

*　　*　　*

Natasha says to me: "I'd been asking questions about how happy they are, how excited they are about the baby, and meanwhile he's telling me we're going to have an affair. And then Melania sits down, and I start asking questions, and it is a *complete lie*. I mean, everything he is saying now in the interview I *know is a complete lie.*"

*　　*　　*

The photo Natasha mentions? It is taken at Mar-a-Lago. Trump is standing between Natasha and Melania smiling like a hyena. It is taken after Natasha says he assaults her. I cannot stand looking at it.

The photo *I* like?

Natasha in the gym, wearing boxing gloves, gleamy all over with sweat and a big ear-to-ear, one fist raised in triumph. And who is beside her? Who has a towel over his left shoulder? Who is grinning like a tiger? World Heavyweight Champion, Mike Tyson. You can see it on Natasha's Twitter—@Tashka9—and enjoy a little chuckle about what she says.

*   *   *

"Norman Mailer is so amazed at how hard Natasha can hit that whenever she stays with him and his wife, Norris, in Provincetown, she and Norman put on the gloves and they spar on the back porch," I write in the *Atlantic*: "Each new boxing trainer tells Natasha that she should turn professional. Her punch is between hospitalization and murder. Her nickname is Boom Boom. *Boom Boom*? One can imagine the rest."

Or maybe one can't imagine it. Because, you see, Natasha's continuing fantasy is to rewind the clock and "to have knocked down Trump." She could have done it too. She was in great shape in 2004. That's the thing. We all wanted to knock him down, but Natasha Stoynoff could really have done it.

23

"THAT'S MY WIFE"

Judge Kaplan excuses Natasha, and for the rest of the afternoon, and for an hour the next morning, former president Donald J. Trump, his once overhandsome face coated in bright apricot makeup the thickness of Elizabeth I's death mask, appears in the courtroom on the very star-hatching machines that send the six-time bankrupt real estate hustler to the White House—viz, TV screens. If Mark Barnett, the mastermind behind *The Apprentice* could take a flyweight and create a wise, trustworthy, wealthy, intellectual heavyweight, then the star of that show should have no trouble convincing an upstate jury that my lawsuit is a "big fat hoax."

The screens are in the jury box, on the attorneys' tables, and mounted above the pews for the spectators.

THE COURT: This is sworn testimony given by Mr. Trump. May I have a transcript, please.

MS. KAPLAN: Yes, you may, your Honor.

——*This is a videotaped deposition of the defendant, Donald J. Trump, taken by Robbie Kaplan at 10:22 a.m., Wednesday, October 19, 2022, in a rundown gilt room at the Mar-a-Lago Club,*

1100 South Ocean Boulevard, Palm Beach, Florida. It concludes at 3:50 p.m. with an hour's recess for lunch which Trump is too pissy to provide to Robbie, Shawn, and Matt.

It is a staggeringly brilliant performance. I am not talking here about Trump. I am talking here about Robbie Kaplan. She flatters Trump. She scorns Trump. She soothes Trump. She traps Trump. And Trump, like the Cyclopes falling for Odysseus's tricks, stumbles into most of them.

But—!

Robbie is fair. For example, she warns Trump three times she is about to show him a photo of me.

And, Friends, look what happens:

ROBBIE: In your June 21st statement that's marked as Exhibit 20, you say: "I've never met this person in my life."

TRUMP: Yes.

ROBBIE: You have *since* seen a photograph that shows you with Ms. Carroll on a receiving line—correct?

——By the way, Robbie knows it was not a "receiving line." Not a "celebrity charity." Not a "coat line." It was an NBC party. But she uses Trump's own description of it, so he understands which photo she is talking about.

TRUMP: Along with a lot of other people.

ROBBIE: So, the answer to my question is, "yes," that after you made the statement, you became aware that there's a photo of you with Ms. Carroll in a receiving line, correct?

TRUMP: At some point.

ROBBIE: Okay.

TRUMP: I saw there was a photo on a receiving line, yes.

ROBBIE: Okay. Let's mark the photo.

—EXHIBIT 23 IS MARKED FOR IDENTIFICATION

ROBBIE: You have in front of you a black and white photograph that we've marked as DJT 23. And I'm going to ask you: Is this the photo that you were just referring to?

(*Trump looks at it closely.*)

TRUMP: I think so, yes.

ROBBIE: And do you recall when you first saw this photo?

TRUMP: At some point during the process, I saw it. I guess that's her husband, John Johnson, who was an anchor for NBC. Nice guy, I thought. I mean, I don't know him, but I thought he was pretty good at what he did. I don't even know the woman. I don't know who—it's Marla.

ROBBIE: You're saying Marla is in this photo?

TRUMP: That's Marla, yeah. That's my wife.

ROBBIE: Which woman are you pointing to?

————*Friends, he is pointing to yours truly. MS. ALINA HABBA, ESQ. ENTERS THE FRAY.*

HABBA: No! That's Carroll!

TRUMP: Oh, I see.

ROBBIE: The person you pointed to was E. Jean Carroll.

HABBA: (*Pointing to Ivana Trump*) *That's* your wife.

Friends, I do *not* need to tell you, do I?

Before Robbie shows Trump the photo, she establishes the fact that he was sitting "behind the Resolute desk in the oval office" when he proclaimed to *The Hill:* "She's not my type."

Apr 25, 2023

Pictured are photos of **Marla Maples** and **E Jean Carroll** in their younger days. The similarities between the two are staggering......So much for tRump claiming **E Jean** is not his type.

282   2.1K   7K   208K

*   *   *

ROBBIE: One of the other things that you said about Ms. Carroll at the time appears in your June 24 statement, which is DJT 22, and what you said there is: "I'll say it with great respect. Number one, she's not my type." When you said that Ms. Carroll was not your type, you meant that she was not your type physically, right?

TRUMP: I saw her in a picture. I didn't know what she looked like, and I said it—and I say it with as much respect as I can, but she is not my type.

ROBBIE: And, again, when you say "type," you just referred to looking at photos. So you mean physically she's not your type?

TRUMP: Physically she's not my type, and now that I've gotten indirectly to hear things about her, she wouldn't be my type in *any* way, shape, or form.

ROBBIE: But when you were talking back on June 24, you were referring to her not being your type physically; correct?

TRUMP: I saw a photo of her.

ROBBIE: Okay.

TRUMP: And the only difference between me and other people is I'm honest. She's *not* my type.

ROBBIE: I take the three women you've married *are* all your type?

TRUMP: Yeah.

Regarding Trump's stream-of-conscious, four-hundred-odd-word October 12, 2022, statement about me, part of which says: "It is a hoax and a lie like all the other hoaxes that have been played on me for the past seven years. . . ."

ROBBIE: CNN reported that you used the word "hoax" more than 250 times in 2020. Does that sound right?

TRUMP: Could be. I've had a lot of hoaxes played on me. *This* is one of them.

ROBBIE: How would you define the word "hoax?"

TRUMP: A fake story, a false story, a made-up story.

ROBBIE: Something that's not true?

TRUMP: Something that's not true, yes.

ROBBIE: Sitting here today can you recall what else you have referred to as a hoax?

TRUMP: Sure. The Russia Russia Russia hoax. It's been proven to be a hoax. Ukraine Ukraine Ukraine hoax. The Mueller situation for two-and-a-half years hoax. The lying to the FISA court hoax. The lying to Congress many times hoax by all these people, the scum we have in our country! Lying to Congress hoax, the spying on my campaign hoax. They spied on my campaign, and now they admit it. That was another hoax. I could get a whole list of them. And this is a hoax too.

ROBBIE: This—when you say *this*?

TRUMP: This ridiculous situation that we're doing right now! It's a big, fat hoax! She's a liar and she's a sick person in my opinion. *Really* sick. Something wrong with her.

ROBBIE: Okay. In addition to the Russia Russia Russia hoax, the Ukraine Ukraine Ukraine hoax, the Mueller hoax, the lying to FISA hoax, the lying to Congress hoax, and the spying on your campaign hoax, isn't it true you also referred to the use of mail-in ballots as a hoax?

TRUMP: Yeah. I do. Sure.

HABBA: Objection.

TRUMP: I do. I think they're very dishonest. Mail-in ballots. Very dishonest.

ROBBIE: Isn't it true you yourself have voted by mail?

HABBA: Objection.

TRUMP: I do. I do. Sometimes I do. But I don't know what happens to it once you give it. I have no idea.

And so on and so on . . .

*　　*　　*

During Natasha's testimony, Mike Ferrara plays the *Access Holly-wood* tape for the jury. Now Robbie asks Trump about it:

*　　*　　*

ROBBIE: Are you familiar—I'm sure you are—with something that's often referred to as "the *Access Hollywood* tape"?

TRUMP: Yes. I am . . . And you know what I said then, and I say it now: Locker room talk. That was locker room talk. That's what goes on.

ROBBIE: And you did say in the video that you, quote, moved on her heavily; correct?

TRUMP: Excuse me?

ROBBIE: You do say in the video that you quote—

TRUMP: Yeah.

ROBBIE:—moved on her heavily?

TRUMP: I did say that, yes, absolutely.

ROBBIE: And you do say in the video that as part of trying to have sex with this woman, you took her furniture shopping; correct?

TRUMP: We actually *did* look for furniture, yes.

ROBBIE: So that was true? You actually took this woman Nancy furniture shopping?

TRUMP: I think so. I mean, it's been a long time ago. How long is that? Long time ago. But I think so. I do think so.

ROBBIE: Is that the only occasion when you took a woman shopping?

TRUMP: I think so.

* * *

ROBBIE: And you say—and again, this has become very famous—in this video: "I just start kissing them. It's like a magnet. Just kiss. I don't even wait. And when you're a star, they let you do it. You can do anything, grab them by the pussy. You can do anything." That's what you said, correct?

TRUMP: Well, historically, that's *true* with stars.

ROBBIE: True with stars that they can grab women by the pussy?

TRUMP: Well, if you look over the last million years, I guess that's been largely true. Unfortunately, or *fortunately*.

ROBBIE: And you consider yourself to be a star?

TRUMP: I think you can say that. Yeah.

NOTE 1

That the jury gets to hear Trump deny my accusation numerous times, call me a liar, a whack job, a sick woman, a hoax-puller, a disgrace, an operative of the Democratic Party, a woman with something wrong with her, 100% not his type, etc., etc., is almost beside the point.

NOTE 2

Trump tells Robbie that *she* is not his type either. This delights Robbie no end.

24

THE TACOPINA FASHION AWARDS

Well, Friends, I see I have been jamming in the witnesses. And, what with the boxing, the smiling, the reheating of the kids' nuggets, the "40 zillion hands," the death of Dr. Edgar P. Nace, Jackie Kennedy editing manuscripts in Bergdorf Goodman dressing rooms, and the big fat hoaxes, I have mushed it all together and missed half the dates. Do we even know if we are on day five, day six, or day seven?

OK. So:

Today is day seven.
Thursday, May 4, 2023.
Yesterday was day six, Wednesday, May 3
when we heard about the mother
chasing her hat,
and that the Carrolls "didn't talk about such things," and
"She's a disgrace!" and "That's my wife."
On day five, Tuesday May 2,
we heard a whisper:
"He raped you."
On day four, Monday, May 1, we heard
I should have screamed.

On day three, Thursday, April 26, we heard
I
could
have screamed.
On day two, Wednesday, April 25, we heard
I did not scream.
And on day one, Tuesday, April 24, we start
"The Trump Rape Trial."

*   *   *

Before Robbie Kaplan calls our next witness, I should probably tell you that I am starting to fall asleep during the witnesses' testimonies.

This is how relaxed I am becoming.

Not totally, not all the way relaxed, but in the morning after the rising, the washing, and the drinking coffee, I am drawing back the curtains now. I am taking five or six seconds to look at the misty gray light of the Lower East Side, and I am smiling as I slip on my sunglasses when Robbie and I arrive at the Daniel Patrick Moynihan United States Courthouse. The silvery haze of the morning makes the cameras of the world press—twice as many now that the Ed Sheeran Copyright Trial is about to reach a verdict in the same federal courthouse—look like fluttering dragonfly wings.

And I am now recognizing and nodding to the people lining the way holding up huge signs: WE BELIEVE E. JEAN. Robbie goes in the "All Attorneys" entrance, and the youngest Carroll Team attorney, tiny, serious, former Miss Porter's School pupil, the Row-and-Loro-Piana'd bride-to-be Emma DeCourcy (yes, I am staying at the Sixty LES under her name), takes me into the building and stands in line with me chatting about the Prada skirt we both saw on the RealReal and "that great Chanel jacket" and "the fantastic Dior coat"; and she waits as I disrobe in front of the reporters who are shooting me through the glass windows.

I hand the security official my old Fendi briefcase (a 1988 Christmas gift from my husband John Johnson—the first person in "the photo" Trump recognizes). I unbutton and remove my coat. I unbuckle and remove my belt. I undo and remove my jacket. I unbuckle the straps on my high heels and remove my shoes. I put everything into a Flexcon container. I walk through the backscatter X-ray scanner. I put on my shoes and buckle the straps. I put on my jacket and do it up. I put on my belt and buckle it. I carry my coat and my briefcase to the *next* security check, and Tall Rick, the redheaded, former, but still-famous NYPD homicide detective, who has been escorting Emma and me, stops jawing with the court security guys who are all former NYPD, bids melodious adieu to his comrades, and, while he commences jawing again with the *new* security guy at the electronics check, I hand over my phone for the day.

We walk down the marble hallway past Shawn G. Crowley's portrait. We arrive at the elevator. We ride up to the twenty-fifth floor and Judge Kaplan's courtroom. We join the reporters, podcasters, bloggers, influencers, spectators, wives of Trump lawyers, etc., etc. in the security line and I hand over my briefcase and coat. I unbuckle and remove my belt. I undo and remove my jacket. I unbuckle the straps on my high heels and remove my shoes. I put everything into a Flexcon container. I walk through the backscatter X-ray scanner. I put on my shoes and buckle the straps. I put on my jacket and do it up. I put on my belt and buckle it. I pick up my briefcase and coat, take three steps to adjust my shoes, walk into the vestibule of the courtroom, turn right, open an oak door with a shiny brass plate saying, "Witness

Room" and enter Carroll Headquarters—a paradise of peanut butter and jelly sandwiches, chocolate chip cookies sent by my sister Barbie and her friend Jane Michel, piles of protein bars, bunches of bananas, bags of apples, galaxies of grapes, pretzels, popcorn—a banquet! A smorgasbord! And the best coffee in the world because it is *the only* coffee in the world. I hug Helen with the Eyelashes. I hug Rachel Tuchman who is rapidly losing weight after delivering her baby, Leila, and closing in on her goal of being "the Hot Mom" at Disneyland in the bike shorts, tight T-shirt, and mouse ears. I hug the two paralegals, Ali (headed to Duke University School of Law) and Katherine (headed to University of Virginia School of Law), who are smarter than 98.9 percent of the attorneys in Manhattan. I hug Trevor Morrison, former dean of New York University School of Law. I hug Joshua the Man with the 583 IQ. I hug Shawn, Matt, and the Duke of Ferrara. Everyone is stoked. Everyone is on fire. The sun breaks through. The window turns blue. I take a peanut butter sandwich, plop myself in a chair, and watch Robbie reading Joshua's and Trevor's latest draft of a reply to an "urgent" Trump team motion as she downs a bottle of watermelon-flavored water.

*   *   *

Before Judge Kaplan arrives and asks Andy the Deputy Clerk to "get the jury," the lawyers mill about on the runway. Robbie Kaplan came out of the womb milling. Mike Ferrara is excellent at milling, Shawn G. Crowley is too cool to mill, Alina Habba, Esq. is a good miller, but Joe Tacopina is the greatest man in New York. And by "milling," I mean walking up and down the runway in front of the empty jury box, being pleasant, looking sharp, railing one another, talking about one thing while thinking of something else, and so on.

Tacopina is leaning a left buttock—as pumped as a tether ball—against the jury box as I come down the runway in my old brown Bergdorf jacket. The one I buy in 1993, and I have the Oscar de la Renta pleated cream skirt I get on the RealReal for $148.

"Miss Carroll," says Tacopina, smiling.

I stop.

"You're beating me at the dressing game," he says.

I step back.

"Mr. Tacopina," I say.

I give him the up-and-down.

"The competition is stiff," I say. "You wear $6,000 suits."

"I don't! I don't!" he cries.

"OK," I say, "$5,999 suits."

I forget to check if he is wearing the $3.2 million Patek Philippe Tiffany-blue Nautilus.

"No! No!" he cries, his eyes two merry whirligigs.

"Yes. Yes." I say. "We all read about it in *GQ* magazine. The men's *fashion* magazine. They say you wear $6,000 suits."

"They don't cost $6,000!" says Tacopina, laughing.

He opens his jacket to show me the signature of his celebrated tailor, because—*Of course*! *Of course*! *Of course*!—his suit *is* bespoke.

And, Friends, just let me tell you: Until you have seen the lining of a Tacopina jacket, you have never seen the aurora borealis.

I laugh.

Because it's like a Guy de Maupassant story. Tacopina's suit doesn't cost $6,000. I will eat my size 11 shoe if it doesn't cost *more* than $6,000.

25

THE WOMAN YOU DON'T WANT TO MESS WITH

DAY SEVEN

May 4, 2023

THE COURT: Your next witness?
MS. KAPLAN: Plaintiff calls Carol Martin.

——Carol enters the courtroom and looks down the runway like she has arrived at the state fair and is overwhelmed by the grandeur of the blue-ribbon pigs.

THE DEPUTY CLERK: Ms. Martin! (*Waving*) If you would please take the stand.
MS. MARTIN: (*Turning, looking in the deputy clerk's direction with a low, charming laugh at herself*) Oh!
THE DEPUTY CLERK: Right this way, ma'am . . .

——Carol veers in the direction of the courtroom artists, pulls her shoulders back, lifts her chin, and, with genial determination, proceeds down the runway in smart black trousers and black sweater by Vince. "Undies by Carter," Carol later tells me.

THE DEPUTY CLERK: And if you could just step around and up on the witness stand?

——*Carol steps up on the stand, nods affably to Judge Kaplan, tries to push back the heavy chair, and is turning about and lowering her shanks . . .*

THE DEPUTY CLERK: If you could please remain standing . . .

——*She shoots upright—the hardest, most unshakable witness in the history of civil justice.*

THE DEPUTY CLERK: And raise your right hand.

——*Carol raises her hand. And, with her famous low viola Carol Martin voice gives such an earnest "I do," I am dumbfounded when Tacopina tries to knock her out of the ring before lunch.*

THE DEPUTY CLERK: Thank you. Please, be seated. If you could please state your name and spell your first and last names for the record.

THE WITNESS: Sure. After I pull up the chair a little bit . . . (*Good luck, Carol! The chair is so cumbersome it would be easier to parallel park a posthole digger on West Tenth Street!*) My name is Frances Carol Martin. F-R-A-N-C-E-S, C-A-R-O-L, M-A-R-T-I-N.

*   *   *

In the history of Judge Kaplan's courtroom, nobody wants to be here *less* than Carol Martin—well, maybe Prince Andrew, Duke of York, who absolutely definitely wanted to be in Judge Kaplan's courtroom less, and settled, in February 2022, for a sum rumored to be between $3.6* and 16.3 million† with Virginia Giuffre *out of court* for sexually assaulting her when she was a teenager.

It is not that Carol is afraid. Old Carol has been striking blows against, well, what have you got?—Patriarchy? Racism? Sexism?—since the days of oversized blazers with power shoulders. No, Carol Martin does not scare. She was the first Black woman to anchor a major evening news program in New York, and you know what Carol eats for breakfast? Carol enjoys an amusing bowl of oatmeal topped with glass shards from all the ceilings she's shattered. Carol does not give two flying figs about testifying about Donald J. Trump.

But Carol has a family and a granddaughter to protect, and if the jury is safeguarded in their anonymity to prevent *them* from being harassed, threatened, poisoned, stabbed, smeared, bribed, kidnapped, roasted, scorched, run over, etc., etc., Carol is worried about her granddaughter, and she has told Robbie she does not want to be here. She has told Shawn and Mike and Matt and Noam Biale, her personal attorney, she does not want to be here. She tells me she does not want to be here about seven hundred times.

And, yet, here she is because we have known each other since the mid 1980s, because in the '90s we become close friends when we work together and both have TV shows on America's Talking (which becomes MSNBC), because a day or two after the attack in Bergdorf's I see Carol at work, standing outside the studio, and though Lisa Birnbach and I had only twenty-four hours

---

* *The Daily Beast*, August 7, 2022.

† *Time,* February 17, 2022.

before we ended our phone call with vows never to speak about it again, I see Carol standing there—*just standing there*—and that's it.

I never needed a hug so badly in my life.

We drive to her house. Her daughter, Courtney, is not home from school yet. Her husband, Joe, a television director—he would soon become Oprah's director—is not expected till later. Carol and I and her dog, Cisco, sit in her kitchen.

I tell her everything.

Carol holds both my hands very tightly in hers and says, "Tell no one. Forget it! He has two hundred lawyers. He'll bury you."

And *that* is why Carol is in court today. That is why she was subpoenaed. That is why she had to hand over every text, every email she has written in the last ten years. And let me ask you, friends:

How would *you* like it if all *your* emails and texts were turned over to Donald Trump, and Joe Tacopina could not wait to cross-examine you?

Robbie takes Carol through her direct testimony and then . . .

THE COURT: Everybody ready? All right. Cross-examination, Mr. Tacopina.

MR. TACOPINA: Thank you, your Honor.

CROSS-EXAMINATION

BY MR. TACOPINA:

Before Tacopina starts in, here is a picture of Carol and Brian Williams anchoring the 12 o'clock news. Born and raised in Detroit, Carol goes to Wayne State, works for a couple of years

MediaAttic Radio
@media_attic

Carol Martin and @11thHour anchor Brian Williams on WCBS in 1990.

©2NEWS AT NOON

0:02

as a reporter for the *Detroit Free Press*, starts her television career as a producer and on-air personality in Washington, DC, at the local NBC station, is hired away by WCBS in New York, and begins her door-crashing, gender-cracking rise to anchorwoman. Like I said: oversized blazers with power shoulders.

Now here's Tacopina:

Q. Good morning, Ms. Martin.
A. Good morning.
Q. You were asked by Ms. Kaplan on your direct examination about having to turn over and produce some text messages and emails.
A. Yes.

Q. Okay. Suffice to say you did not expect at the time you were writing those e-mails for those to see the inside of a courtroom.

A. No, certainly not.

Q. They were personal.

A. All of them, yes.

*   *   *

Now, to the *reporters* in the courtroom, the salient fact of Carol's testimony was her telling me not to go to the police:

> Ms. Martin testified that Ms. Carroll had asked if they could talk after work. They drove to Ms. Martin's home and sat in her kitchen.
>
> "'You won't believe what happened to me the other night,'" Ms. Martin recalled Ms. Carroll's telling her. "'Trump attacked me.'"
>
> "I was completely floored," Ms. Martin said.
>
> Ms. Martin said that Ms. Carroll had never used the word rape and that she instead said she had been fighting with Mr. Trump.
>
> "It was a very disconcerting thing to hear," Ms. Martin said. She said she had advised Ms. Carroll not to tell anyone or to go to the police because Mr. Trump had a lot of lawyers who would "bury her."
>
> "I am not proud that that's what I told her," Ms. Martin testified.[*]

---

[*] Benjamin Weiser and Lola Fadulu, "Regretted Advice," *New York Times*, May 4, 2023, updated May 5, 2023.

But to Tacopina? He does not care what happened in Carol's kitchen. His case rests on Carol's texts. And what with her 370-word counts, her throat-grabbing openings, her cliff-hanging conclusions, her dizzying emojis, her dazzling intelligence, her real-time tantrums, her hilarious descriptions of the aches in her back, pains in her knee, dryness of her eye, her advice for the GOP, her surreal grasp of the ungraspable, and her loathing of Donald Trump, Carol's texts and emails are as good at capturing the plot of what Vinson Cunningham of the *New Yorker* calls the "mind-shredding global catastrophes" than almost anything I know. (And, yes, she *does* calls me a "narcissist," and "scary" and "crazy" to my face many times. It is why I love her.)

And though there is not one syllable written by Carol over the last ten years that mentions, implies, suggests, or imagines a "conspiracy" to "make up a story" to "fake a rape," Tacopina, who understands the circus aspect of a trial almost as well as his client, acts like he's found *gold.*

"Okay," he says, bouncing on the balls of his feet and all but rubbing his hands together. "I'm going to discuss a few of them with you, okay, Ms. Martin? I will show them to you."

And off he goes reading snippets of Carol's texts and emails:

"I cannot bear to listen to Trump. I feel unsafe under his rule."

"I hate Donald Trump more than words."

"This man needs to be put away. God help us, but he is so unhinged"

"I hate this man who is running our world, spreading his stank all over."

"Are you traumatized by the election of Donald Trump? Here's the program for you."

"Oh my God, make it stop."

"He is out of his freaking mind. This is terrifying."

"I don't understand why that wasn't *my* prerogative to make these comments," says Carol, from the witness chair.

She is wearing a very attractive pair of pearl-framed glasses. And her hair, well, Carol and I are continually amazed at her hair. We do not understand how the older Carol gets the younger and lustier her hair looks.

"I'm not saying it's not your prerogative, Ms. Martin," replies Tacopina, rippling his upper arms to keep his triceps from atrophying.

"I don't understand why they are being offered as evidence," says Carol.

Everything Carol says sounds somehow invigorating. It is her voice. Like Yo-Yo Ma pulling a bow.

"Yeah," replies Tacopina, "you just don't *have* to understand it, unless the court rules otherwise. I'm just going to ask you some questions and you can give me honest answers. Okay?"

And here is the jewel:

Tacopina gets nowhere!

He nudges.

He pushes.

He jabs.

He clinches.

He flings a few classic left hooks.

He slugs away at Carol like Ahab riding Moby Dick. Except it is *not* a great white whale. It is a Black female icon. And the more he flails at Carol in front of a jury composed of three white members and six members of color, nine mostly upstaters all together, at least half of whom probably watched Carol on TV as they were growing up, the faster Trump and Tacopina become the most vulnerable persons in the courtroom.

And this is when a strange idea strikes me. It is such a strange idea, I bat it away. It comes back. I bat it away. It returns.

It is crazy.

It is completely crazy.

I look at the jury.

I look back at Tacopina.

He is rolling his shoulders, his eyes glowing like lights on a smoke detector, and I think: "*Why* is he doing this? He is the personal attorney for a former president of the United States. He represents Trump in the Election Interference-Hush-Money-Stormy case. He represents Trump in this sexual assault and defamation case. He is one of the top attorneys in the world, his intellect is decisive and clear, he would rather die than lose a case, and yet—here he is slugging away at a . . . grandmother? Telling a Black woman, 'You just don't *have* to understand it?'"

And for half a moment I wonder if he is concussed like a boxer who has had too many fights. I wonder the same thing when he is beating up on *another* grandmother. Of course, he could have pulled Jessica Leeds's fingernails out, and she would not have budged, but Tacopina looked small and spiteful beating up on her (instead of righteous and true); and I cannot say for certain the strange idea did not occur to me then. If it did, I brushed it away and Tacopina went right on working out on her like Sylvester Stallone in the *Rocky* meat locker scene.

But right now?

With Carol Martin on the stand?

I see a jury with four older persons, two of them women of color. I see again six members of color all together. Would not a smart attorney—and Tacopina is one of the smartest—want to challenge Carol Martin on the salient questions, and then get Carol Martin and her calm, supportive, powerful presence off the fucking stand and out of the fucking courtroom as quickly as possible? Even Judge Kaplan, the chap whose sole aim in life seems to be to run a fair trial, halts Tacopina's right-and-left combinations long enough to give him the definition of "argumentative" from *Black's Law Dictionary*.

Am I missing something? Am I completely nuts? Because here is my strange idea: Could mighty Joe Tacopina be secretly trying to throw this case?

Friends, if you have any doubts about what I just said—and, of course, you *do*, you do have doubts—I am going to ask you to sit on them. I am not saying he *is* throwing the case. But in light of happened afterward, I am saying I am amazed the idea occurs to me so soon. And you may think so too when the time comes.

26

OUR SECRET WEAPON

On Oct 12, 2022, Donald Trump makes a many-worded statement on Truth Social which I will not repeat here, because why sue someone for publishing nasty lies and then turn around, and, like a blockhead, reproduce the nasty lies in a book?

So.

This case is not just—("*just*!")—for sexual assault. It is also for defamation, hence:

Judge Kaplan thanks Carol Martin.

Robbie Kaplan sits down.

Robbie tells me in the car leaving the courthouse: "Carol Martin just won our case. Pew! Pew! Pew!" Superstitious Robbie never makes a positive forecast without letting God know that Robbie knows that God will hail destruction upon Robbie *personally* for predicting a win, so she always adds the spitting sounds, "Pew! Pew! Pew!" It is the old Russian peasant practice of spitting three times when a good thing happens to ward off the Evil Eye. Robbie picks it up when she spends a semester in Moscow when she's an undergrad at Harvard.

Shawn G. Crowley stands up and calls the next witness.

Young, cheerful, and deadly, our next witness is discovered by Robbie, Shawn, Mike, Matt, and the Carroll Team when they find her laboring—humble, uncelebrated—in the ivied oblivion of Northwestern University.

*　　*　　*

Friends, I am excessively fond of Northwestern.

When I was a sophomore at Indiana University, my boyfriend, the Olympic gold medal butterflyer and cover of *Sports Illustrated* Mike Troy—I know, I know, you expected me to say Fred Schmidt the Olympic gold medal winner and leading man on my list at the beginning of this book. But *this* is Mike Troy, and just be happy I do not fling any more world-famous athletes in here, because I can, don't ya know. Well, Mike and I—and, yes, I was retaining at the time I am writing about one hundred percent possession of my maidenhead—run off for the weekend to Chicago in Mike's lime-green 1956 Ford, Rocinante.

Our aim? The Playboy Club!

It is 1963.

One problem: I am twenty. I must be twenty-one to enjoy this zenith of culture and refinement.

Northwestern University is in Evanston, Illinois. Evanston is fourteen miles north of Chicago. We drive to Northwestern University. I pop in the Pi Beta Phi sorority house, greet the sisters, introduce myself, borrow an ID, change into my high school senior prom dress—an ice-blue Grecian chiffon number—Mike changes into his dark-blue suit in the rec room, and, laughing at each other in mutual admiration at how wonderful and ravishing we are, we wave goodbye to the Pi Phis, the gates of the City of Big Shoulders are thrown open, the door of the Playboy Club is unbarred, our IDs are examined by the "butler" at the entrance, the champagne is uncorked, and we have one of the great nights of our lives.

Little do I dream that in twenty years, I will become the first female contributing editor to *Playboy*.

And our witness?

She is Dr. Ashlee Humphreys, the soon to be famous Northwestern sociologist and pioneering social media professor, who—thanks to Robbie, Shawn, Mike, Matt, and the Carroll Team putting her on the stand—a couple of months following our trial will testify in the Ruby Freeman and Shaye Moss defamation case against Rudy Giuliani.

I do not need to remind you that Ruby and Shaye win $148 million, do I?

*   *   *

I will now try to tell you what Dr. Humphreys and her team of grad students do. What Dr. Humphreys and her team do is they take a malicious statement, calibrate how many people see it on television, in newspapers, in online articles, on social media, etc., etc., count how many people are likely to believe it when they see it, and then they determine how much it would cost the person who is maligned to repair the damage to their reputation with the people who saw the message and believed it. Taylor Swift, Robert Downy Jr., Jane Fonda have all employed reputation repair campaigns. You could not have lived through the last election season without seeing reputation repair campaigns everywhere.

And now, Friends, you can forget my simplified explanation, because here is Shawn G. Crowley leading Dr. Humphreys through the end of her direct testimony:

Q. So to summarize, Professor Humphreys, what was your conclusion about how far or how wide Mr. Trump's statements spread?

A. So my conclusion about how wide it spread in the impressions analysis was that it had between 13.7 million impressions and 18 million impressions.

Q. And again, that was the number of times that the October 12 statement was viewed?

A. Correct.

Q. And what was your conclusion about how many people who saw that statement likely believed it?

A. So my conclusion: There was on average 21 percent of people likely to believe it, and that gives you between 3.7 million and 5.6 million impressions.

Q. And what was your conclusion as to how much it would cost to repair Ms. Carroll's reputation amongst the target audience, the people who saw the statement and likely believed it?

A. So on the low, low end it would be three hundred and sixty-eight hundred thousand dollars, and on the high end it would be $2.7 million.

THE COURT: Did you mean to say $368,000?

THE WITNESS: Yes.

Q. And 2.7 million?

A. That's right.

MS. CROWLEY: One moment your Honor.

(*Counsel confer*)

MS. CROWLEY: No further questions.

THE COURT: Let's take our break. 15 minutes.

It is at about this point I wake up and look around and see a rosy, blond woman on the stand. And have to go back and read her testimony on the court transcription screen.

*   *   *

So apparently, this is the *new* way I deal with stress. Before: I could not sleep at all. Now: I cannot stay awake. And because I *am* awake, Friends, let us smile at my strange idea of Tacopina—you know, that thing I mentioned this morning when Carol was testifying. About Tacopina throwing the fight. I mean, who am I—Daphne du Maurier? There is no mystery here. Can we just forget I said it?

After all, when Tacopina is a prosecutor with the Brooklyn district attorney's office, how many cases does he win? Thirty-nine out of forty. When Tacopina starts representing gangsters and dirty police officers, how many cases does he win? More than he loses, I can tell you that. And when Tacopina turns full-on, round-the-clock, on-your-TV, big-time criminal defense attorney, who does he represent? Big-time criminals. And why do big-time criminals hire Tacopina? Because Tacopina gets big-time criminals off. And why does Trump hire Tacopina? Trump hires Tacopina *because* he beats up on grandmothers. Beating up on grandmothers works for Tacopina, or Tacopina would not beat up on grandmothers. Case closed. I must have been off my rocker to think—well, let us not go into it.

*   *   *

But still . . .

27

THE JURY FALLS IN LOVE

Remember that fifteen-minute break Judge Kaplan called a few minutes ago?

Well, the oddest thing is happening. Tacopina and Ferrara are hugging! Alina Habba, Esq. is punning! Shawn G. Crowley is smiling. Breeze is being shot by Robbie! Andy the Deputy Clerk is laughing at one of Matt's jokes—*laughing*. It would not surprise me to see them all break out in a cancan.

Judge Kaplan appears and ascends his stately perch, and, I kid you not, lets loose with a quarter of half a smile (equivalent to running off in a mad frolic through the begonias) as he asks Andy the Deputy Clerk to "get the jury." The jury arrives. Court resumes with the next witness. Judge Kaplan has asked the jury to stay late. They should be irritated, tired, crabby, sick of one another, hungry. But not this jury. You know what this jury is doing?

This jury is falling in love.

Robbie Myers, the beautiful former editor-in-chief of *Elle*, is in the witness chair and every single jury member, including the Tim Pool Guy and his acolyte the Shepherd are leaning forward and gazing at her azure brilliance. She is wearing all black. And it clings to her slender figure—Robbie Myers is a former state champion diver—with All-American precision. She is exquisite.

She is a dream woman. The jury has never seen anything quite like her before. And yet one or two of them may be wearing something Robbie featured in the fashion pages of *Elle*. They may have seen her on their movie screens, in the outfits their daughters are choosing, in the pages of the novels they are reading—Robbie Myers is the eternal, exciting, ephemeral representative of Glamour, with a capital G, and they cannot get enough of her.

She speaks in a light, low, shimmery voice. There seems to be an invisible magnet between her and the jury, a harmony. And what is she telling them? Well, Friends, she is not telling them how she and I first meet in 1985 when she is a bright, young associate editor at *Rolling Stone* and I write the famous Billy Idol cover story in which Billy calls me a cunt three or four times in the opening paragraph.

No. She is telling them what it is like to run the largest fashion magazine in the world for seventeen years. She is telling them about advice columns. She is telling them about me.

W. Perry Brandt, the terror of Kansas City commercial litigation, boyishly, shyly, commences an unbearably gentle cross, concludes with a heartbreaking smile, Shawn G. Crowley has no further questions, and she is gone.

And in the space of about twenty-four minutes, Robbie Myers has accomplished what the last two weeks of trial have been unable to accomplish. She has left the jury wondering why I have not won the Nobel for writing the greatest advice column of all time. And with this, the plaintiff rests—

Uh, well, not quite.

28

"I'M COMING BACK TO CONFRONT THAT WOMAN"

Robbie Myers, bathed in light all her own, walks up the runway, departs the courtroom—I say Robbie *Myers*, not Robbie Kaplan, though Robbie Kaplan has a light all *her* own too—and the grand assembly of belligerents gathers for one of the final sidebars with His Honor, Judge Kaplan.

The question to be debated: Am I a perjurer?

*　　*　　*

Friends, you keep a diary, right? Well, I keep a diary too, and on the witness stand a few days ago I testify that "I do not write bad things in my diary." Why? Because "if I don't write it down, I don't have to think about it."

Tacopina is impeaching that.

Impeaching means he intends to convince the jury that I am lying my jaws off. Hence, Helen with the Eyelashes and Rachel the Hot Mom have been spending their wild precious lives being bored out of their skulls reading and looking for "bad things" in my journals, and now the judge is preparing the jury to hear about the calamities, failures, blights, curses, low blows, wrecks, and woes of my life.

His Honor tells the jury: "You are about to hear a 'stipulation,' which is a fancy word for an agreement between Ms. Carroll's team and Ms. Carroll on one hand, and Mr. Trump and his team on the other. The facts to which they stipulate are deemed established for this case's purposes and you must accept them as true."

Mike stands up and tells the jury about the diaries, that one is approximately 234 and the other 266 pages in length, with "multiple short entries on each page," and admits that, yes, Tacopina is correct. "Negative entries" *have* been discovered, indeed:

1. One night I write that I am "distraught" over political developments (2020).
2. I mention the death of Cande's husband, David, on February 17 (2020).
3. An afternoon backache causes a remark. (Ditto.)

The jury withstands my ruthless villainy with majestic poise, and Mike says:

MR. FERRARA: Your Honor, Plaintiff offers this stipulation, which is marked as 78.
THE COURT: Mr. Tacopina, so stipulated?
MR. TACOPINA: Stipulated, your Honor. Yes.
THE COURT: Any other evidence on behalf of the plaintiff?
MS. KAPLAN: No, your Honor. Plaintiff rests her case.

And so, Friends, and I am admitting that tears spring into my eyes as I write this, after four years pursuing justice in the New York State Supreme Court, the United States District Court for the Southern District of New York, the United States Court of Appeals, Second Circuit, the DC Court of Appeals, and a return to the federal court for the Southern District of New York, with

the DOJ butting in every chance they get the last three of those
years,

   I
   Rest
   My
   Case.

*　　*　　*

Now the question is: Does the *defendant* rest?

Judge Kaplan, noting the "news reports out of the British Isles
attributing to Mr. Trump various statements with respect to his
possible presence here before this trial ends," wants to know if
Trump will, in fact, leave his golf course in Doonbeg, Ireland,
fly to New York and testify so that he (Judge Kaplan) can run
a fair trial and give the defendant "every chance" to be heard by
the jury.

The administrative staff of the District Court, Southern District of New York wants to know if Trump will leave his golf
course in Doonbeg, Ireland, fly to New York and testify so that
they can provide extra security and personnel.

Robbie Kaplan wants to know if Trump will leave his golf
course in Doonbeg, Ireland, fly to New York and testify because
she can't wait to get him in the witness chair, tear his head off,
and feed it to him.

Tacopina wants to know if Trump will leave his golf course
in Doonbeg, Ireland, fly to New York and testify because he has
been assuring Judge Kaplan he will *not* be leaving his golf course
in Doonbeg, Ireland and coming to New York and testifying.

And me? I just want Trump to *stay* on his golf course in Doonbeg, Ireland. Because, if you will allow me to say a "bad thing"
and put a "negative entry" into this memoir, I believe that the
man who is so persuasive that his tweet, "Big protest in D.C. on

January 6th. Be there, will be wild!" results in a mob attacking the United States Capitol in 2020, will take the witness stand, wring the undecided bosoms of our upstate jury, and terrify them into letting him off.

*   *   *

"He won't be able to stay away," says Robbie.

She makes this pronouncement on January 9, three and a half months before the trial, during dinner in the marble-columned dining room of the extremely hip Riggs Hotel, in Washington, DC, the night before Joshua argues before the DC Court of Appeals that Donald Trump's duties as president did not include calling me too ugly to rape. Shawn G. Crowley is with us, and she says, while dispatching a haunch of beef (she will run five or six miles tomorrow before breakfast), "Trump will not testify."

Robbie and I make a bet.

I bet Trump will not testify. If he actually shows up, I will pay for a first-class, round-trip ticket to Montana so Robbie can fish the Fire Hole. If he does *not* show up, Robbie will buy me a first-class, round-trip ticket to Montana so I can pick wildflowers in the Spanish Peaks.

*   *   *

Who is the most shocking person to show up in *your* life?

My most shocking person shows up in the Spanish Peaks. And, yes, Friends, brace yourselves for *another* chap in an athletic uniform, because who shows up? 6'5" flaxen-haired, sapphire-eyed Tom Van Arsdale of the famous Van Arsdale twins—gods of Indiana University, tall, twangy-voiced stars of the Knicks, the Suns, the Pistons, the Royals, the Celtics, uh, I beg your pardon. Do these names ring a bell, Friends? Do you follow the NBA? Tom is the basketball star, and I am the cheerleader—the mid-century Taylor and Travis, and here we are at my Pi Beta Phi pledge dance:

In all our cornfed-splendor.

The dress alone—a home-ec project of the girl who lives down the hall from me—is worth all the trouble I just took finding this photo for you in an old issue of *Esquire*. The ribbon: French blue. The thing hanging down my neck: a fake hair twirl. And speaking of "down the hall," Tom and Dick once fall asleep in my Smithwood dorm room during freshman year Sunday-afternoon visiting hours (this is 1962 and men are not allowed in women's dorms except on designated Sunday afternoons), and I tiptoe about three dozen girls down the hall and allow them, through a crack of my door, a peak at Tom's and Dick's magnificent forms stretched out on the two beds, their giant feet hanging off the ends. In *Esquire*, I write: "It was the high point of my freshman year."

O! I simply adored Tom Van Arsdale!

So, about seventeen years after this photo is taken, Steve Byers (see the list on page 5) and I are living on the Ralph Paugh ranch on the Madison River, outside Ennis, Montana, and across the road from our old farmhouse is the most stupendous view of the Spanish Peaks you ever saw in your life. And my sorority sister Nancy Kesler Logan—a Miss Chicago!; her talent was underwater ballet—and her husband, Michael Leff, a plastic surgeon, are visiting, and the four of us, with Steve's and my dog, Bloody Mary, a suave bull mastiff, hike up, up, up through the waves of yellow and violet wildflowers deep, deep, *deep* into the Land of the Grizzly. We pitch a tent, set up camp, and feel we are so "deep in the peaks" nothing could amaze us except a maybe million mountain lions, and the first night all we see is a UFO, and the second day, we spot—far across a basin—a guide on horseback, leading two pack horses and two riders.

And we are sitting there in the lilies, all lined up like bowling pins on this little hillock, observing the two pack horses, the guide, and the two riders and saying, "Boy! Are they lost!" and "Wow!! It'll take 'em three days to ride outta here," and so on and so forth. And we are all sitting there watching, and Bloody Mary sits up and *really* looks at them, and Nancy puts down her Snickers bar and slowly stands up and looks at them, and, of course, because Nancy is a daughter of the Great Sioux Nation and possesses extraordinary powers of sight and hearing, I copy Nancy and stand up and look at them; and I can see that the guide on his horse is definitely leading two people, and that one is a man and one is a woman, and Nancy starts walking toward them and so I start walking toward them and Nancy starts running and so I start running, and Bloody Mary starts barking and leaping, and, Friends, let me tell you, it's Ashley Wilkes coming home to Tara in *Gone With the Wind* with Melanie running toward him and Ashley Wilkes running toward her and Melanie running and opening her arms and Ashley Wilkes running and dropping his pack and Melanie throwing herself in his arms, except Nancy pulls Tom Van Arsdale—Yes! *Tom Van Arsdale!* By Gawd!—out of his saddle, and, as Tom's very pretty wife is smiling in flabbergasted elegance, Nancy drops Tom into the flowers, and we both fall upon him like mountain lionesses.

*   *   *

I like remembering these moments with Tom Van Arsdale in the Spanish Peaks, and with Mike Troy at the Playboy Club, because this memoir is about a trial against a not-nice man, and every once in a while I must give myself a treat.

*   *   *

So. Where was I? The "diary issue" has been settled. The plaintiff has rested. Nothing remains to be done except for Tacopina to ask Judge Kaplan to strap on his sturdiest hiking boots and give my case a running kick out the door.

Or, *in legal terms:* Tacopina makes a Rule 50 motion for "judgment as a matter of law." I.e., Trump wins because no reasonable jury could find Trump liable. Tacopina has been filing these kinds of dirty belly-aching motions and letters throughout the trial at a pace not seen since Oliver Wendell Holmes sent out his daily laundry, and Joshua Matz, the Man with the 583 IQ, Trevor Morrison, the dean, and Kate Harris, the baseball phenom—clerks for Supreme Court justices Kennedy, Ginsburg, and Sotomayor respectively—are replying to Tacopina's blizzard of beefs with such a hail of brilliance, we are winning nearly every decision.

Without even a flick of an eyelash, but with something sounding like an amused snort, Judge Kaplan denies Tacopina's motion and turns his attention to the fat old man on the golf course in Doonbeg, County Clare, Ireland.

Friends, you can't fall down in a pub in County Clare without being helped to your feet by one of my distant cousins. The whole place is simply crawling with Carrolls!

But there he is, the former president, windy, pudgy, ruddy, high-hatted, zipped tightly into a red jacket, and wearing one glove like Michael Jackson, yelling to the world press that he is coming to New York to slap Lady Justice's blindfold off.

"IT'S A DISGRACE! I'LL BE GOING BACK EARLY BECAUSE A WOMAN MADE A CLAIM THAT IS TOTALLY FALSE! IT WAS FAKE! IT'S A DISGRACE THAT IT'S ALLOWED TO HAPPEN! IT'S CALLED FALSE ACCUSATIONS AGAINST A RICH GUY! OR, IN MY CASE, AGAINST A FAMOUS, RICH, AND POLITICAL PERSON THAT'S LEADING IN THE POLLS BY 40 POINTS!"

JUDGE KAPLAN: Does the defendant wish to present a case, or do you now rest?

MR. TACOPINA: We rest, your Honor.

JUDGE KAPLAN: All right. Now, Mr. Tacopina, I know it is not perhaps an everyday occurrence to do so, but I'm going to ask you some questions about that.

MR. TACOPINA: Sure.

JUDGE KAPLAN: As I think we covered previously: First of all, the legal effect of your decision that Mr. Trump waives his right to testify in his defense in this case—is that right?

MR. TACOPINA: Yes, sir.

JUDGE KAPLAN: And have you communicated with him personally?

MR. TACOPINA: Yes, sir.

JUDGE KAPLAN: About that?

MR. TACOPINA: Yes, sir.

JUDGE KAPLAN: And you are representing to me, as an officer of the court, that he has personally, after consulting with you and being advised by counsel, elected voluntarily to waive his right to testify in this case?

MR. TACOPINA: Yes, sir.

——Wait! Tacopina has advised Trump not to testify? I cannot believe my ears!

JUDGE KAPLAN: How recently have you spoken to him about that?

MR. TACOPINA: Two minutes before I came in to court this morning.

——I am stunned! Floored! Tacopina counseled Trump not to testify!

JUDGE KAPLAN: (*Turning to Robbie*) Now, any other inquiry the plaintiff would like me to make in this circumstance?

MS. KAPLAN: Nothing further, your Honor.

JUDGE KAPLAN. I am absolutely committed to this case, as in every case, to ensure, to the best of my ability, that every party has a full and fair opportunity to pursue or defend against a claim asserted by or against that party. In the interest of justice, I will allow, until *10:00 p.m. on Sunday,*[*] the making of a motion on behalf of Mr. Trump to *re-open* his case for the purpose, and the sole purpose, of testifying as a witness in this case. I am not saying that I will grant it. If it is made, I will consider it, and I will give him appropriate consideration in all circumstances. He has *a right to testify*, which has been waived. But if he has second thoughts I will, at least, consider it. And maybe—we will see what happens. If no such motion is filed by 10:00 p.m. Sunday, that ship has irrevocably sailed. Do you understand?

MR. TACOPINA: Yes, sir.

JUDGE KAPLAN: Will you communicate that, please, to Mr. Trump?

MR. TACOPINA: I will and thank your Honor for that consideration.

*   *   *

Friends, I am perplexed.

Nobody in their right mind wants to be cross-examined by Robbie Kaplan, I get it. The minute Robbie has you under oath, you are a goner. Remember when she rips Trump's brain out through his ears at his deposition? That is Robbie warming

---

[*] The deadline is soon changed to 5 p.m. at Robbie's suggestion, so she and the Carroll Team will have time to prepare.

up. Can you imagine what happens when she has Trump on the stand for six, seven, eight hours—but still:

Come *on*.

All Trump has to do is show up on Monday and convince one upstate jury member he did not assault me—one!—and we have a mistrial. And if Mr. Bankrupt can convince nearly half the country to vote for him because he is a business "genius," win the presidency in 2016, be impeached twice, lose the 2020 election by seven million votes, still convince 70 percent of Republicans that he wins by "a landslide," and come storming back to take the presidency in 2024—(but, of course, not he nor anyone knows this at the time), he should have no trouble convincing one little upstater that I am a disgrace.

So, either Tacopina, who is very smart, is making a very dumb mistake advising Trump not to testify or . . . Tacopina is inadvertently saving the country from an abuser, and Tacopina is the hero of my story.

29

THE WALK

his waiting. *Please.* There is no court tomorrow because it
is a Friday. There is no court on Saturday. There is no court
on Sunday. And guess what Monday is, Friends? Monday is closing arguments. *Closing arguments*! How can I make
it through three days till closing arguments? I *cannot* make it
through three days till closing arguments. *Hell,* I cannot make it
through three hours. And Tuesday? Do you know what happens
on Tuesday? The case goes to the Tim Pool Guy and his acolyte
the Shepherd and they will sit at the big oak table with their fellow jurors with their notebooks and their coffee and their pens
and their bottles of water and their prejudices and their sandwiches and their secret sex lives and, well, do you think I can wait
the days and days and days and days it will take for the Shepherd
to decide my case? No. I cannot wait. It is too much waiting. I
cannot do it. It's impossible. I cannot wait. It's unbearable.

*   *   *

So how I make it till Monday and closing arguments, I cannot
tell you, except that I walk.

In a pair of navy-blue, size 36 reg, 100% cotton, long-sleeved
mechanic's coveralls with concealed, heavy-duty snap closures,
two front pockets, two hip pockets, two chest pockets, and a rule

pocket on the right hip (Red Kap, Amazon, $46.99) I walk the streets of Manhattan. Here is the place I can endure the waiting because every one of the eight million New Yorkers living here and walking the streets with me is also waiting for something and, despite Herman telling me not to leave Sixty LES without telling him, and despite it being very cold in the morning and very hot in the afternoon, I walk around waiting with the eight million New Yorkers, feeding from a bag of mixed nuts; and what with the nuts and the hot and the cold and the walking and the eight million of us all waiting, and the not telling Herman, and the little boxes of chocolate that Mary Trump sends me, and the stopping in Ted Baker on Sunday and buying a beautiful double-breasted jacket the color of a blue jay's egg, I make it to Monday morning.

30

BEHOLD! THE MALE *SPECIMEN!*

The subject of these illustrious memoirs—appearing in double-breasted blue jacket, black pleated skirt, black cashmere turtleneck, black tights, irresistible thirty-year-old black velvet Donna Karan heels—having made it through the three days, a tad puffy, perhaps, constipated from the many bags of nuts, but bobbed to the hilt, straight-backed and determined as ever, sits at the Plaintiff's Table. (Capitalizing the furniture now that these items are specific places in Manhattan.)

And who is *not* at the Defense Table?

*   *   *

"There were *two* people in that dressing room back in 1996," Mike Ferrara is saying to the jury on Monday afternoon. "*One* of them testified. One of them did not!"

A stirring line.

I hear it the first time on Sunday morning when I stop by the sixty-third floor of the Empire State Building on my three-day walk, and tap on the glass of Mike's office.

He jumps up, steps out from behind his desk, and looking lean as a wolfhound, opens the door and says:

"E. Jean, you wanna hear the rebuttal?"

"Egads!" I say, "just let me grab a bagel!"

And I biff off to crash Robbie's orgy outside the Ruth Bader Ginsburg Conference Room where she's set out a binge of blintzes, babka, bagels, bialys, lox, potato latkes, caviar cream cheese, chopped liver, scrambles, rye breads, and schmears from the fabled temple called Russ & Daughters; and as the tired, the hungry, the sapped, and sleepless Carroll Team—watched over by a special god—crawls toward the buffet like the squadron swarming the shore in the D-Day scene in *Saving Private Ryan,* I take two bagels, slather them in something that tastes like creamy, sunny, silky, melted cheese, and dash back to Mike.

* * *

Now, Friends. When Mike says "rebuttal," he is talking about the thirty-five-minute address he will give to the jury.

First, Robbie delivers our closing argument.

Second, Tacopina delivers Trump's closing argument.

Third, Mike rebuts whatever paranoid tripe Tacopina just shellacked the courtroom with.

That is the program.

* * *

I offer Mike one of the bagels; he declines. I take a tufted chair, Mike adopts a stance in front of his immense windows, lifts one foot (the waiting and walking must be undoing some of my lazy visual habits, as I would never have noticed this before), shakes it slightly, lifts the other foot (I'm talking a tenth of an inch here), shakes it (a toe flick), lifts the other foot, shakes it, lifts the other foot, and so on, the lifting and the shaking being what runners do before a race.

And in college Mike Ferrara is a runner. A quarter-miler known as "the sexy blur."

"Huh?" says Robbie when she hears this during a break in trial, "You were called the 'sexual blur' in college?"

"The *sexy* blur," says Mike.

"Ah!" says Robbie, "I thought you said 'the sexual blur' and my whole college life flashed before my eyes!"

Such highly satisfactory discourse—along with the Hall's menthol throat lozenges, Mike's panegyrics to the length and sleekness of Shawn G. Crowley's legs, Shawn G. Crowley's ripostes about the length and ephemerality of Mike's Supreme Greatness, and so on and so forth, keep us fresh while waiting for the jury to come back from breaks.

And now planting both feet semifirmly on the sixty-third floor, in his old New Balances and plaid flannel shirt, without looking often at his notes, the eloquent "Blur" elevates his voice, and, inspiring awe—I have never had anyone orate a rebuttal on my behalf before—chops Tacopina up like a tomato for lamb lasagna.

I have no other word for it. Powerful. Around the twenty-seven-minute mark, Mike leaves the rebutting behind, raises his voice, and enters into armed conflict:

"Mr. Tacopina didn't call *Mr. Trump* to testify. And *you* (to the imagined jury) should conclude it's because he would have *hurt* his case if he had. Mr. Tacopina told you that Ms. Carroll *lied* when she testified to you. But Donald Trump never took the witness stand at all! *He didn't even show up in court*!"

"Bravo!" I cry.

"It was *Ms. Carroll* who respected the justice system enough to walk into this courtroom, swear an oath, look all of you in the eye, and subject herself to two days of cross-examination.

Donald Trump did not do that"—lifting his voice to a very loud pitch—"*He could not do that*!"

"I love it! I love it!" I cry.

"What does *that* tell you? What does your common sense tell you? If someone accused *you* of rape and you didn't do it, you would *run* to the courtroom!"

"Ohhhhhh!" I leap up.

"*You* would look the jurors in the eye!" roars Mike.

"Yes!" I shout.

If I open the windows, Tacopina could probably hear us out in Connecticut.

"*You* would tell them it never happened!"

Mike's voice is so booming that Shawn G. Crowley, whose office is next door, abandons her digs, and, looking charming in *her* plaid flannel shirt and Nikes—she was a miler in college—stands for a moment outside the glass of his office, stares at Mike as if he is Patrick Henry addressing the Virginia Convention, raises one eyebrow in the quickest, slightest—woman to woman—sign to me, a sign that says, "Behold! The Male Specimen!" and, with an arch smile, returns to her office.

"Mr. Trump did *not* do that!" shouts Mike.

I yell:

"No! He didn't! No! He didn't!"

"So," says Mike.

He drops his voice so low that about only half the people on the sixty-third floor can hear.

"*You* should draw the conclusion that *that's* because he did it!"

I shout, "He did!" and clutching my paper plate which had the bagels, I continue shouting as Mike roars the last line over my shouts:

"Because he assaulted Ms. Carroll!"

*　　*　　*

OK. That was Sunday morning. Now it is Monday afternoon, and, Friends, I wish you could have heard Robbie Kaplan! For the first time in American history, a federal jury hears a summation of the evidence of sexual assault and defamation against a former president of the United States. No clamor. No "ten-dollar words," as Hemingway calls them. Robbie simply piles fact upon fact upon fact upon fact upon fact, and shows the jury that if I lied, then all the other witnesses had to be "in on the conspiracy, and they had to lie too."

And Tacopina?

*　　*　　*

He is magnificent!

He is hushed. He is Al Pacino in *Godfather* I. He is noisy. He is Al Pacino in *Godfather* II. He is apoplectic. He is Al Pacino in *Godfather* III. Tiny body suit! Unlocked door! Impossible to have sex standing up! No police report! No medical report! Lots of parties! Going to parties! Going to *all* the parties! Hungry for attention! Anderson Cooper! George Conway! *Law & Order*! Gonna get rich off a book! Gonna take down the president!

In a nearly two-hour, one-man show worthy of an audition for an Off-Broadway production of *Hairspray,* all of which I watch with feelings of the deepest horror, Tacopina delivers to the jury a "Revenge Plot" with charts and timelines, and, trust me, Friends, next to a box score, nothing is more interesting to a jury than a timeline.

The five highlights on Tacopina's timeline are:

(1) Donald Trump becomes president. (2) Lisa Birnbach, Carol Martin, and I loathe Trump. (3) We make up a story—or,

in plain English, steal "a rape story" from an old 2012 *Law &
Order*—so we can sell *millions* of books and get Trump kicked
out of office. (4) George Conway entices me to sue Trump which
leads to my (5) *enjoying* myself at a *party,* joking on Twitter, saying I am fabulous, and other appalling dissipations.

*   *   *

I hate to tell you, Friends, Tacopina kills.

*   *   *

And what is Mike Ferrara doing while Tacopina is awakening
moral indignation in the upright, upstate bosoms of the jury?

Mike, Matt, and the Carroll Team are checking transcripts,
confirming evidence, composing counterarguments, and writing
rejoinders in a hailstorm of Post-it notes as Robbie is steadily
standing up and objecting. The following events then take place:

- Tacopina asks the jury "to please—*please* have the courage
  to do what is right here," and sits down.
- Judge Kaplan says, "Members of the jury, we will take
  twenty minutes."
- The jury exits.
- Mike rewrites the rebuttal.
- The jury returns.
- Judge Kaplan says, "We will now hear the rebuttal
  argument on behalf of the plaintiff. Mr. Ferrara, you may
  proceed."
- Mike stands up and says:

"Hi, everyone."

*   *   *

It is not yesterday's ringing, thrilling, roaring, racing Sexy Blur.

It is gentle Mike, the widower who knows tragedy, the man who lost his beautiful wife, the single dad with two kids.

"Trump needs you to believe that everyone is lying because they're in this grand conspiracy to take him down. But there is just no evidence of that. Yes, many of our witnesses are registered Democrats and they have no love for Donald Trump. It's true. That doesn't make them unique and that's not evidence of a conspiracy.

"Ms. Martin and Ms. Birnbach have built their careers as writers and journalists based on their viewers and readers trusting them. They're *not* going to throw away their reputations and livelihoods on some scheme to take down Donald Trump.

"But Mr. Tacopina is asking you to believe that Ms. Carroll, Lisa Birnbach, and Carol Martin hate Donald Trump *so much* they're willing to lie to you. Commit perjury. Risk going to jail. Risk their reputations and their careers as trusted journalists to drum up some hair-brained scheme to take down Donald Trump.

"So let's step back for one minute.

"The Trump team's theory is that Ms. Carroll, Ms. Martin, and Ms. Birnbach, three intelligent, successful people, modeled their secret-secret scheme on an episode of *Law & Order*, one of the most popular shows on television because, yeah, why not model your *big conspiracy* on an episode of television that only six *million* people have seen. Who's going to notice? Other than those six million people? It makes no sense. Put aside how silly it is. If these three people were going to make up an accusation? *This* is the best they could do?"

(Matt Craig comes up on the fly with the "one of the most popular shows on television. . . . Why not model your big conspiracy on it? . . . Who's going to notice? Other than those six million people?" lines.)

"If these three women were going to make up a lie, why would they say the assault happened in a *department store*? They could make up a more private place than that. They could agree on a more specific time period. They could say that E. Jean screamed, not that she laughed. But they didn't say those things to you because that's not the truth. What they told you was the truth, good or bad. This isn't a conspiracy to take down Donald Trump, it is evidence of what actually happened. Donald Trump assaulted Ms. Carroll.

"Of *course* the defense argument has always been that Ms. Carroll made all of this up and it never happened. Okay. But if that's Trump's defense, why did Mr. Tacopina ask all those questions about whether Ms. Carroll screamed? About whether she was laughing? About whether she willingly went into the dressing room with Mr. Trump?

"Those questions are about whether Ms. Carroll *consented* to what Trump did to her. And Mr. Tacopina agreed that this isn't a case about consent. Consent is not his defense. So then *why* does it matter? If consent is not the defense, why does it matter if she screamed? Why does it matter if she laughed? Why does it *matter*? She walked into the dressing room *first*. Okay. I thought Trump said he was never there, and he had no idea who this woman was.

"Those questions were a distraction. As Mr. Tacopina agreed, consent is not the defense. Donald Trump claimed this never happened, he has no idea who this woman is. He doesn't go to Bergdorf's. That's what he said. And those denials were lies.

"You are *not* being asked anything about consent. You are being asked to decide whether an assault happened at all, and you know the answer to that. It did. And I really can't stress this enough: If you find yourselves in the jury room talking about whether Ms. Carroll consented, *then she wins.* Because it means you have concluded she was in that dressing room with Donald Trump's hands on her.

"Mr. Tacopina also argued that Ms. Carroll is lying to sell a book, and that this lawsuit is a money grab. Well, that's totally wrong. First, my partner Ms. Kaplan spoke to you for ninety minutes earlier, and she never asked you once to award Ms. Carroll some ridiculous amount of money and I'm not going to do that either.

"Second, Ms. Carroll told you that this lawsuit isn't about the money. I asked her if she's hoping for a large payout from this case and she answered: 'It's not about the money, it's about getting my name back.' That's at page 316 of the transcript. If Ms. Carroll is hoping for a huge payday, why would she tell you, the jury, who will decide the issue, that it isn't about the money? She wouldn't. What she told you is the truth. This lawsuit is about far more than money to her, it is about getting her life back.

"And the book? I mean, Ms. Carroll told you the book was a dud! It didn't sell! And remember the evidence about how Ms. Carroll published the 'Trump chapter' from the book? That chapter about Trump and a few other chapters were published online and in the printed edition of *New York* magazine. Right? So, in other words, Ms. Carroll gave away, *for free,* the chapter about Trump! She wouldn't have done that if she was making up a story to get people to buy her book. This is *not* a money grab."

(Kate Harris, the baseball phenom, currently Justice Sonia Sotomayor's clerk, is the one who *did* care enough about the money to remember—I certainly didn't remember—that I received no money for the Trump chapter, that the $7,000 check went to my publisher, St. Martin's, to pay my massive book advance ($75,000) which, by the by, has *still* never earned out, and so that I did, in fact, give it away "for free," instead of trying to make "millions of dollars." Indeed, like any journalist, the main thing I remember is not that I received no money for the excerpt, but that it was the second most popular story in *New York* magazine in 2019. *Hell*, why am I telling you? You probably read the chapter online. Right? Did you buy the book after that? Ha! Tell *that* to Tacopina. No need to tell me. I have seen the sales figures.)

"Now, the defense spent some time talking about how Ms. Carroll said she's fine, or great, or fabulous, on many occasions since the assault. Ms. Kaplan talked about this, how Ms. Carroll minimizes difficulties. And you heard testimony from Dr. Lebowitz and Ms. Carroll's sister Cande explaining why Ms. Carroll does that, why she has such a hard time checking in deeply with her own emotions.

"But I also will admit I just don't get the argument. Is the defense saying that because Ms. Carroll was attacked she could never be happy again? That she can never shop in Bergdorf Goodman's again? That *can't* be the argument, right? If I get mugged outside of my office, am I supposed to never go to work again because it is too triggering? If a loved one passes away and you manage to get on with your life and find happiness again, does that mean you didn't care about the person you lost? Of course not."

(Mike's wife, an attorney, a famously captivating woman, passed away. I did not get a chance to meet her, but I hear their love was so sweet and strong as to be almost unheard of between two mighty New York lawyers, and Mike and their children, Logan and Max, have been carrying on with heartbreaking cheerfulness and spirit.)

"Ms. Carroll is entitled to find happiness again in her life, to focus on the positive things in life and work, to be the happiest, best version of herself. But it feels like the defense has an idea of the perfect rape victim. And in their version it goes something like this:

"The perfect rape victim doesn't flirt. The perfect rape victim screams. The perfect rape victim never goes back to where they were raped. The perfect rape victim tells the police but otherwise never discusses the rape publicly. The perfect rape victim burns whatever clothes they were wearing. The perfect rape victim never laughs again, never jokes around. The perfect rape victim never again has success in their career. The perfect rape victim never looks at their rapist again. The perfect rape victim never tries to hold their rapist accountable, never gets their day in court. And, the perfect rape victim is never happy again.

"That's the defense's out-of-date, out-of-touch view. It is as wrong as it is offensive.

"The long and short of it is this, ladies and gentlemen: Donald Trump's entire defense rests on calling everyone a liar. He needs you to believe Ms. Carroll is a liar, Lisa Birnbach, Carol Martin, liars. Natasha Stoynoff and Jessica Leeds, he has to call them liars. Even Robert Salerno and Cheryl Beall, I guess they're lying, too, when they talk about seeing Trump in or near the store. All of them apparently willing to break the law and risk ruining their lives to bring down Donald Trump.

"Each of our witnesses took the stand and swore an oath to tell the truth. Their testimony is consistent, and it is overwhelming. And the guy calling them a liar is the only one of them who didn't testify, who couldn't swear an oath in this courtroom without admitting he assaulted Ms. Carroll.

"This was never going to be a 'he said, she said' case. We had too many witnesses for that. But now, at the end of this trial, we see there wasn't even 'he said,' because Donald Trump never looked you in the eye and denied it. Find him liable for assaulting and defaming E. Jean Carroll.

"Thank you."

*　　*　　*

My heart is beating so quickly, I want to stand up, dash around the courtroom, and gladden the hearts of the spectators, the courtroom artists, the judge's wife, the journalists, my sister Barbie, my niece Lauren, and the jury.

I remain in my chair, however, leaning forward, beaming at Mike, as Judge Kaplan says:

THE COURT: Thank you, Mr. Ferrara. (*Addressing the jury*) Ladies and gentlemen, 10:00 tomorrow morning. I will give you my instructions, and you will get the case. Don't talk about it, don't read or listen to anything about it. Thank you. Counsel remain, please.

——(*JURY NOT PRESENT*)

THE COURT: Be seated, folks, please. Now, was there something else that somebody wanted to bring up, or not?
MS. KAPLAN: Not from our side, your Honor.

THE COURT: Mr. Tacopina?

MR. TACOPINA: No, your Honor.

THE COURT: OK. See you tomorrow morning.

And we are adjourned until May 9—never forget that date!—at 10 a.m.

In Rape Trial, Jury Must Now Decide if It Believes Carroll or Trump

Donald J. Trump never showed up for the trial, nor did his lawyer call witnesses. Their case was simple: The writer E. Jean Carroll had made up her story.

31

A LITTLE EXPOSURE THERAPY

Norman Mailer won two Pulitzers, two National Book Awards, the George Polk Award, the Emerson-Thoreau Medal, and in 2007, Mr. Mailer was honored with not the Booker, not the Nobel, not the Hugo, not the PEN, but the stupendously preeminent Bad Sex in Fiction Award.

Until the pandemic, this noble prize was bestowed annually upon the world's great writers by the bright Brits at the *Literary Review*. Gabriel Garcia Márquez, Salman Rushdie, Joyce Carol Oates, Haruki Murakami, Jonathan Franzen, etc., etc., etc., have all been short-listed. John Updike won the Lifetime Achievement Award.

I am about to give you a look at Mailer's winner because today is Tuesday, May 9—the day I told you never to forget!—the day the jury gets the case, and we are gathered in the courtroom, with the world press spilling out of the "overflow room," awaiting Judge Kaplan's arrival and his instructions to the jury.

And, Friends, trust me: When Judge Kaplan delivers his instructions to the jury, you will hear descriptions of intimate acts that might make you want to stop reading.

So what I am about to try here is a bit of "exposure thera-py"—i.e., gently introduce you to descriptions of intimate acts in a safe and controlled way with the hopes of reducing your urge to stop reading when we get to Judge Kaplan's instructions. All right? OK? Ready? Go get your reading glasses. Here is Norman Mailer's 2007's Bad Sex in Fiction winner:

> Klara turned head to foot, and put her most unmention-able part down on his hard-breathing nose and mouth, and took his old battering ram into her lips. Uncle was now as soft as a coil of . . .

Well, Friends? What do you think? A good bracer? Will it help you confront the urge to stop reading when we get to Judge Kaplan? I love Mailer, and I like the comical "Uncle," but I mean, really, don't you think Natasha Stoynoff should have gone a few more rounds with old Norman? And knocked some of these words out of his head? Speaking of words, I am sorry. You bought a nice memoir by an old woman about a trial. And now here you are being asked if you are strong enough to hear instructions to the jury.

What do you say, Friends? Are you *inured*? Are we done? Did the exposure therapy work? Did I gird your loins? Or do you *need* Nick Cave's marvelous medal winner? "I entered her like a pile-driver?" * No? Okey dokey.

*   *   *

---

* *The Death of Bunny Munro*, published in 2010 by Farrar, Straus, and Giroux.

The most erudite and literary of all federal judges, Judge Lewis A. Kaplan—the man who explains to Tacopina in a sidebar on day three of the trial that Jonathan Swift uses "satire and irony"—is approaching the courtroom. He will explain the "ten questions" on the "verdict form" and instruct the jury on the two claims of my case: battery[*] and defamation.

---

[*] Unlawful use of force or violence on another person.

32

JUDGE KAPLAN INSTRUCTS THE JURY

Good morning, folks. I hope everybody had a relaxing evening. The record will reflect the jurors are all present. Members of the jury, we have reached the point in the trial where you are going to begin your final function as jurors.

"Now, if you look on the verdict form, you will see the first question is whether Ms. Carroll proved by a preponderance of the evidence that Mr. Trump raped her. It's a yes/no question. Ms. Carroll must prove each of two elements by a preponderance of the evidence. The first element is that Mr. Trump engaged in sexual intercourse with her. The second element is that Mr. Trump did so without Ms. Carroll's consent by the use of forcible compulsion. So let me define each one of those terms.

"'Sexual intercourse' means any penetration, however slight, of the penis into the vaginal opening. In other words, any penetration of the penis into the vaginal opening—regardless of the distance of penetration—constitutes an act of sexual intercourse. Sexual intercourse does not necessarily require erection of the penis, emission, or an orgasm.

"Now, of course, I hope you will forgive me for this very explicit language, but I have no alternative—nobody has in this case—in discussing the elements of the alleged battery.

"I also used the phrase 'forcible compulsion,' and what that means is intentionally to compel by the use of physical force.

"If you find that Ms. Carroll has proved by a preponderance of the evidence both of those two elements, you will answer Question 1 'yes.' If you find that Ms. Carroll has not proven either of the two elements of rape by a preponderance of the evidence, you must answer 'no' to Question 1, and go on to Question 2, which deals with the second of the three alternative bases for the battery claim.

"The second theory of battery corresponds to something called sexual abuse. Sexual abuse has two elements. In order to establish that Mr. Trump sexually abused her, Ms. Carroll must prove each of two elements by a preponderance of the evidence.

"The first element is that Mr. Trump subjected Ms. Carroll to sexual contact.

"The second element is that he did so without Ms. Carroll's consent by the use of forcible compulsion. So let me define 'sexual contact' for you. Sexual contact for this purpose means any touching of the sexual or other intimate parts of a person for the purpose of gratifying the sexual desire of either person. It includes the touching of the actor by the victim, as well as the touching of the victim by the actor, and the touching may be either directly or through clothing.

"Now, I just used the term or the phrase 'sexual or intimate part' in defining sexual contact. For this purpose, a 'sexual part' is an organ of human reproduction.

"So far as intimate part is concerned, the law does not specifically define which parts of the body are intimate. Intimacy, moreover, is a function of behavior and not just anatomy. Therefore, if any touching occurred, the manner and circumstances of the touching may inform your determination whether Mr. Trump touched any of Ms. Carroll's intimate parts.

"You should apply your common sense to determine whether, under general societal norms and considering all the circumstances, any area or areas that Mr. Trump touched, if he touched any, were sufficiently personal or private that it would not have been touched in the absence of a close relationship between the parties.

"I mentioned also that the touching, if any, of any sexual or intimate parts must have been for the purpose of gratifying the sexual desire of either party. Sexual gratification is a subjective determination that may be inferred from the nature of the acts committed and the circumstances in which they occurred. There is no requirement that actual gratification occur, but only that the touching, if there was any, was for that purpose."

——*I do not need to interrupt here, Friends, and say the justice system was created by men, for men—do I?*

"The second element of this theory is forcible compulsion. I defined that for you a couple of minutes ago when I told you the elements of rape, and here, as there, it means intentionally to compel by the use of physical force.

"If you find that Ms. Carroll has proved by a preponderance of the evidence both of the two elements of sexual abuse that I just referred to, then you will answer 'yes' to Question 2. If you find that Ms. Carroll has not proven either of the two elements of sexual abuse by a preponderance of the evidence, you must answer 'no' to Question 2 and proceed to Question 3. And if you will forgive me for a minute, I'm going to get a drink of water."

——*Good idea, Judge! Following your excellent example, I would like to deliver to every reader a tall glass of Mother Nature's purest tears from the burbling mountain stream behind my cabin.*

"The third alternative of battery is something called forcible touching.

"Forcible touching occurs when a person intentionally, and for no legitimate purpose, forcibly touches the sexual or intimate parts of another person for the purpose of degrading or abusing that person or for the purpose of gratifying the actor's sexual desire. It has five elements.

"The first element is that Mr. Trump touched a sexual or intimate part or parts of Ms. Carroll. I have already defined the terms 'sexual or intimate parts,' and you will apply that definition here on the issue of forcible touching.

"The second element of forcible touching, as the name implies, is that the touching of any of Ms. Carroll's sexual or intimate part or parts, if any occurred, must have been forcible. Forcible touching includes squeezing, grabbing, pinching, rubbing, or other bodily contact that involves the application of some level of pressure to the victim's sexual or intimate parts. Any bodily contact involving the application of some level of pressure to another person's sexual or intimate parts qualifies as forcible touching.

"The third element of forcible touching is that the forcible touching, if any, was intentional. 'Intent' means conscious objective or purpose. Thus, a person intentionally forcibly touches the sexual or intimate parts of another person when that person's conscious objective or purpose is to do so.

"The fourth element of forcible touching requires that the forcible touching, if there was any, of Ms. Carroll by Mr. Trump must have been for the purpose of degrading or abusing her or for the purpose of gratifying Mr. Trump's sexual desire. I have already defined the term 'sexual gratification,' and you will apply that instruction here in deciding whether Ms. Carroll has proved that Mr. Trump forcibly touched her for the purpose of gratifying his sexual desire. If you do not find that the forcible touching of Ms. Carroll, if there was any, was for the purpose of gratifying Mr. Trump's sexual desire, you must consider whether the forcible touching, if any, was for the purpose of degrading or abusing Ms. Carroll.

"The fifth and final element is that the forcible touching, if there was any, was committed without consent. Forcible touching takes place without a person's consent when it results from any circumstances in which a person does not expressly or impliedly acquiesce to the actor's conduct.

"If you find that Ms. Carroll has proved by a preponderance of the evidence all five of these elements of forcible touching, you will answer Question 3 'yes.'"

THE BUSBY BERKELEY BALLROOM

How do I feel sitting here at the Plaintiff's Table listening to these instructions? I feel like everybody feels when they hear about sexual assault. *I do not want to hear about sexual assault.* I feel numb. I feel hot. I feel I want to flush my head down a toilet. I feel powerless. I feel helpless to help whoever Judge Kaplan is talking about.

But, Friends, we have made it through the worst of it.

The jury may look like they have been hit by an extremely large board, and a pen may have dropped and rolled on the floor, but the Upstate Nine are still upright. Judge Kaplan goes on to explain Questions 4 and 5 about "compensating Miss Carroll" for any "injury," and then, sensing the cloying pall in the court-room—and I do not know if His Honor is a Yankees or Mets fan—invites everyone, in the spirit of the seventh-inning stretch, to get to their feet, "sit or stand as ever you wish," proceeds to read Trump's October 22 statement ("This Miss Bergdorf case is a complete con job . . . hoax and a lie . . . complete scam . . . ," etc., etc., etc.) and explain Questions 6 through 10 about the def-amation: Was Trump's October 22 statement defamatory? Was it false? Did he make it with actual malice? Was I injured by it? Did he make it out of hatred, ill will, spite, reckless disregard?

The answers to these questions will, if Twitter is right, bring down the wrath of an Angry God and send me, the skank, the slut, the cunt, con job, the liar, the fraud, straight to hell. At last Judge Kaplan says:

"When you retire, you are going to select one member of the jury as your foreperson. That person will preside over your deliberations and speak for you in open court when, and if, that becomes necessary. The foreperson will send out any notes.

"Now, let's talk about the verdict."

Can you take this much longer, Friends?

"When you reach a verdict, the foreperson is to write a note saying 'verdict.' Put it in a sealed envelope. Do not label the envelope. Hand it to the officer who will be right outside the jury room. The officer will bring it to me, and I will get the people who need to be here."

Following a sidebar to settle Tacopina's beefs about four changes to His Honor's instructions,* the jury is told they will receive a "clean laptop" containing all the images of evidence on it, plus a DVD player, and Andy the Deputy Clerk swears in a US Marshal:

"You do solemnly swear that you will keep the jurors impaneled and sworn in this cause together in some private and convenient place. You shall suffer no one to speak to them, nor shall you speak to them yourself without

---

* The day before Judge Kaplan reads his instructions, Joshua Matz runs figure eights around W. Perry Brandt when the Carroll and Trump teams argue for changing/approving Judge Kaplan's instructions to the jury— and I am talking line by line.

direction of this Court, unless it be to ask them if they
have agreed upon the verdict, so help you God."

THE MARSHAL: I do.
ANDY, THE DEPUTY CLERK: Thank you.
JUDGE KAPLAN: Ladies and gentlemen, you will now retire
and deliberate your verdict.
TIME: Ten minutes before High Noon.

And off they go to decide my fate.

*   *   *

Walk up the runway. Exit the courtroom. Pass the thick oak
door of the Carroll HQ with its glistening brass plate blazon-
ing: "Witness Room." Pass the security check. Turn right at the
backscatter X-ray. Walk by the elevators, walk by the Ladies' and
Gents'; and, Friends, you better be lookin' *good* because you are
now entering the Busby Berkeley Ballroom. I do not have the
foggiest idea what the room is actually called.

But it looks like the set of just about any Busby Berkeley dance
number you ever saw—white-and-black marble, the whole
room, white-and-black marble and granite; walls, ceiling, floor, a
veritable glaze of white marble, streaked with inky black; a floor
so polished you think you can see up your own skirt; tap the heel
of your shoe and the vibrations bounce off the marble walls; hum
a tune, it reverberates off the ceiling twenty feet above. The great
director drinks a martini with his daily bath, marries six times,
and is carried on a stretcher into his own trial when he is pros-
ecuted for second-degree murder in Los Angeles, in 1935, for
causing an automobile accident in which two people die. The
first two juries hang. The third acquits him.

*   *   *

The Busby Berkeley Ballroom is where the Carroll Team and its friends and family gather each lunchtime during trial. Robbie's wife, Rachel Lavine, a vivacious earring swinger, an outrageously, hilariously opinionated attorney and politician, coFounder and chair of the Progressive Caucus of New York State Democratic Committee, instrumental in getting a moratorium on fracking in New York, and so on, tells me how my bangs are doing, savages the Trump team, brings Robbie messages from their son, Jacob, and makes sure I get all the cookies I want when the Kaplan Hecker support staff arrives with the Yaddo-grade boxed lunches enclosing the delicious egg salad sandwiches, the chicken parm heroes, the vegan lobster rolls, the French-onion-and-I-do-not-know-what sandwiches, the tomato and prosciutto sandwiches, the pastrami on ryes, the Caesar wraps, the bagels, the lox, the turkey, the tuna, the bacon, the cheese, and the fries. But today? With the jury deciding my case?

You think I can eat?

Oh, yes, Friends, I can eat. I do not *taste* what I eat, have no idea *what* I am eating; someone picks up whatever it is I am eating which I accidently drop on the marble floor, hands it to me, and I go on eating it.

"When will we get a verdict?" I say.

"Not soon," says Shawn G. Crowley.

"It won't be quick," says Mike.

"He was president of the United States," says Matt.

"So—" I say, "*late* this afternoon?"

Shawn G. Crowley, wearing her second-best suit, the pretty dark-blue tweed with the white piping and short skirt, has been a waiter on many verdicts.

She smiles.

Shawn G. Crowley shares my pain.

"E. Jean," she says, "do not expect anything till Thursday."

Thursday! Today is Tuesday.

"Dean!" I cry to Trevor Morrison, the former dean of the New York University School of Law.

"Friday afternoon," says Trevor.

"Robbie?" I say.

Robbie waits three days for the jury in her *Charlottesville* case. She waits three *months* for the Supreme Court's decision on *Windsor.* Robbie has too much history to guess.

"I don't know."

I look at Joshua.

I am exhausted from not knowing anything.

Joshua, a treasure chest of reassurance, gazes into my eyes with ripe candor, pushes up his glasses, pauses, and says:

"Monday."

*   *   *

Because my phone is taken as I enter the Daniel Patrick Moynihan United States Courthouse every morning, I cannot see when the NBC, ABC, CBS, FOX, MSNBC reporters standing outside on the Daniel Patrick Moynihan pavement are saying *they* expect a verdict. I walk around the Ballroom. I look inside the unclaimed box lunches. I make a daisy chain out of the bobby pins I find in my bag. I flick the crumbs of whatever it was I ate off the bosom of my jacket. I look out the windows. I brush the suede on the toe of my old Donna Karan shoe. I pull out my mirror and see what my bangs are doing. I leave the Ballroom. I pass the Ladies' and Gents', go by the elevators, turn right at the backscatter X-ray scanner, take a nice seat on a oak bench, and, figuring I have a couple of days to wait, and feeling sleepy and stupid, stretch out my legs, cross my arms, close my eyes, and I am lolling and tumbling like Alice in Wonderland down a lovely hole, when I feel a gentle touch on my shoulder.

"E. Jean . . ."

I open my eyes.

I see a blazing pair of turquois-blues landscaped with shrubbery.

"Helen?"

"See that door?" She nods at a large oak door about three feet from where I am sitting. My legs are, in fact, lolling out in front of it.

"*That's* Trump headquarters . . . come on," she says. "Let's sit in *our* room," and I tumble to our door with the brass plate blazing, "Witness Room," and enter.

*   *   *

Amidst the coats, the briefcases, the peanut butter and jelly sandwiches, the protein bars, the Dunkin' Donuts cups, the vat of cold coffee, the document boxes, the bananas, and the watermelon water, I pull out a chair near the round table.

"Ahhhhhh," I say, "just the ticket—"

I put up my feet.

Helen sits down near the window, her blond hair hanging like spun sugar in the sunlight.

I peep into the book Mary Trump sent me. It has cats posing as famous works of art.

"This . . . sun!" I say, drowsily.

Helen puts up *her* feet.

"What?" she says.

"The sun . . ." I say. "Wonderful . . ."

Helen tilts her head back. Her hair looks so luminous.

"I shouldn't fall asleep," says Helen.

She down-lashes.

Pulling the all-nighters reading my journals.

A cat dressed as the Mona Lisa.

"So cute," I say.

I want to show Helen the cat.

"Really," I say, "ador . . ."

I am too lazy to lift the book.

Silence.

My eyes close.

*　　*　　*

BOOM!

The door opens.

It's Mike.

"There's a verdict!"

*　　*　　*

I mean a joke is a joke, but there *is* a limit.

"Getouttahere!"

"HAHAHAHAHA!"

"No joke," says Mike, frightened.

He shifts to one foot and looks like the flamingo in the *Alice in Wonderland* croquet game after the Queen uses him as a mallet.

"We've got a verdict," he says. "It came at two twenty. Judge Kaplan says we're to be in the courtroom to hear it read at three o'clock."

Within seconds the Carroll Team is assembled and staring at one another in the Witness Room. No one can decipher it. No one knows what it means. It is so quick. So incredibly quick.

Everyone is jabbering. Nobody is saying anything. I suggest we all hold hands. We all hold hands.

Shawn says in a low voice:

"It's too fast. They didn't have time to attach damages."

This knocks us all flat.

"Well, somebody should say a prayer," I say.

Joshua says a prayer.

I have no idea what the *hell* Joshua prays because it is in Hebrew, but he tells me later it is the Traveler's Prayer, and I look it up and see that Joshua has asked God to protect the Carroll Team from ambush, robbers, and wild beasts.

And we travel from the Witness Room into court and walk down the runway.

*   *   *

Lewis A. Kaplan had told the jury in his instructions that if they "had a verdict between 12:15 and 1:30"—i.e., during lunch—the foreperson was to "write the note, give it to the officer, and I will know that, and we will move as fast as we can."

At least *somebody* could see the possibility of a quick verdict.

*   *   *

There is a Great Shoving. A spot in Judge Kaplan's courtroom is harder to get than a Supreme Court seat.

THE COURT: Good afternoon. I have received a note reading in its entirety "Verdict."

ANDY, THE DEPUTY CLERK: Shall I get the jury?

THE COURT: Just give me a minute. (*Casting a stern look at the spectators and press*) Assuming that there is in fact a verdict and, for that matter, even assuming there isn't—which doesn't seem very likely—*decorum* will be maintained in the courtroom. *No* shouting. *No* jumping up and down. *No* race for the door. Just remain seated and quiet. There are further things that have to happen in that event.

(*Another stern look*)

All right. Let's get the jury.

*   *   *

Friends, would now be a good time to tell you about the evidence we did *not* present at trial?

34

JEFFREY EPSTEIN'S "TORRID DETAILS"

EVIDENCE WE DO NOT INTRODUCE

Michael Wolff, the journalist who says he was "Trump's best friend" and also that Trump is "a moron," writes the bestseller *Fire and Fury* about Trump, and has released several tapes of his interviews with Jeffrey Epstein. On many of those tapes Epstein talks about Trump.

Wolff writes in the last chapter of his book *Too Famous: The Rich, the Powerful, the Wishful, the Notorious, the Damned* that Trump "regaled" Epstein with details about the Bergdorf attack.

And there was another Trump aspect he [Epstein] seemed to be rushing back to the United States for—if only to gossip about. The journalist E. Jean Carroll had, in the past weeks, described in a new book and in an article in *New York* magazine how in the mid-nineties Trump had raped her in a dressing room in the department store Bergdorf Goodman. Epstein told one of his callers that he had seen Trump shortly after this happened and Trump had regaled him with the torrid details. Trump's move now, Epstein theorized, would be to deflect from this story by reviving the rape charges against Bill Clinton. He was eager to discuss with Bannon.

WHY IS THIS EVIDENCE NOT INTRODUCED?

Robbie is interested in Wolff's interviews for sure, but even if she could solve the hearsay difficulties, she decides that the two words "Jeffrey Epstein" are so flamingly prejudicial, Judge Kaplan will never allow it. She wastes no further time on it.

35

THE WHITE HOUSE
PRESS SECRETARY

EVIDENCE WE DO NOT INTRODUCE

On October 6, 2022, at a Hampton Inn, deep in the heart of Kansas, Robbie, with Matt helping, deposes Stephanie Grisham, the thirty-second White House Press Secretary. The deposition is about what happens in the Oval office when the *New York* magazine story hits, and some *very* interesting things happen in the Oval office when the *New York* magazine story hits, but I cannot quote from the deposition transcript.

It is under seal.

But I *can* tell you that Robbie speaks with Stephanie Grisham shortly after Robbie reads Ms. Grisham's book *I'll Take Your Questions Now: What I Saw at the White House.* And I *can* tell you this is a quote from Ms. Grisham's book.

I was in the Oval Office with Jared, Dan Scavino, and a few others when the Carroll claims came up. Trump was doing his usual routine when accused of misconduct:

"She's a liar," "She's gross," "Do you think I'd be with that?", on and on, mostly attacking her physical appearance rather than the "I would never do that to my wife" line.

Then, at one point, sitting at the Resolute Desk, the president shot me an unusual look. It's hard to explain, but it was like he was staring me down or piercing my soul. "You just deny it," he said. "That's what you do in every situation. Right, Stephanie? You just deny it," he repeated, emphasizing the words.

But as for the thing Ms. Grisham tells Robbie that is not in her book, the thing that Trump says back to her in June, 2019, when Ms. Grisham is handling press questions about the New York story and my accusation, the thing that many on the Carroll Team think "proves" our case? You will have to ask Ms. Grisham.

WHY IS THIS EVIDENCE NOT INTRODUCED?

Miss Grisham presents some of the strongest evidence for *Carroll v. Trump*. But Robbie thinks that because Trump claims my cause is "political" and because he tells the world—in an official White House statement—that I am being "paid" by the Democrats to sue him, hauling Stephanie Grisham, Trump's former White House press secretary, to New York and putting her on the stand, will *absolutely* look political, and our case is *not* political. It is personal.

Stephanie Grisham is not called.

TRUMP'S BERGDORF SHOPPING TIPS

EVIDENCE WE CANNOT INTRODUCE

On day 7 of the trial, after the jury hears Professor Ashlee Humphreys testifying about the many ways Trump's October 22 statement bludgeons my reputation, Judge Kaplan announces there will be a fifteen-minute break, and when the jury is not present, Shawn G. Crowley rises and says to Judge Kaplan that we have an "evidentiary issue."

Judge Kaplan asks what the evidentiary issue is.

Shawn says the evidentiary issue is "a book authored by Mr. Trump that we would like to introduce."

JUDGE KAPLAN: What book?
SHAWN G. CROWLEY: It's called *Think Like a Billionaire,* and we would like to introduce a small portion where he talks about shopping and buying gifts from Bergdorf's.

WHY THIS EVIDENCE WAS NOT INTRODUCED
Judge Kaplan does not allow it.

"FURTIVE LUNCHTIME ROMANCE"

EVIDENCE WE WISH WE COULD INTRODUCE

Of course, the Carroll Team speaks with people from Bergdorf's and elsewhere, and these people say it is "not a secret" that trysts take place in Bergdorf's dressing rooms.

No one, however, will testify in court.

But during the trial I receive a note from Merrill Markoe, the writer (the *New York Times*, *Rolling Stone*, *Esquire*, etc., etc.), winner of three Primetime Emmys for Outstanding Writing for a Variety Series, former head writer at *Letterman*, and now author of a brilliant Substack.

Merrill has been following the trial and remembers that her friend Nell Scovell, the television and magazine writer, creator of *Sabrina the Teenage Witch*, and currently a *Vanity Fair* contributor, is hired by Graydon Carter right out of Harvard to be the first staff writer for *Spy* magazine—the first magazine to fact-check Trump's finances. (Bloated.)

Nell's stories in *Spy* get a lot of attention because her observations are sharp, accurate, and funny. The story Merrill remembers is a 1987 piece called "Furtive Lunchtime Romance."

What is it about? It is about the notorious places New Yorkers go for their "afternoon delights." And who is on the cover? Donald Trump.

On Nell's list are the private rooms on the mezzanine of Tiffany's; the screening room in the Brill Building; the downstairs bathrooms at Bottega Veneta (convenient to leather goods), also . . .

Number five on the list: a changing room in Bergdorf Goodman.

WHY THIS EVIDENCE IS NOT INTRODUCED

We are in the middle of trial and do not have time to interview and introduce new witnesses; but even as I write this, the Carroll Team believes that Nell's story strongly corroberates our case.

38

A JOY SO WILD

Joshua has said his prayer. Robbers do not set upon us as we travel to the courtroom. Judge Kaplan has warned the press and spectators that "*decorum* will be maintained." Now Andy, the Deputy Clerk, gets the jury. We stand. The jury enters.

I bow my head, lift my eyes, and give them the nervous glance that a Roman gladiator gives to the emperor. Not one of them looks at me. Not one of 'em!

"Well, I'm finally glad to see the Jury is looking at me."*

Gary Gilmore says this to *his* jury after they take an hour and twenty minutes to bring back a verdict of "Guilty."

Judge Kaplan wastes no time getting underway.

THE COURT: Jurors all present. Members of the jury, who is the foreperson?

——Juror 81 rises. Number 81! My heart leaps! One of the three women! She is rising! She is standing up! I cannot help it, a surge

---

* *The Executioner's Song*, Norman Mailer's second Pulitzer. When Gilmore is given the death penalty he is allowed to choose how to die. He says, "I prefer to be shot."

*of hope floods my chest. A sturdy, fair-haired businesswoman
in her late forties, with exceptionally good posture, Juror 81
has maintained a serious expression (and a serious wardrobe of
corporate sweaters and jackets) throughout the trial.*

THE COURT: Yes, ma'am. Has the jury in fact reached a
verdict?

THE FOREPERSON: We have.

THE COURT: Would you please pass the envelope to Andy.
Thank you.

*——Juror 81 passes the envelope to Andy. Andy opens it, looks at
it, and passes it up to Judge Kaplan on his perch. Judge Kaplan
reads it, and passes it back down to Andy. One more second of this
and I will be unable to obey His Honor's rule about staying "seated
and quiet."*

THE COURT: The clerk will publish the verdict.

*——Andy begins reading it aloud. I am between Robbie Kaplan
and Shawn G. Crowley. We clasp hands.*

THE DEPUTY CLERK: As to battery, did Ms. Carroll prove, by
a preponderance of the evidence, that **Question 1.** Mr. Trump
raped Ms. Carroll? **Answer: No.**

*——I hear the "No." I hear the "No." I definitely hear the "No."
My brain blasts it right out my ears again.*

THE DEPUTY CLERK: Question 2. Did Mr. Trump sexually
abuse Ms. Carroll? **Answer: Yes.**

——A joy so wild it shakes my whole frame, springs up from my feet, and, having nowhere else to go, booms out the top of my head.

THE DEPUTY CLERK: Question 4. Ms. Carroll was injured as a result of Mr. Trump's conduct? **Answer: Yes.**

——I am squeezing Shawn G. Crowley's and Robbie's hands so hard, Robbie's hand turns a cold alabaster shade.

THE DEPUTY CLERK: What is the dollar amount that would fairly and adequately compensate her for injury—
THE COURT: For that injury.
THE DEPUTY CLERK: *For* that injury or those injuries: **Answer. $2 million.**

——My ears are ringing with the euphoric blasts of Shawn G. Crowley's ecstatic breathing. I do not hear the amount.

THE DEPUTY CLERK: Did Ms. Carroll prove, by clear and convincing evidence, that, as to **Question 7.** Mr. Trump's statement was false? **Answer: Yes. Question 8.** That Mr. Trump made the statement with actual malice? **Answer: Yes.** Did Ms. Carroll prove, by a preponderance of the evidence, that, **Question 9.** Ms. Carroll was injured as a result of Mr. Trump's publication of the October 12, 2022, statement? **Answer: Yes.** If **"yes,"** answer a dollar amount for any damages other than reputation repair program: **$1 million.** If **"yes,"** insert a dollar amount for any damages for the reputation repair program only. **$1,700,000. Question 10.** In making the statement, Mr. Trump acted maliciously, out of hatred, ill will, spite, or wanton, reckless, or willful disregard of the rights of

another? **Answer: Yes.** If "**yes**," how much, if any, should Mr.
Trump pay to Ms. Carroll in punitive damages? **$280,000.**

———*Not a single syllable of this reaches me. The joy vibrating in
my heart—and, Friends, it vibrates still as I write these words—
makes it impossible to hear Andy. He could be announcing to the
courtroom that Robbie has just been appointed to replace Merrick
Garland as attorney general, or that Mike Ferrara and Shawn
G. Crowley have fallen deeply in love. I hear none of it. I am
watching Robbie's right hand. She is trying to hold a pencil and
write down numbers. The pencil is jumping about.*

THE COURT: And it has affixed to it the juror numbers. Is
there a request for a poll, Mr. Tacopina?
MR. TACOPINA: Yes, your Honor.
THE COURT: Poll the jury, please, Andy.

———*The jury is polled. The Tim Pool Guy answers, "Yes" as loudly
as the other eight. Judge Kaplan delivers a "thank you" oration. I
mean, I do not hear a bit of it, my heart is thumping too loudly,
but I hear afterward it is wonderfully frightening because at the
end of it Judge Kaplan advises the jury that for their own safety
not to identify anyone they served with on the panel, and not to
identify themselves—"Not now. And not for a long time." Then
he thanks the Defendant's Table and the Plaintiff's Table for
not killing each other, which I do not hear either because I am
endeavoring not to do any of the following things:*

> Shouting.
> Jumping up and down.
> Racing for the door.

I am trying my best, Friends, but I am ready to burst. I cannot say that I *would* have consulted legal advice about knocking myself out with chloroform, but after spending the whole trial trying to find my voice, and now the whole verdict trying to silence my voice, I *do* hear the words: "I don't think I have anything else to say. Good job all around. Thank you, folks," and the Carroll Team stands, turns, and starts up the runway.

Tacopina steps out and presents his hand as if he is conferring the Stanley Cup on me.

"Miss Carroll," he says, with a smile, "congratulations."

I take his hand.

"He did it," I say. "And you know it."

*   *   *

The Carroll Team exits the courtroom. We turn left. Ali and Katherine, the paralegals open the door with the blazing brass plate, we enter, and, despite the fragile splendor of my age, despite the fact that old women do not win lawsuits, I let out a shout so loud that it must reach Judge Lewis A. Kaplan in his robing chamber, because everybody shushes me. There is a second of silence—a half moment of realizing that we won—and *everybody* explodes.

*   *   *

Carol Martin is balling the jack down Hudson Terrace near Fort Lee, running errands in her big old Subaru, when she gets a call from her attorney, Noam Biale.

He says calmly:

"They're about to announce the verdict."

Carol jerks the wheel, arcs off into a little park at about 40 mph, does not see a parking space, stops where she is, throws the brake, staggers out of the car like a pilgrim who has rolled across the continent to hear The Word, and lies down upon a bench!

(Carol has never lain down on a bench in her life.)

Having prepared for the eminent peril, resting her phone on her chest, she closes her eyes, and waits. A minute. Two minutes. Three minutes. God knows how many minutes till her phone leaps and fires and whirrs and rings and pings on her chest. She picks it up. A banner alert from the *New York Times* flashes on her screen as she hears Noam shout:

"Carroll wins!!"

A swirl of joy hits Carol so hard, it probably *would* have flattened her if the great State of New Jersey had not supplied her with that park bench. I am thinking of putting a plaque on it:

CAROL MARTIN DID NOT WANT TO BE HERE
BUT SHE'S GLAD SHE WAS

*   *   *

Lisa Birnbach is in the courtroom when the verdict is read. She does not know it yet, because, of course, her phone is being held in Security, but when she retrieves it from the guard, and stops being insanely elated for two seconds and turns the thing on, she sees Lawrence O'Donnell has called.

One of the traits I like about Lisa is she is enthusiastic about things. Lawrence wants her on tonight at ten o'clock, and Lisa simply continues being elated until about nine forty-five p.m. She slaps on the makeup—Lisa is one of those people who are better on TV than in real life—and is so completely brilliant when she goes live at ten p.m., that when I watch the next day, I learn all the things that happen when the verdict is read that I was too happy to see.

*   *   *

An Off-Broadway play is in dress rehearsal. Actors are playing a tense scene. A young production assistant dashes out on the stage and cries:

"Carroll won!"

Everyone bursts into applause. The house lights flash like it's *Midsummer Night's Dream.*

*   *   *

The sound of the photographers yelling, "E. Jean! Robbie! This way! E. Jean! Over here! Robbie! E. Jean!" as they run alongside the car taking photos, fades as we roll away from the Daniel Patrick Moynihan United States Courthouse and turn at—well now, I am not sure what street we turn onto with Robbie and me in the back seat and Robbie yakking on her phone, but it begins the greatest ride of my life—and, Friends, I have driven with Hunter S. Thompson at 110 mph at midnight with the headlights *off.*

When Robbie is happy she jaws on her phone. And right now Robbie is about as full-tilt jubilant as it gets, talking to everybody she knows at the top of her lungs nonstop, never pausing for breath straight through the traffic jams of Chinatown, the tourists in SoHo, and the culturati in the Village. And me?

I am sitting back in the seat with a wicked grin of joy thinking: "This is your town, Donald Trump, and I just beat the shit out of you."

*   *   *

Robbie and I arrive at the Empire State Building, ride up to the sixty-third floor, open the door of Kaplan Hecker and music comes blasting out and people come running from all directions shouting and dancing and the music is roaring and the champagne corks are popping and I am dancing and hugging everyone and everybody is shouting as in a whole mad swoosh we all ride the elevators down to the street again and rush eagerly through the twilight together toward I am not certain where, across some sort of little green park and then dance up a lot of stairs to the most fantastic rooftop party in the world where every single one of my favorite foods is floating past on huge platters held up by waiters, and everyone is bursting with joy and Mary Trump shambles in—*leaves her apartment!*—and we hug about thirty times, and yell with wild glee in one another's ears and Lisa Birnbach has to leave early to go do *Lawrence*, and Carol is probably still laid flat on her bench, and Mike gives a speech, and Shawn gives a speech, and I do not remember if Matt gives a speech, and Robbie gives a speech and I give a speech, and I have been so elated for so long, I can no longer stand up and take three Advil when I get back to the Sixty LES, and go to bed.

Now if there is one thing I do not like going on, it is TV. I am not good at it. I *think* brilliantly, *write* smartly, and *speak* stupidly, to steal a line from old Vlad.

Back in the day I was good at it, no longer. However, I am still so happy that being forced to go on all four morning shows with Robbie and tell how happy I am does not diminish my happiness.

"Tell us, E. Jean, what do you plan to do now?"

"Well, I'm going to go home and throw the ball for the dog."

"E. Jean, now that you've won, what are you going to do next?"

"Well, I'm gonna go home and buy some *premium* dog food for my dog."

"What does the future hold for you, E. Jean, now that you are the first person since he was president, to make Donald Trump pay for his lies?"

"Well, I'm gonna go home and adopt a dog for my dog."

I am so happy to be done with the shows and so happy that I won I get into bed early with the most delighted smile in the world, and while I am sleeping Trump has his CNN *Town Hall* and cracks everybody up with jokes about sexual assault and repeats every single thing that a unanimous federal jury just declared he has to pay me $5 million for saying, and, after I wake up? I sue him again.

And this time Trump does not make the same mistake. *This* time he shows up at trial.

39

THE DOGS OF WAR

This is a photo of the "dog I adopt for my dog" I promised on the morning shows. Her name is Miss Havisham. She is a Great Pyrenees. The smaller dog—a light heavyweight at eighty-four pounds—is Guffington Von Fluke, a pit bull. He is the dog I got the dog, Miss Havisham, for. Guff will turn out to be one of the stars of the second trial. Vagina T. Fireball, the black-and-white cat, is not in this photo. (Like T. S. Eliot, I think the names of dogs and cats should bow to the magical dignity of their animal life.) Trump talks about her at the CNN *Town Hall*. Gets a big laugh. You may hear more about the beasts when the beautiful Alina Habba, Esq. cross-examines me.

All four are rescues, including "Alina."

So when January comes a'blowin' in, and a blizzard hits a few hours before I am to leave my mountain cabin, drive out to the Hamptons, and start prepping to meet Donald Trump in court the morning of January 16, 2024—and when the snow does not stop, and when I am burning about 49,388 calories an hour trying to dig my car out, Friends, do not think that I do *not* consider harnessing Miss Havisham and Guffington Von Fluke to a sled and mushing my twelve bags and me down the mountain, across the George Washington Bridge, and through the woods to our secret Hampton's prep lair.* The idea occurs to me about thirty times.

Robbie sends Lloyd, instead.

Lloyd is a pleasant, sweet-tempered, patient young lad of sixty with a very *very* bad Dunkin' Donuts jones. He is the owner and proprietor of a massive GMC trucklike machine—a man who yearns to "get in shape," and whose downfall is consuming low-tab dinners while waiting for his clients. And me? I possess a giant sled which seats six. I load the sled with my bags and haul the

---

* Robbie, more superstitious than a major league pitcher throwing a no-hitter, insists we prep in East Hampton because we prepped for the *first* trial in East Hampton, and so we must—despite the blizzard—prep for the second trial in East Hampton.

sled up up up up to Lloyd, who waits between two snowbanks about a 170 yards from my cabin. I make four trips with that sled.

*   *   *

Journalists do not often get unshackled access to a person, let alone unshackled access to a person about to undergo for the second time a high-stakes trial, where the person takes the stand and testifies about the worst days of her life while the most famous man in the world, whom the jury will decide if he *causes* the worst days of her life, is sitting right in front of her denying every word she says so loudly the jury stares at him in fright. But Friends, *you* are in luck.

I am about to unzip the bags I haul up to Lloyd and let you take a peek.

*   *   *

For one night in the Hamptons and a three-and-a-half week stay at the semi-swank Marmara Park Avenue Hotel ("evoking the feeling, spirit, and spontaneity of the world's most storied metropolis") on East Thirty-second Street for trial, and, in expectation of rain, hail, sleet, snow, slush, gusts, floods, gales, and freezes, we have in the six-year old, two-handled Global Huntress cinder-gray nylon bags measuring 27.2 x 13.9 inches each:

BAG ONE

> *3 Uniqlo umbrellas in white, gray, and black*
> *3 Pairs of Uniqlo knit gloves—white, brown, black*
> *10 Belts*
> *3 Red Top mechanics coveralls in navy, white, and red*
> *1 iPod layered in the mechanic's coveralls*

9 Pairs of shoes:

   The old black-and-white Vivienne Westwoods

   The old black Donna Karan velvets

   Two pairs of Amazon's finest: Franco Sarto Mary Jane high-
     heel pumps in "tobacco gloss" and "black gloss," size 11, $79
     each

   Another Amazon special: "Pointed toe" Mary Jane high-heel
     pump in "seal brown suede," size 11, $135

   And from the first trial, the Jimmy Choo navy-blue pumps,
     the Manolo Blahnik crème brûlée pumps, and the Black
     Reformation block-heels

BAG TWO

7 Tartan scarves from Scotland which I plan to give each of my
   lawyers as presents, in memory of my Ma, a McKinney

4 Patterned silk scarves

8 Pairs of Hanes "Max Cushion" cotton crew socks

5 Sets of Uniqlo long underwear in black

5 Wacoal wire-free T-shirt bras #852189 in orchid, black,
   fudgesicle, pink nectar, and whatever the skin color is
   called

6 Merino ribbed sweaters in cream, gray, brown, beige, black,
   and white at $29 each from Uniqlo, which the artful Rory
   Satran of the Wall Street Journal will refer to as "quiet
   luxury knits," in a supple story titled "To Take on Trump, E.
   Jean Carroll Wears Luxurious Layers"

8 Pairs of Wolford panty hose from the first trial, all in excellent
   shape

4 Pairs of my special black tights, the fabled Peds Women's
   Super-Opaque Comfort Tights that I get on Amazon for
   $7.50 each

2 *United States military flight suits. I wear these flight suits
    for trial prep. I wear these flight suits with my army US
    Army Cold Wet Weather Gen 1 Woodland Gortex parka
    for walks. I wear these flight suits at all times except when I
    am wearing my "quiet luxury knits" in the Daniel Patrick
    Moynihan United States Courthouse. And, one day, I plan
    to buy and wear a "landing suit"*
1 *Mac Air layered between the sweaters*
My old Fendi briefcase that John Johnson gives me in 1987

BAG THREE

T-3 hot rollers
Comb
Bobbie pins
Hair clips
Head bands
Ribbons (black, brown, navy, white)
3 Mirrors—regular, 3X, 10X
Deodorant
Safety pins
Sewing kit
Colgate Optic White Toothpaste
Colgate Whitening Mouthwash
Toothbrush
Oribe Shampoo for Beautiful Color
Oribe Conditioner for Beautiful Color
Oribe Gold Lust Dry Shampoo
Oribe Superfine Strong Hair Spray
Oribe Dry Texturizing Spray
4 Miniature jars of Vaseline (purse, desk, bedside, bathroom)
Eyebrow plucker

Makeup
  Chanel Cream foundation
  Charlotte Tilbury eye shadows in grays
  Nars blush (Orgasm)
  Thrive Liquid Lash extensions
  Givenchy Rose Perfecto #201 lipstick

Do I need to point out that Lisa Corvelli arrives every morning with *her* Pony Express–size bags full of beauty archeology and that the superb housekeeping staff of the Marmara is probably *still* finding the primers, highlighters, low lighters, bronzers, blushers, glossers that Lisa and I throw madly around the room in wacky comradeship one morning, when we suddenly have only ten minutes to get me downstairs to join Matt, so we can pick up Robbie, go to court, and meet the great screaming frenzy of the press, and I have one eye that looks like Barbra Streisand in *Funny Girl* and one eye that looks like Glenn Close in the bathtub scene in *Fatal Attraction*.

BAG FOUR

  Notebooks, pens, batteries, cords, chargers, flashlight, etc., etc.
  Boots—black, swashbuckling Cole Haans, never wear 'em
  1 soup bowl
  1 salad bowl
  1 glass jar
  1 tablespoon, fork, teaspoon, knife
  2 jars Mount Hagen instant coffee from New Guinea
  And, as I never believe Manhattan has enough food:
    1 loaf Dave's 21-grain bread
    2 jars Once Again organic crunchy peanut butter
    1 jar organic cherry jam

2 bags of organic dry-roasted almonds
1 roll Bounty towels
1 box Kleenex

This concludes the viewing of the four bags that I haul up to Lloyd on *first* sled trip.

The next eight bags are large garment bags gorged with clothes—and, Friends, I admit it. I am a bit above myself because the *New York Times* names me one of the Most Stylish People of 2023 along with Beyonce, Gwyneth, and Taylor, and I do not want to let them down. So:

BAGS FIVE, SIX, AND SEVEN (THE COATS)

The creamy, *big-shouldered Giorgio Armani vintage pea coat I will wear double-belted.*[*]

The corpse-brown *vintage (late '80s) Prada wool coat that I will never wear.*[†] *Like Lydia Bennett buying bonnets, I think I may as well buy it because there are "two or three much uglier" ones. I give it to Shawn G. Crowley at the end of the trial, and on Shawn? The coat looks omniscient. Like it has been waiting forty years to meet Shawn G. Crowley.*

The ice-blue *Harris Wharf London wool trench coat.*[‡]

The burgundy *Theory wool trench coat. (I am actually afraid to look up how much I fork over for it.)*

My dear *long white coat.*

---

[*] The RealReal for $195.

[†] The RealReal for $Too Much.

[‡] The RealReal for $*Wayyy* Too Much.

Old Mr. Softy—*the Adam Lippes coat which I wear the first day of the first trial.*

The rakish *Yeohlee coat—Prussian blue!—from Bergdorf's I purchased thirty years ago.*

My dark-indigo *cashmere officer's greatcoat, which I buy at H&M in 2002 and sew gold buttons and epaulets on in 2024 so I can look like the Duke of Wellington trouncing Napoleon at Waterloo.*

BAGS EIGHT, NINE, TEN, ELEVEN, TWELVE—THUS
BRINGING THE TOTAL, FRIENDS, TO THE FULL DIANA
ROSS DOZEN

These five happy garment bags hold the scrubbed and cleaned outfits you remember from the first trial, with one addition—an otter-brown Richard Tyler double-breasted blazer which I buy in LA in 1997. I want to wear it with the Oscar de la Renta pleated cream skirt that Joe Tacopina says I am beating him "at the fashion game" with. This blazer is as close to being hugged by my childhood teddy bear as I can get.

For traveling in Lloyd's powerful machine, and continuing the whole "we shall fight on the beaches, we shall fight on the landing grounds, we shall never surrender" thing I have going on, I wear my *third* flight suit, a British Royal Air Force pre-owned in sage green, and my extremely old US Army Cold Wet Weather Gen 1 Woodland Gortex parka.

Four days later, I am wearing the sage-green British Royal Air Force flight suit when, in the Ruth Bader Ginsburg Conference Room on the sixty-third floor of the Empire State Building, I have the meltdown.

When Saint Joan Didion traveled, she packed two skirts, two jerseys, a pullover sweater, stockings, a nightgown, slippers, prescriptions, baby oil, cigarettes, bourbon, typewriter, etc., etc., but she did not pack a watch and "didn't know what time it is."

I pack eight coats, nine pairs of shoes, three umbrellas, a jar of organic cherry jam, and six Merino ribbed sweaters, but I do not pack a brain.

*   *   *

The meltdown happens Friday afternoon, January 12. The trial starts in four days, on Tuesday, January 16. Robbie Kaplan, Shawn G. Crowley, Matt Craig, Helen with the Eyelashes, and Emma DeCourcy from Miss Porter's are prepping me. And where is the Duke of Ferrara? Robbie has moved Mike over to a big case representing Tiger Woods. We are at the enormous white conference table. I can see the six states out the window, but I miss seeing Mike.

Robbie is standing at a lectern with her bottle of watermelon water and her stack of evidence.

"Miss Carroll," says Robbie. "How did you feel when you saw this?"

I look at it.

Robbie nods expectantly at me with a big, hopeful bob of her head.

Waves of shame swamp over me.

I loathe myself.

"It's fucking scary," says Shawn G. Crowley, in a low voice. "Take your time."

*   *   *

Facebook
You're not friends on Facebook
3 mutual friends including
and

Add friend   Profile

MAY 23 AT 11:33 PM

I'm so very sorry; my friend said he wants to kill you and I cannot stop him. Rest in peace cunt

MAY 25 AT 3:24 PM

Pile of shit u are!

Robbie puts her bottle of watermelon water down with a bang.

"E. Jean!" says Robbie, frustrated.

*   *   *

In November 2019, I sue Trump for defamation in the Supreme Court of the State of New York. This suit is called *Carroll I.* In September 2020, Trump, facing the deadline to provide a DNA sample, gets the DOJ to save his bacon, and the case moves to Judge Lewis Kaplan in federal district court in Manhattan. Judge Kaplan rules the DOJ must butt out. In December 2020, the DOJ, claiming that Trump was absolutely acting as president when he calls me too unattractive to rape, appeals Judge Kaplan's decision to the United States Court of Appeals, Second Circuit. In September 2022, the Second Circuit throws the decision to the DC Court of Appeals.

In November 2022, New York passes the Adult Survivors Act. It goes into effect on Thanksgiving. I am the first person to file, at a few minutes past midnight, and I sue Trump for the 1996 assault and for defaming statements he makes in October 2022. This suit is called *Carroll II.*

On April 25, 2023, *Carroll II* goes to trial, and the anonymous upstate jury of three women and six men holds Trump liable for inserting his fingers into my vagina without my consent and for making false and malicious statements about me.

I am masticating the *Carroll I* and *Carroll II* casserole for you, Friends, because when we go to trial next Tuesday—and we are going to trial because two things happen. *Primo,* The DC Court of Appeals throws *Carroll I* back to Judge Kaplan and Judge Kaplan sets the trial date; and *segundo,* the Fox News starlet Alina Habba, Esq.'s last-minute, joke-shop, Hail Mary emergency appeal to the Second Circuit claiming Trump's total, universal, eternal *presidential immunity* is chewed to gristle by Joshua Matz, the Man with the 583 IQ. When we go to trial, as I say, next Tuesday, the sexual abuse and defamation claims have *already* been decided by the jury in *Carroll II.*

So next Tuesday's trial is not a do-over. Next Tuesday's trial is about the damage—and *only* about the damage (if any)—done to me by Trump's statements from the White House and the remarks he makes after leaving office, viz: the CNN *Town Hall,* campaign statements, etc.

The good news is this trial will be short and straightforward. Robbie will simply show the new jury evidence of what happens when Trump says terrible things about me.

"Miss Carroll," she says, paging through her exhibits looking for a message which might elicit a more enlightening answer than my last one—the order of Robbie's questions will change fifty-two times before trial—"how did you feel when you saw this?"

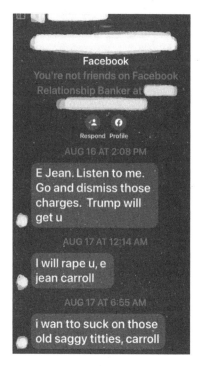

I look at it.

I look back at Robbie.

"It's *your* testimony, E. Jean," says Robbie. "The jury will want to hear how this message affects you."

I look again at the Relationship Banker at a Manhattan Bank's message. I am humiliated because I can't stop picturing what he is saying he will do to me. Shame just rolls and rolls and rolls and rolls over me, and, what is worse, this isn't even one of the *really* bad messages.

"E. Jean" says Shawn G. Crowley, softly. "You're under a lot of stress. Just tell us what you feel as you read it."

I help the team collect this evidence that is gushing into my Twitter, my mail box, my Facebook, my "Ask E. Jean" letters, my life. I gather it and sweep it into Google Docs titled "Avalanche of Offal" and "Ugh," and into folders on my desktop labeled "Threats," and send them to Emma DeCourcy.

I become acutely aware everyone is staring at me. They are waiting with the reassuring smiles they reserve for a mentally de-caying patient who can't remember where her spoon is. *This* is why I am ashamed. I am frightened I cannot talk.

Exasperated, Robbie sorts through her exhibits trying to find something repulsive enough to make me speak:

"Tell us, Miss Carroll," she says, pulling up a new one. "How did you feel when you received this?"

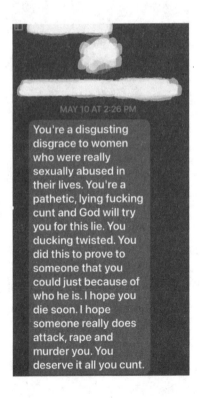

MAY 10 AT 2:26 PM

You're a disgusting disgrace to women who were really sexually abused in their lives. You're a pathetic, lying fucking cunt and God will try you for this lie. You ducking twisted. You did this to prove to someone that you could just because of who he is. I hope you die soon. I hope someone really does attack, rape and murder you. You deserve it all you cunt.

*   *   *

Now, Friends, I'm an upbeat girl. You might say I'm a *very* upbeat girl. I like to laugh. You can hear my laugh bouncing off the mountaintops up here in the forest, in my cabin—my cabin. It's got a fireplace. It's on an island. A river runs in front and a creek runs in back, and, since Trump's first White House statement on June 21, 2019, saying I "should pay dearly," waves of hatred run through my cabin, a hundred messages a day, a thousand a day, twenty or thirty posts per minute, liar, fraud, psycho, cunt, death, bitch; people hate me, they really, *really* hate me.

This kind of thing can get a girl down.

P.S. I see Jackdaniels Melissa called. Luckily I missed it.

*   *   *

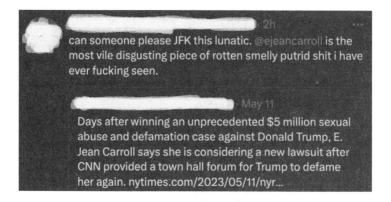

can someone please JFK this lunatic. @ejeancarroll is the most vile disgusting piece of rotten smelly putrid shit i have ever fucking seen.

Days after winning an unprecedented $5 million sexual abuse and defamation case against Donald Trump, E. Jean Carroll says she is considering a new lawsuit after CNN provided a town hall forum for Trump to defame her again. nytimes.com/2023/05/11/nyr...

What is my brain supposed to do with "please JFK this lunatic"? It tries. My brain tries. My brain only lets me see certain words. I see the date, May 11, for instance. Right after Trump's CNN *Town Hall*. But my brain is never *quite* fast enough. I have *already* seen the words and the alarm goes off. My nervous system is on red alert. I have seen *all* the words. I go back. I reread the words my brain thinks it didn't let me see to see if I read the words the first time, and, of course, I *had* read them the first time; they had come sneaking and crawling in when I did not even know I was looking.

People say, "Well, get off social media."

I am a journalist. I live for breaking stories. I post breaking stories. I jaw with my fellow journalists. I am not getting off social media.

So my brain just sops it up.

It is just a "condition," as Tom Wolfe calls it.

I go cold.

I go hot.

I duck.

Next message, please.

*   *   *

There is what they call "dead silence" in the Ruth Bader Ginsburg. There is dead silence in the Ruth Bader Ginsburg because I am sitting in my chair, loaded with unburnt flight fuel. Or fight fuel. Or I do not know which kind of unburned fuel, but I feel I must weigh seven hundred pounds. Everything is sad and ragged. Everyone is looking at me with concern. How can we go to trial if I can't talk? How will the jury hear about the damage?

I see the fear in everyone's eyes.

Their alarms have put *their* nervous systems on red alert. Robbie advises me to set up a Zoom with Dr. Leslie Lebowitz as soon as possible and sends me back to the Marmara Park Avenue Hotel with four bags of popcorn, a bag of chickpea puffs, some Pink Lady apples, a mushroom sandwich, and a big falafel.

"E. Jean," she says. "Please take it easy."

But I cannot take it easy in the Marmara because Trump is all over TV saying he is "going to go to court and tell the world

I have never met this woman," and the room is so dark I cannot see, and it is heated by hot blowers which make my eyes sting, my skin flake, my nails break, and my nose run, so I wrap up in two of the tartan scarves, put on my parka, and walk around New York eating the popcorn and buying humidifiers.

*   *   *

I am supposed to talk to Dr. Leslie Lebowitz about not being able to talk about the damage, so I start the Zoom the next day with Dr. Leslie Lebowitz by telling her the bizarre three-part dream I have about Trump.

Boy! Is Dr. Lebowitz thrilled about my dream!

It is as if she just watched *The Terminator*! She suggests that when I take the stand and Trump is sitting right in front of me at the Defendant's Table, and when the moment is right, I should look Trump in the eye, I should give him a look that says—Well, Friends, I am not going to tell you what my look is going to say, but it is exactly the look he deserves.

As for the not being able talk about the damage, Dr. Leslie Lebowitz sneaks up on me. She tells me *not* to talk about it. But if I could just do her a favor, just give her an example of just one of the messages I cannot talk about she would appreciate it. So I read one to her, and what with all her creating the sexual trauma protocols for the United States Air Force and United States Department of Veterans Affairs, even Dr. Leslie Lebowitz *herself* is taken back for a moment.

And then she says:

"E. Jean, you can't talk because you *see* the gun in your mouth. You *see* and *feel* the guy raping you anally, and it shuts everything down. Your senses heighten. Your muscles tense. Your heart rate increases. You start to sweat, and you lose language."

And then she gives me excellent advice:

"You're a reporter, E. Jean," she says. "Go to the body. When Robbie shows you a tweet and asks how it makes you feel, report the reaction of your body: 'I'm having difficulty breathing. I feel sweaty. I can't get my eyes to focus.'"

"Stick to the facts!" I say.

"Yes!"

"I can do that!" I cry.

And, Friends, what with Dr. Lebowitz's advice, and John Blonde, Robbie's Super Man Executive Assistant, arriving with two bags of lamps from his own apartment, along with the bottle of green Chartreuse sent to my room by Robbie and Matt, I must say, all in all, I do not feel *absolutely* doomed.

40

A FULL AND FAITHFUL REPORT OF THE MEMORABLE TRIAL OF *CARROLL V. TRUMP*

DAY ONE

Tuesday, January 16, 2024

OPENING ARGUMENTS

BY MS. CROWLEY AND MS. HABBA:
Right after Donald Trump's attacks from the White House—*the White House!*—in June 2019, Ms. Carroll bought bullets for the gun that she inherited from her father.

Ms. Carroll was completely unaffected by negative feedback and was *basking* in the limelight.

Literally within minutes, people started posting *horrible* things about Ms. Carroll, *amplifying* Trump's own threats.

People who do not support President Trump *heaped praises* on her and stopped in the street to support her.

Her pit bull now guards her property.

Her *friend* is Mary Trump!

She is afraid that someday somebody is going to make good on their threats and come after her in person.

She is friends with *Kathy Griffin*! I would not *allow* my team to put a picture up of her holding a likeness of President Trump's severed *head*!

Donald Trump's horrible lies did more than destroy E. Jean's sense of safety. They ruined her professional reputation, a reputation for honesty and integrity that she spent years, decades, her whole career building up as a journalist and advice columnist.

Ms. Carroll is now more famous than she has ever been in her life, which was her *goal*.

You will hear that *as* Donald Trump faces trial over how much money it will take to get him to stop defaming Ms. Carroll, *he keeps doing it*. He sat in *this* courthouse. You saw him. He sat in this courthouse this morning. And while he was sitting here he posted defamatory statements, more lies about Ms. Carroll and this case. By our last count, 22 posts, *just today*. Think about that. Think about that when you consider how much money it will take him to *stop*.

It's up to you now, the jury, to see through this charade, and tell *her* it is enough!

* * *

The above story about the life and death of my career comes from the opening arguments presented to the jury by the brilliant Shawn G. Crowley and the beautiful Alina Habba, Esq. the first day of trial, Tuesday, January 16, 2024, in Judge Lewis A. Kaplan's courtroom with the oak, the jury box, and the famous runway.

It is a dark, blistering, snowing, sleeting, freezing day in New York. The headlines this morning are "Trump Wins Landslide in the Iowa Caucuses" and "Joe Tacopina Withdraws from Representing Trump in His Criminal and Civil Cases."

Tacopina declines to say why.

*   *   *

Before the opening arguments—which I hope I have shown no prejudice in presenting, Friends—we have jury picking. And before the jury picking, Alina Habba, Esq., looking like the captive Haydee in *The Count of Monte Cristo*, with her "large black eyes shaded by lashes, complexion of purist olive, and teeth like pearls," and her partner Michael T. Madaio, a large, promising young fellow stuffed into a small gray suit looking like he's just been elected vice president of the Boosters Club in Zenith, tell district judge Lewis Kaplan that he, His Honor, does not "have jurisdiction to proceed forward with this trial."

"Overruled," says Judge Kaplan.

Next, Habba and Madaio try to "preserve the right to have this case overturned, if *Carroll II* is overturned by the Second Circuit."

"Overruled," says Judge Kaplan.

Next, Madaio and Habba accuse Judge Kaplan of being "prejudicial" and that he should allow in the Anderson Cooper tape.

"Overruled," says Judge Kaplan.

Next, Habba asks for an adjournment so Trump can go to Melania's mother's funeral in Florida.

"I am not stopping him from being there," says Judge Kaplan.

Next, Madaio complains about gagging the parties. "It's *completely* unnecessary to gag both sides during the course of this trial!" he cries out passionately.

"There *is* no gag order," says Judge Kaplan.

And so on, till Judge Kaplan tells Andy the Deputy Clerk to call for the prospective jurors. But Andy the Deputy Clerk says the jury department will not be ready for several minutes, and, while waiting, Judge Kaplan asks the attorneys from both sides how long their cases will take to go on, and what witnesses they are calling.

"A lot of it is up in the air, your Honor," says Habba.

"*None* of it is up in the air," says Judge Kaplan.

*   *   *

Friends, you have seen Trump, right? You have seen him around. Here and there. A handsome man. Tall, blond, still with the streak of the old Tab Hunter about him, his hair combed into a plume-like Tippi Hedren in *The Birds*—but trust me, Friends, you have *never* seen Trump like this. Swiveling around in his chair at the Defendant's Table, nodding, twinkling, clasping his hands in happy woe, and smiling at the prospective jurors like Pamela Harriman at a cocktail party.

O! Trump loves being here! Loves it! Loves it! From where I am sitting, which is right in front of him, his every gesture looks to me like a win in a game of tit for tat. Who can buy campaign coverage like this!? Who could *look* like a bigger victim!? Iowa is good, but *this* is heaven! The more he sits here, the more money he raises. The more money he raises, the more races he wins, the more races he wins, well . . . I really do not have to tell you how happy I think Trump is, do I?

Outside the courtroom, of course, he says the opposite, he

scowls and sneers and says it's a "disgrace." He says it's a "witch hunt." He says Judge Kaplan is "totally biased," that this trial is a "hoax" and "election interference never seen before," and so on and so forth. But trust me, he loves it.

*   *   *

It is after Trump slathers each prospective juror with his smile or his twinkle or his nod, that I give Trump "the look."

*   *   *

He and I are alone—each at our massive table. I am at the Plaintiff's Table. Trump is behind me at the Defendant's Table. How far behind me? About seven and a half feet, closer than the length of a pool table, closer than a king-size mattress. If I turn my head slightly, I see him. If I reach back with my arm, I will be within two feet of grabbing him by the hair.

Our attorneys are squabbling at a sidebar with Judge Kaplan, drawing up the final nine jurors. No courtroom artists, press, spectators are in the courtroom.

I seize the moment and turn completely around in my chair, *completely around* in my brown silk Oscar de la Renta dress and white blazer and lance him in the eyes. It takes him a beat to realize I am serious and he looks at me with a flash of attention. His pupils are the color of blue masking tape. I commit myself. My eyes hold his eyes. Me and Trump. I look at him. He looks at me. It is the most intense moment of my life. My look says the thing I want to say. He tilts his head. He gets it. He got it. He got it good. I turn back around and face Judge Kaplan and the attorneys at the sidebar, never to know what Trump was thinking.

OK. OK. He was probably thinking *he* intimidated *me*—

*   *   *

For the next two days I will be in the witness chair, eighteen paces from him (trials are always duels) testifying about the wounds he gave me. He will never meet my eyes again.

*   *   *

After a scrap over a prospective juror who is unvaccinated—Habba, in good rioting mood, with her marvelous "anything goes" attitude, and Madaio, with his thick, stolid manner—fight for the unvaccinated juror, but go down in defeat when Judge Kaplan mentions that their own client, not to mention the plaintiff and the judge himself are all "vulnerable," i.e., *old*—and after a knees-up free-for-all straight out of Charles Dickens's Buffs and Blues about "Biden supporters" and "Trump supporters," and a new attorney for Trump lumbering into the fray—an enormous, black-haired, chewed-up-looking chap who introduces himself to the judge with:

"Your Honor, Boris Epshteyn, the president's in-house counsel and member of the bar in good standing."
—the jury is sworn in and seated.

*   *   *

Friends, you ask: Is it a *good* jury?

Well, it is a *very* good jury for Trump because it is *seven* men and two women. And it is a good jury for us because the ice and snow closed the roads in the upstate Trump counties and the only beings who *can* show up today are dyed-in-the-wool New Yorkers with the hearts of polar bears and the balance of Brian Boitano who can make it across the ice and snow to the Daniel Patrick Moynihan United States Courthouse, so take your choice.

Here are the *Carroll v. Trump* Nine: **(A)** a squarely built re-tired track supervisor for the New York City Transit Authority who gets his news from Channel 7; (**B**) a teacher from Germany who wears a smartly fitted coat with a pretty faux fur collar who is taking some time off from the International School in New York where she works and who does not follow the news because she is busy studying "the history of America"; (**C**) a twenty-six-year-old newlywed with an associate's degree in business who gets his news from Facebook and Instagram and is currently working in property management and maintenance, as does his bride; (**D**) a man from Ireland who works in cybersecurity sales with a subscription to the *New York Times*; (**E**) a professional violinist from Barcelona, with a doctorate, who gets his news from various Spanish newspapers; (**F**) an emergency medicine physician who gets his news from "a composite picture from different sources such as the *New York Times* and the *Wall Street Journal*; (**G**) a shiny publicist who gets her news from "major TV broadcasts and newspapers"; (**H**) a respiratory therapist who gets his news from YouTube; (**I**) a man who does postproduction for TV and gets his news from "print, local news stations, online, all of it."

These nine souls, some still wrapped in their outdoor scarves, hear Judge Kaplan explain the case. They also hear Shawn G. Crowley's opening argument. Also Alina Habba, Esq.'s opening argument and Judge Kaplan saying, "Okay, we will resume at 9:30 a.m. tomorrow." And off the nine souls go to board a private elevator which will drop them under the Daniel Patrick Moynihan United States Courthouse, where they will climb into a secret vehicle which will speed them through the snow to an undisclosed location at which they will debouch and disperse to their unknown homes, where they will tell no one that they are one of nine souls who will decide the outcome of this month's Trial of the Century.

*   *   *

DAY TWO

Wednesday, January 17, 2024

MS. HABBA GOES TO LAW SCHOOL

——*Rise, coffee, wash, Dave's 21-grain bread, hair, makeup, brown blazer, Oscar skirt, Marmara lobby, Carroll Team, Robbie, Daniel Patrick Moynihan United States Courthouse, popping photographers, X-rays, more X-rays, Secret Service, witness room, jury late, banana, green tea, peanut butter, down the runway, trial resumes.*

Before the jury is called, Habba rises and, for a third time, thwacks it out with Judge Kaplan about the funeral of Amalija Knavs, Trump's mother-in-law. After calling him "insanely prejudicial" she says:

HABBA: I am asking your Honor to have the kindness that my client *deserves* to be with his family tomorrow and not to have to miss trial that he has a *right* to be here for. There is a jury watching. It is prejudicial.

TRUMP: (*Big, brawny nod.*)

JUDGE KAPLAN: Indeed Ms. Habba. The right that he has, according to the Supreme Court of the United States, is the right to be present either in person or by counsel, and nothing is stopping him from doing either. The application is denied. I will hear no further argument on it.

TRUMP: (*Under his breath*) Nasty man!

HABBA: Your Honor.

JUDGE KAPLAN: None. Do you understand the word? None. Please, sit down.

TRUMP: (*Rolling his head, anger blowing out of his eyes in red glints.*)

HABBA: Your Honor, if I may.

JUDGE KAPLAN: I said: Sit down.

TRUMP: (*Slamming his fist on the table*) Man!

HABBA: I am not arguing on that, your Honor.

JUDGE KAPLAN: What else do you want to discuss?

HABBA: I don't like to be spoken to that way!

*   *   *

Friends, I begin the report of day two with this exchange to show you how mistaken you are about the effervescent and industrious Alina Habba, Esq.

Everything you think about Alina Habba, Esq. is crap. For instance, Alina Habba, Esq. is not dumb. You doubt me? Naw. Naw. Her sass conceals high art under its Diamond-Big-as-the-Ritz glitz. Trust me, Friends. In the end, you will agree with me. You will have never in your lives seen anyone butch it out like Alina!

*   *   *

I am sworn in, take the witness chair, and grapple with its tonnage, pulling it forward by gouging my heels into the carpet.

Robbie, the once-in-a-generation attorney superstar, gives a respectful nod to the jury, takes up her position at the oaken lectern like Alexander the Great landing in Persia, and begins with "Ms. Carroll, can you please say your name and spell it for the court reporter." (None of the old Joe Tacopina "Good morning" folderol.) And smoothly, swiftly, she moves through my childhood, career, the magazines, *SNL*, the show, the books, the advice column, etc., etc., and then like the great narrator of facts that she is, she sharply plunges me and the jury into darkness. And we enter my lurid world of hate, threat, death.

She introduces document after document into evidence* which tie Trump's statements to the vile stream of horror running through my daily life, and, with only thirteen objections from Habba that are overruled, five objections from Habba that are sustained, three statements I make that Habba gets stricken, a lecture from Judge Kaplan to Habba about how to behave in court—"When you speak in this courtroom or any other courtroom in this building, you will stand up!"—and sixty or seventy snorts, whines, sighs, grunts, sneers, groans, arm-flappings, table thumpings, and loud mutterings from Trump, the morning break arrives.

How does it feel testifying before Trump with his Sandra Dee hair shining smack in my face?

I imagine it is like how a nun feels—stay with me here, Friends—when she is saying her rosary aloud. She feels God is watching her. And the more she feels God is watching her, the louder and more confidently she tells her beads. That is what it is like.

Except I do not have a rosary and it is not God watching me; it is the emperor from Hans Christian Anderson, and I am the kid who sees the emperor has no clothes. That is what it is like.

Except the guy *I* am looking at in court *does* have clothes, but nothing is *in* the clothes. That is what it is like.

Except I am not a kid, I am an eighty-year-old woman doing something that millions and millions and millions and millions of people on this planet *wish* they could do—I am telling Trump the truth *to his face*.

---

* Robbie introduces fifty-three documents into evidence in less than three and a half hours—a fact that Judge Kaplan will soon mention to Alina Habba, Esq. when she cannot figure out how introduce *anything*.

That is what it is like.

*   *   *

We break for lunch and when the jury leaves the courtroom for the nice meal provided by the Daniel Patrick Moynihan United States Courthouse cafeteria, Shawn G. Crowley rises, glances at Trump, turns back to Judge Kaplan, and says:

MS. CROWLEY: Judge, I just want to place on the record, *again,* that notwithstanding your instruction right before we started, the defendant has been making statements that, *again,* we can hear at counsel table. Some of the jurors are sitting closer to him than we are. He said: "It is a witch hunt." "It really is a con job." And, when the last video was played,* he said, "It's true." So we would just ask your Honor to remind the parties that they are not supposed to make statements to, or indirectly to, the jury.

THE COURT: Mr. Trump has the right to be present here. That right can be forfeited, and it can be forfeited if he is *disruptive,* which what has been reported to me consists of, and if he disregards court orders.

———*And for a world needing badly to escape, and hungry for news, here comes the court tidbit of the day: Judge Kaplan, with his long, doleful face and head of sensational white hair, a steel rod of a man, famous for his "taking no nonsense," glares down from his dais at the apricot mythomaniac:*

---

* A video starring an angry, but slick-looking Trump calling me a liar, which Trump publishes the day after the unanimous jury in the *first* trial holds him liable for defamation.

THE COURT: Mr. Trump, I hope I don't have to consider excluding you from the trial, at least from the presence.

MR. TRUMP: (*His head down like a bull, he eye-forks His Honor.*)

THE COURT: I understand you're probably very eager for me to do that.

MR. TRUMP: (*Throwing up his hands like he is catching a baby*) I would love it!

THE COURT: I *know* you would. You just *can't* control yourself in these circumstances apparently. Thank you.

*   *   *

Michael Madaio, his suit looking smaller than ever after lunch, tells Judge Kaplan that he, Judge Lewis A. Kaplan, has been displaying "a general hostility toward the defense throughout the case," and therefore Donald J. Trump submits that Judge Lewis A. Kaplan should go fuck himself, or to use Madaio's more musical term, he wants, under Ethical Canon 3, to make an application for "recusal to the court."

Judge Kaplan glances down at Trump, the curse of the legal profession.

"Denied."

*   *   *

Soon after, the front of the courtroom is made additionally glamorous by Alina Habba, Esq. taking over the trial lectern, her cheekbones jutting like tulip bulbs, her dark eyes on me like the queen about to give Snow White the apple.

And, Friends, as she begins her cross-examination of yours truly, please remember that what I am about to tell you is only how I, a lowly cross-examinee, view her from the witness chair, but it appears that Trump's most beautiful attorney may be a total loss when it comes to legal procedure, such as introducing a document into evidence, or citing a line of transcript, or impeaching a witness, though I know *you* will not be so cold-hearted as to judge Alina Habba, Esq.'s performance as a "trial attorney." No. You *already* know she doesn't know doodly-squat about the law.

But her confidence?

It's a dilly! Her talent? *Extreme.* I mean, you try and cross-examine me with Donald Trump making a noise like sewage escaping a leaky pipe and Boris Epshteyn scoffing and hissing commands at *you.* She hits me with everything. All at once. A numbskull in legal matters, a *genius* at cross, *that's* Alina Habba, Esq.! Her questions are attacks, her assumptions are slanders, her time frames are relative, her topics are salacious, and her style riveting. She is brilliant! I'm telling you. At one point, when Robbie is standing and objecting, Alina Habba, Esq. smiles at the jury like Tiffany Haddish in *Girls Trip,* then turns to Judge Kaplan and asks:

"Why is *she* objecting?"

His Honor replies:

"This is not my law school examination."

But do not take *my* word for it, let Trump himself give you the highlights of Alina's cross:

*   *   *

"It was a very interesting day. You probably noticed. It's a *big* story. The witness today—a person I never knew—a totally rigged deal, this whole thing is RIGGED! ELECTION IN-TERFERENCE!!!!!!—Well, they found out today that she got rid of a lot of evidence, as you probably noticed. MASSIVE amounts of evidence! And in addition to *that,* she had a rifle or a gun—because she said she bought bullets. . . . or rifle bullets—"

Here Trump frowns.

(*Is* it a rifle? Or—?)

He is standing in front of eight brass standards implanted with eight giant American flags in the lobby of Trump Tower, after court, with his hair rolling across his forehead like Barbara Stanwyck in *Ball of Fire*. Not wasting a second more on the "gun-rifle puzzle," he pulls himself together and goes on:

"—the opposite, I guess, of her gun. And was it *licensed*? *NO! IT WASN'T LICENSED*! So I guess she's got a difficult PROBLEM. That's going to be her problem. But she has a gun or a rifle. She didn't really explain which, she might have *both* because she said she bought rifle bullets and it's *totally* unlicensed . . .

"So the *big* take today is she *deleted* and destroyed *MASSIVE* amounts of evidence and we think *both* trials should be thrown out! Because it's *ridiculous*! They should be thrown out! And *I*, frankly, am the one who suffered damage!"

Saint Sebastian tied to a tree and shot with arrows could not look more pathetic.

"*I'm* the one who should be given money! Given damages!!!!"

*   *   *

On second thought. Let's not take Trump's word. Let us look at my testimony—Robbie Kaplan's direct examination and Alina Habba, Esq.'s cross—to find out what *really* happened, re the "massive" deletion of "evidence," and the gun:

DIRECT EXAMINATION

BY MS. KAPLAN:

Q. How often did you receive messages threatening to kill you?

A. Often.

Q. Let's go with the two groups. Messages like the ones we have been looking at up to now that did *not* contain threats of violence. (*Viz: a timeline of scabrous messages directly connected to Trump's statements which we could safely show the jury without causing them to lean over the railing of the jury box and throw up on the runway.*) How many messages like that do you think you've received to this day?

A. Oh, thousands. Thousands.

———*I've had three or four thousand in a single day.*

Q. And the new category that we're now talking about— messages that *do* threaten violence. How many messages like that do you think you've received to this day?

A. Hundreds.

Q. When was the very first time, Ms. Carroll, that you recall seeing a message threatening you?

A. I remember almost the exact time. It was around 11:30 on the night of June 21. I was in a very small, very cheap hotel on Tenth Avenue. I walked into the room. I couldn't wait to see the news and check out what was happening. I had been unconnected. And the room was so small, there was no desk. There was a board that you flapped down from the wall, so I flopped the board down. I put my computer on the board. I opened it up. I immediately went to Twitter where I get breaking news and I saw:

> *"You lying whore." "You lying scag." "You lying slut." "You lying psycho." "You lying scumbag."*

My brain just froze. So to make myself feel good, I went to my "Ask E. Jean" email, thinking that I would feel better if I could read some support. And I opened it up, and, yes, there was a really lovely email saying, "You go girl!" And then I opened up the next "Ask E. Jean" letter, and I looked at it, I read it, and I ducked.

Because the image of what the person was saying caused me to believe that it was going to happen *right now.* I thought I was going to get shot. And what the hard part was, I couldn't get the curtain across the window closed. I was sitting in a room with an open window at eleven thirty at night. And it's—when I see the words, the image comes into my mind, and I believe it's about to happen *right now.* So I deleted the message to protect myself. Then I stood up and tried to get the curtain closed. Couldn't do it. I had brought some jumpsuits in my bag. I tried to hang them up over the window. And it was—I had never dealt with anything like that.

——Friends, this is the first deletion. Later I will tell the jury I am sorry for making them sick when Robbie shows them more threats.

Q. And I think as you were telling the story, Ms. Carroll, you said it was June 2l. Is that June 21, 2019?

——June 21, 2019, is the day Trump issued his first statement from the White House.

A. Yes.
Q. Did you get more than one message that night?
A. Yes.
Q. Threatening you with violence?
A. Yes.
Q. And did you—what did you do with the other messages?

A. Two of them I remember, I immediately deleted because they sent *images*. One was a car accident with a very dead woman on the pavement with some of her brains coming out her head. And the other one was a woman who had obviously been murdered, blood on her neck and her chest.

MS. HABBA: Objection, your Honor. It's inflammatory.
THE COURT: We'll strike the last sentence. The question was: "What did you do with the other messages?"
THE WITNESS: Yes, I deleted them.

——*I also delete five or six more the night of June 21 but nobody asks me.*

*   *   *

So there is Trump's "massive amounts of evidence" that I "get rid of." Now let us look at Habba's cross:

CROSS-EXAMINATION

BY MS. HABBA:
Q. Do you *know* what discovery is?
A. Yes.

——*But hang on a moment . . . I wonder if the most distinguished and illustrious graduate of Widener University Commonwealth Law School, a superb institution which accepts only 65 percent of its applicants, knows what discovery is, because her client delivers almost zero.*

Q. Do you *understand* that you had a *duty* to preserve documents?

A. I preserve every single one of my (Twitter) posts. I never deleted.

Q. What about e-mails in your inbox?

A. No.

Q. No you did not delete those?

——*Alina Habba, Esq. with her off-beat erotic magnetism, in her fitted pants and high heels, looks very pretty when she is chock-full of threats.*

A. No. I did not.

Q. So do you have, in your inbox *all* the messages relating to death threats that you spoke about today?

——*Her hot black eyes are on me.*

A. No. I deleted them early on because I didn't know how to handle death threats. I had no idea. I thought deleting them was the smartest, best, quickest way to get it out of my life.

Q. What about the e-mails *supporting* you, Ms. Carroll, do you keep those?

A. Some, yes. Most.

Q. Did you delete any of those after this, your first lawsuit against the president?

THE COURT: Which is the first lawsuit?

MS. HABBA: *This* is the first lawsuit.

A. I'm not sure. The Ask E. Jean address where they come in, I tend to delete questions to me about—that I *know* I won't use

in the column, but I don't believe I deleted anything supportive.
I think I had an entire file, people who send supportive
messages. I file it all in one place.

*——In other words, I may have deleted a question or two sent
to "Ask E. Jean" asking about the correspondent's love life, career,
friendships, purpose on this planet, etc., etc. which I knew I would
not use in the Elle column because I had recently run a similar
letter about the same topic.*

Q. Ms. Carroll, do you CONTROL your e-mail?
A. Yes.
Q. Can you provide me those email—Well, actually I won't let
you do that. Does anybody *else* control your email?

*——Is this a trick question? What do you think, Friends? The
Iraqi-American queen bee, with her 556,000 Instagram followers
and her $3,586,350 million from Trump and his Save America
PAC for "legal consultation," is swaying behind the lectern with
witchy anticipation.*

A. Nobody.
Q. Would anybody else have *deleted* the messages after we were
in ACTIVE litigation?
A. I don't think they would.
Q. So only *you* could have done that, is that correct?

——The tulip bulbs of her cheeks gloat into flowers.

A. Yes.
Q. Ms. Carroll, are you aware that it is *illegal* to DELETE
evidence after a *subpoena* has been issued?

————*Only Alina Habba, Esq. could be crowing over deleted emails that would have destroyed Trump's case.*

MS. KAPLAN: Objection, your Honor.
THE COURT: Sustained. Jury will disregard the question.
MS. HABBA: Your Honor.
THE COURT: You're not instructing the jury, counsel.
MS. HABBA: I was not going to. Your Honor, at this moment, I feel I have to ask for a *mistrial*! The witness has just admitted to DELETING evidence herself! Which are part of her claim for damages! And I haven't *seen* them! She has *no* evidence of them. She hasn't turned them *over*!!!
THE COURT: Denied. The jury will disregard everything Ms. Habba just said.

Of course, over the weekend Habba files a written motion for a mistrial, Judge Kaplan denies it, and later he issues a thirty-page opinion explaining that he denies it chiefly because the motion "made no sense." He writes that at the time I deleted the death threats I received after Trump's June 2019 statements, I was not considering suing Trump.

> "It was not until attorney George Conway in mid-July 2019 explained to her the idea and the process of litigation that she first truly considered suing Mr. Trump," said Kaplan. "Mr. Trump offered no evidence to the contrary. Accordingly, Ms. Carroll had no duty to preserve any [electronically stored information] before mid-July 2019."

*   *   *

But Trump is right about one thing. That gun. It *is* an unlicensed Double Nine—an old High Standard .22 revolver, nine chambers, which fires a .22 "long rifle" bullet which I inherited from my dad.

*   *   *

DAY THREE

Thursday, January 18, 2024

MY BRAIN DIET

Berries
Leafy greens
Walnuts
Almonds
Hard-boiled eggs
Broccoli
Shredded cabbage
Pumpkin seeds
Black beans
Olive oil

Everything on this list will "improve motor and cognitive functions" and help "slow cognitive abilities with older age," according to the National Institutes of Health, and this is what I feed my poor gasping brain every night for dinner after trial.

I change into a flight suit, leave the Marmara at Thirty-second Street, fly down purple and gray Park Avenue to Whole Foods at Twenty-eighth and Madison, ride the escalator up, load down my cart, speed through self-checkout, fly back down Park Avenue to the Marmara with two bags, off-load the haul in my little kitchenette, open the packages, wash the berries, wash the leafy greens, wash the broccoli, wash the shredded cabbage, dry them in the soft, plush, luxurious Marmara towels, slice the hard-boiled eggs, load everything into a huge bowl, shower the whole mess with olive oil, walnuts, almonds, pumpkin seeds, and a couple of wallops from the can of beans, and chow down.

Even the bottle of Chartreuse made by the Carthusian monks at the Grande Chartreuse Monastery that Matt and Robbie send me is made from a *secret* recipe of 130 brain-sizzling herbs, flowers, trees, and plants, which Jesus himself, if he appeared in their distillery, could not wheedle out of those monks!

And, Friends, my brain and I feel the good effects when Habba spends all morning continuing her cross-examination of me on day three.

*   *   *

Now, *yesterday,* Habba shows the jury that I kill to be "on TV," live to be on magazine covers, and lie to be famous. ("I'm showing she wanted fame!" she says to Judge Kaplan after I keep answering I was on "four shows" and was not going on TV to tell the world about *me.* I was going on TV to tell the world about *him.*)

And today little Alina is still cranking it out. This morning—I kid you not, Friends—she hints to the jury that I am rabid for "fame" because after I accuse Trump, and after *Elle* fires me, I start a Substack! Now, sure, when I was a wild young lady of fifty, I wanted to get noticed for writing a good book. But at eighty-one? BAH! If I drag my withered carcass out of my cabin to *buy* a book and the dogs notice me, I am tickled. This is one of the things that happens when you get old. You get wise.

"And it [the Substack] became popular *immediately*, correct?" says Habba.

"No, it's a slog," I say. "It's hard work."

"But you generate a good amount of income from that, *correct?*"

THE COURT: Questions like this—"what's a "good amount of income?" It's evidence number one.

MS. HABBA: Yeah.

THE COURT: Evidence 101.

Habba *does* get in a couple of good whacks with "promiscuous" tweets which I post on Twitter as short answers to "Ask E. Jean" questions.

"Ms. Carroll!" she says with spangled oomph.

She has just introduced a document into evidence like a pro and is haughty as Lady Catherine de Bourgh.

"Does this tweet that you wrote, say: "A chap is not a mind-reader. Show him what you like or he will soon regret he even *has* a penis."

"Yes."

"What did you *mean* by this?"

"Tell a man what you'd like."

"And what do you mean by "he will soon regret he even has a penis"?

"I am talking about when two people are in love, and they're making love, the lovers can't guess what each other wants unless they *tell* one another."

"He will regret it," says Habba. "*That* sounds to me like what you interpreted President Trump to say was a *threat*, correct?"

Robbie objects.

Habba introduces another tweet about a penis, and Robert Smigel's and Conan O'Brien's *Saturday Night Live* sketch, the one where the cast says the word "penis" forty times, zips through my head as I explain that my *Elle* column was about relationships.

Habba says, "And discussed *penises?*"

Ahhhh, Friends . . .

I miss old Joe Tacopina hopping around, twitching the bunched muscles of his neck. To *him*, I would have replied with another example from my column:

"Oh, for Gawd's sakes! It's just a penis. There are twenty trillion of the things on the planet."

To little Alina I just say:

"Yes, we discussed penises."

And after another hour of asking me how many TV shows I went on again, and how I increased the number of my Twitter followers, and how I have come "a long way from Montana," Habba, who has been so skillful and saucy all day, so nimble at riling up voters and making Trump look like a victim—which you gotta chalk up as a win, though most reporters are blind to it and keep talking about how terrible she is in court—closes with:

"As you sit here today, do you believe you are more well known because of allegations you made against my client, President Trump?"

"Yes. I am more well known," I reply. "And *hated* by a lot more people."

"Your reputation, in many ways, is better today, isn't it, Ms. Carroll?"

"No. My status was lowered. I'm partaking in this trial to bring my reputation back."

*　　*　　*

Professor Ashlee Humphreys takes the stand.

You remember Professor Humphreys, the eternal curse of

Rudy Giuliani?* The young woman from Northwestern, the sociologist who accurately pinpointed the cause and calculated the damages from Trump's defamation during the first trial?

Her testimony today:

"So I first found that Mr. Trump's statements (on June 21 and 22) were seen between 85.8 million and 104 million times across all channels (newspapers, television, socials, etc.). I found that they *did* have an impact on Ms. Carroll's reputation, particularly as a journalist . . . and the cost to repair that damage is between $7.2 and $12 million."

*   *   *

After lunch, Michael Madaio lumbers and labors so long with his cross-examination of Professor Humphreys, it begins growing dark outside, and members of the jury who plainly miss Trump (he is at Mar-a-Lago for the funeral of his mother-in-law), and appear to pine for the time when they can again be beguiled by his grunts and mesmerized by his moans, simply throw in the towel and nap.

Indeed, I cannot tell you for certain if *anyone* in the courtroom, except Barbie, my sister, Lauren, my niece who just got off a plane from London, and the judge's wife, is awake when

---

* Giuliani, thanks to Professor Humphreys, was ordered to pay $140 million to Shaye Moss and Ruby Freeman, the two Georgia poll workers, for defaming them brutally, habitually. In an agreement, reached January 16, 2025, "America's Mayor" gets to keep his apartments, his 1980 Mercedes-Benz convertible, a collection of twenty-six designer watches, and a signed and framed Joe DiMaggio jersey, in return for an undisclosed payment.

Madaio reaches the end of his cross with two of the dumbest questions ever asked in this trial:

"What do you think caused the harm to Ms. Carroll's reputation?"

Professor Humphreys, who looks like the milkmaid in Vermeer's great painting, and is anxious to get back to Chicago and her newborn baby, answers:

"From what I've seen, it was the claim that she was a liar, that she had a political agenda, that she was working with the Democratic party. These were the associations that harmed her reputation:

Q. And who made that claim?
A. Mr. Trump, the defendant.

*　　*　　*

We are deprived of Trump's report on today's trial due to the fact, as I have already mentioned, he is at Mar-a-Logo attending the funeral. He does, however, find time to pull himself together, wipe his tears, put on a brave front, and post a selection of my very frankest answers in *Elle*.

*　　*　　*

Also, at 12:58 a.m. Trump publishes a long, howling screed, Hunter S. Thompson style, out on the edge, bad waves of paranoia, greed, fear, glee, hatred, no hands on the wheel, and, yet, crazy as he sounds, he manages to say everything he loses the first trial for saying.

*　　*　　*

DAY FOUR

Monday, January 22, 2024

Juror Sick with Possible Covid.
Things Look Dire. No Trial.

*   *   *

DAY FIVE

Tuesday, January 23, 2024

Judge Kaplan Issues Continuance.
Things Look Desperate. No Trial.

*   *   *

DAY SIX

Wednesday, January 24, 2024

Another Juror Tests Positive with Covid.
Things Look Doomed. No Trial.

*   *   *

DAY SEVEN

January 25, 2024

Trump Testifies!!

"This Court functioned all the way through the worst
of the Covid pandemic. We conducted over a hundred

jury trials right through the lockdowns and everything else. We have gotten through all that. I'm sure we'll get through all this too."

—Judge Lewis Kaplan

Friends, this is a New York jury. And because New Yorkers, whether born here or forged here, are the most opinionated, impatient, busiest people in the world, and if you need something done, give it to a busy person, all nine jurors—despite two of them testing positive for Covid—are here today. Some are masked, all are upright, and, no way *in God's hell*—whether they love Trump or loathe Trump—are they gonna miss telling their kids and grandkids that they saw the famous old geezer, with his peacock-blue tie *jumping* out in front of his shirt and his hair twirled across his forehead like Bette Davis in *Now, Voyager*, raise his small right hand and swear to tell the truth.

Judge Kaplan will tell them they should not tell *anybody* that they are even *on* this anonymous jury, of course, so I cannot say for sure if they will tell their kids about the seven events that happen *before* Trump swears, but here they are:

First Event: Robbie Myers, former editor-in-chief of *Elle*, my boss for seventeen years, and the most elegant witness to walk Judge Kaplan's runway, returns to this trial and explains to the jury who I am, what I write.

Second Event: Matt Craig, like Jane Fonda announcing the winners at Cannes, introduces into evidence two videos of sworn deposition testimony, both stark dramas— the gripping deposition in which Robbie tears Trump to shreds, and the deposition Trump gives in the New York fraud case—talking about how fabulously, glitteringly, royally rich he is.

Third Event: Shawn G. Crowley, more deeply in love with the Duke of Ferrara than ever, rests my case.

Fourth Event: Alina Habba, Esq., whose courtroom flubups *Saturday Night Live* makes terrible fun of in their cold open over the weekend, moves for a motion that President Trump should be granted judgment as a matter of law, viz, to throw the case out for lack of evidence, saying among other things: "Ms. Carroll has made a number of lewd posts about penises."

   "The motion is denied," says Judge Kaplan.

Fifth Event: In a bizarre move, Habba says she intends to call as her first witness the Woman You Don't Mess With—my friend, the New York Icon Carol Martin—with the intention of impeaching her.

   "Who are you going to impeach?" asks Judge Kaplan, astonished. "Your own witness?!"

   "That's correct, your Honor," says Madaio.

   "I don't think so," says Judge Kaplan.

   "As a witness who is identified as an adverse party, Rule 61," says Madaio, proving that, like suet pudding, he is a force to deal with.

Sixth Event: Stephen Hawking would have *adored* Carol Martin! If Carol Martin hates appearing at the first trial, she *really* hates appearing at the second trial, and she comes down the runway wearing black on black looking ready to crush all matter into her gravitational field.

Friends, *you* could have told Habba and Madaio they would be wasting their time.

> **Seventh Event:** Before Trump testifies, Judge Kaplan makes certain that both parties—i.e., Trump and I—understand that there are no "do-overs," and agree that the trial in May "conclusively decided" that "Mr. Trump forcibly, without Ms. Carroll's consent, inserted his fingers into her vagina."

"*Unnnnnh!*" gasps Trump.

I turn and catch, for a feverish instance, Trump's complexion under whatever cosmetic he is using, going white, then dark crimson.

His Honor says that Trump and I must *also* agree that the May trial "conclusively decided" that Trump's June 21 and June 22, 2019, statements from the White House were false, defamatory, and Trump had a "high degree of awareness that they were false." Therefore, Judge Kaplan says:

"As those issues all were determined previously, Mr. Trump *cannot* offer *any* evidence or make *any* argument before the jury disputing or intending to unwind those determinations."

While the judge is saying this, the big winner of New Hampshire is sitting at the Defense Table with his first-degree-burn, orange-and-red face moaning:

"I never met her."

*   *   *

So, what Judge Kaplan wants to do is "confirm" with Alina Habba, Esq. that Trump's testimony will not contain "inadmissible evidence to the jury."

"I don't know who she is," says Trump under his breath, at the Defense Table.

Habba says she is sorry but she is "not understanding" Judge Kaplan's questions.

"I don't *want* to know who she is," says Trump.

"I want to know," says Judge Kaplan, "everything he is going to say."

"I can't tell you!" says Habba.

"I've never seen her."

"Answer my question," says Judge Kaplan.

"I'm not," says Habba, "testifying for my client, your Honor."

"You *are*," says Judge Kaplan, "making an offer of proof and your client is bound by it."

"Never met her," says Trump.

"This is what my client is going to say," says Habba. "That he did not do it. At the time he denied it for the reason of having to deny it. That he was addressing them (reporters), the questions, because of his accusation. That he never instructed anyone to hurt Ms. Carroll. That is what he is going to say. And also, that he stands by the depositions that *they* (Matt Craig) played, which I am happy they did, frankly."

"And he will say *nothing* else?" says Judge Kaplan.

"That is my understanding, your Honor," says Habba.

"Let me hear from the other side."

Robbie, who is itching to get Trump on the stand and cross-examine him for twenty or thirty hours, but who is too smart to think Trump will even make it through *direct* without imploding, replies judiciously:

"So, your Honor," she says, putting her left hand in her trouser pocket, a sure sign she is about to bargain, "as you were talking and asking the questions of Ms. Habba—we are closer to him than you are—Mr. Trump said under his breath that he intended to say that he never met her and had never seen her before. That's what he was saying under his breath just behind us when Ms. Habba was purporting to say what he is going to say. So I guess if he just says—I mean, we have to figure out what is the proper way to say it . . . We think there is certainly the risk of being *confusing to the jury,* but your Honor certainly knows how to give an instruction."

"Look," says Judge Kaplan to Habba. "You told me in your letters that Mr. Trump is well aware of the strict confines placed on his testimony. Do you confirm that?"

"Yes, your Honor!"

Very gung-ho is little Alina.

"And you say that because you *personally* made him aware of those confine—"

"Excuse me, your Honor," says Habba, pausing to listen to Trump.

"I never met the woman," says Trump. "I don't know who the woman is. I do *not* know who the woman is. I wasn't at the trial. *I don't know who the woman is!* I never *met* this woman!"

"Mr. Trump!" says Judge Kaplan, seated high up on his two thousand pounds of oak. "Keep your voice down!"

"Your Honor," says Habba. "I have now answered many times the three questions. I have literally given a preview into the questions asked—"

"And I have an outstanding question to you," says Judge Kaplan.

"Okay. What is it?"

"Did you make Mr. Trump personally—"

"I never met the woman."

"Yes," says Habba.

"Aware of the confines on his testimony?" asks Judge Kaplan.

"Yes."

"I never met her."

"And will Mr. Trump comply with those confines?" asks Judge Kaplan.

"I don't know who the woman is!!!!!!"

"Outside of having a glass ball," replies Habba, "he will *absolutely—*"

"I'm sorry, Mr. Trump," says Judge Kaplan—a vision of supreme calm one sometimes sees in downhill racers poised on mountaintops just before the start beeps go off—"you are *interrupting* these proceedings by talking loudly while your counsel is talking. That is not permitted."

Trump lowers his head—irises rising—like a bull, gives a great furious look at Judge Kaplan, and says, "I never met her," quietly to Habba.

*   *   *

And what do *I* think while the parties are going back and forth? I think it is strange to be thinking what I am thinking, because what I am thinking is I am glad I did not take out a loan and spend $65,000 on a facelift before trial. Because, *of course,* I visit one of the top plastic surgeons in New York, schedule "eyes" and "jowls," for surgery three months before trial to give my mug "time to heal," and a couple days before I am to be rolled into the operating room and knocked out, I call the thing off. And, Friends, no judgment. If *you* want to get plastic surgery before *you* meet Trump in court, go ahead. But me? I'm *glad* my face is sagging and bagging all over the place.

I am seven and a half feet from him at the Plaintiff's Table, and too bad if he has to look at me in all my fabulous desiccated eighty-year-old glory.

*　　*　　*

——*(Jury present)*

THE COURT: Thanks for bearing with us again, ladies and gentlemen. I hope lunch was better than the cafeteria usually turns out. Ms. Habba, you may call your next witness.
MS. HABBA: Thank you, your Honor. The defense calls President Donald Trump.

——*With his old golfer's shamble, Trump makes his way to the stand without a trace of emotion on his face.*

DONALD JOHN TRUMP, called as a witness by the Defendant, having been duly sworn, testifies as follows:

THE DEPUTY CLERK: Can you please state your name for the record.
THE WITNESS: Donald John Trump.
THE COURT: You may proceed, Ms. Habba.
MS. HABBA: Thank you, your Honor.

DIRECT EXAMINATION

BY MS. HABBA:
Q. Mr. President, you viewed your deposition which was played by plaintiff's counsel at length during the trial. Didn't you?

A. Yes, I did.

Q. Do you stand by your testimony at the deposition?

A. 100 percent. Yes.

Q. Did you deny the allegation because Ms. Carroll made an accusation?

A. That's exactly right. She said something, I consider it a false accusation. No difference.

MS. KAPLAN: Objection, your Honor.

———*Trump cannot say it is a "false accusation" because, as you recall, Friends, this trial is not "a do-over." This "issue," as Judge Kaplan explains about ten times "was determined previously. Mr. Trump cannot offer any evidence or make any argument before the jury disputing or intending to unwind those determinations."*

THE COURT: Everything after "yes, I did," is stricken. The jury will disregard it. Go ahead.

BY MS. HABBA:

Q. Did you ever instruct anyone to hurt Ms. Carroll in your statements?

A. No. I just wanted to defend myself, my family, and frankly, the presidency.

MS. KAPLAN: Objection your Honor.

THE COURT: Objection is sustained. Everything after "no" is stricken. The jury will disregard.

MS. HABBA: I have no further questions. Thank you.

THE COURT: Thank you.

And there, Friends, after five years of denying, denying, denying, after five years of attacking, attacking, attacking, after five years of shouting that the American court system is "broken," that this lawsuit is a "witch hunt," a "hoax," that I'm a liar, a fraud, and a danger to the country, Trump ends one of the greatest campaign appearances ever recorded in American history.

*   *   *

The woman who was *born* to cross-examine Trump stands up.

*   *   *

But Roberta A. Kaplan is too wily to make Mr. Epitome-of-a-Martyr *more* enticing to the jury. They already look flipped out. For or against, makes no difference. They are intoxicated! Dazzled! Gobsmacked!

Force him to acknowledge that the first trial actually took place, then get the hell rid of him. That is the plan. Almost impossible to pull off:

CROSS-EXAMINATION

BY MS. KAPLAN:

Q. Good afternoon, sir. Now, your deposition that we watched earlier today in this trial, took place in October of 2022, correct?

A. I believe so, yes.

Q. And after that, months after that, there was a trial between you and Ms. Carroll that took place actually in this courtroom; correct?

MS. HABBA: Objection.
THE COURT: Sustained.
MS. HABBA: Thank you.

BY MS. KAPLAN:
Q. Sitting here today, Mr. Trump, are you aware that there was another trial between you and Ms. Carroll?
A. Yes.

MS. HABBA: Objection.
THE COURT: Sustained.

Q. Mr. Trump, is this the first trial between you and Ms. Carroll that you have attended?

MS. HABBA: Objection.
THE COURT: I will allow that.

A. Yes.

MS. KAPLAN: No further questions, your Honor.
THE COURT: Any redirect?

REDIRECT EXAMINATION

BY MS. HABBA:
Q. Mr. President, did you have counsel at the last trial?
A. I had counsel.
Q. Did you listen to the advice of counsel at the last trial?

MS KAPLAN: Objection, your Honor.
THE COURT: Sustained.
MS. HABBA: No further questions.
THE COURT: Thank you, Mr. Trump. You are excused.

His Honor tells the jury to enjoy their evening and that they will "probably have the case for decision by lunchtime tomorrow."

*   *   *

DAY EIGHT

January 26, 2024

"WHAT DOES THE 'M' STAND FOR?"

Wow! Alina Habba, Esq. looks so pretty with her dark hair pulled into a low bun—the humble-brag of a beauty!—with her tremendous high heels, and her very tight, white sweater, and her electric-blue pantsuit hugging her round bottom, and her diamonds glittering from her ears, and her excitement mounting (we are just minutes away from closing arguments!), and feeling, no doubt, her oats, she gets into a tangle with His Honor about a tweet she wants to show. His Honor says, "No." Habba says, in so many words, "Yes." His Honor, his eyebrows descending nearly to the top of his glasses, says *"Ms. Haaabba."* And Habba says, "I have to make a record," i.e., a complaint, and His Honor says:

"Ms. Habba! You are on the verge of spending some time in lockup! Now sit down!"

"Shocking!" says Habba to Trump.

And Trump expels air like a jet exhaust.

*   *   *

Judge Kaplan says "Okay. Bring in the jury."

Ready for final arguments, Friends?

Robbie Kaplan steps to the lectern in her stone-gray, custom-tailored, four-button, single-breasted suit over a dark-butterscotch silk shirt, pearl earrings, her blond hair blown into a sleek wave, and, after bidding the smoothest, sunniest, most affable "Good morning, everyone," tears up the courtroom like she's Henry the Fifth at the Battle of Agincourt.

Robbie's summation is so good, with videos of Trump saying terrible lies about me not only *after* the first trial holds him liable for defamation, but with videos of him saying horrible lies about me *during* this trial—"Play it!" Robbie calls out over and over.

Robbie's final argument is so good—she takes the deposition from his New York fraud trial, in which Trump yammers away embellishing his riches, and uses it in *this* trial to show the jury how wealthy he is—"He said his brand alone is worth $10 billion, Mar-a-Lago, $1.5 billion, the Doral, $2.5 billion. . . . That's $14 billion right there, ladies and gentlemen!"

Her summation is so good she points out that Trump doesn't even "bother to *show up*" for the first trial, which is only about sexual assault. But for *this* trial? This trial where the issue is "how much money he has to pay—*here he is.*" And what does that mean? It means that the *one* thing that Donald Trump cares about is *not* truth. *Not* law. "The one thing Donald Trump cares about is *money.*"

Robbie's close is so good, in other words, Trump, his face dark vermillion, flaming, boiling with anger, gets up in the middle of it and walks out.

*   *   *

Ten-minute break.

Trump returns.

Jonah Bromwich reporting from the trial for the *New York Times,* says:

> "This is my first time watching this trial at all, and the tiny amount of distance between Trump and Carroll is worth dwelling on. It's almost impossible to imagine the energy in the room itself. These two people, with their history, sitting that close to each other."

*   *   *

Habba rises for her summation, takes the lectern in her electric-blue suit and her baby-blue–high heels with bows, and, among other things, she tells the jury she is "honestly *mortified*, ladies and gentlemen, that I have to repeat this in front of you. I apologize."

And then she introduces the penis tweets.

Such a superb voice! So loud! So deliciously arrogant! She also brings up that I "hang up a bunch of pants over a window, but don't call the police," that after I accuse Trump, I am happy to have "the fame, the praise I always craved," that I "do *not* suffer emotionally from the president's statements," that I like my "new brand," that the reason I bring the lawsuit is to "improve my status," that I make "rounds on the media! Rounds on the media!" That I am rotting in a "cabin desperate to crawl back" to the glamour of New York. That when she asks me *on the stand* if I "planned on doing TV after this," I do not say no. That I "attended parties!" That I am "living the life of the rich and famous, hanging out with celebrities like Kathy Griffin!" And that—and here she offers to the jury one of the greatest jewels of argument ever tendered in a United States courtroom—Rob Reiner once tweeted about me.

*   *   *

No break.

Judge Kaplan says, "We will hear rebuttal argument. Ms. Crowley, you may proceed."

Friends, you remember her sharp tan suit from the first trial, right? Miss Shawn G. Crowley, like God, Herself, hath no qualms, and is wearing it again today. Halfway into her rebuttal, she turns to Donald Trump, fastens her eyes on him, throws out her arm, points in his face, and shouts, "The sexual assault happened! And Donald Trump has no right to say otherwise!"

Trump, blazing at the effrontery, looks away.

Madaio, almost struck dumb, staggers to his feet.

"Objection!"

"Overruled."

"He is lying!!" cries Shawn.

"Objection."

"He is breaking the law!!" cries Shawn.

"Objection, your Honor. It is on appeal!"

"There are ways for people to lawfully respond to an allegation that is true," says Shawn. "You could say nothing. You could say, 'This is a private matter and I'm going to address it privately.' You could say, 'This happened a long time ago and I'm sorry for it and it is not the man that I am today.' You have certainly seen those types of statements from public figures before."

Because I am turned to watch Shawn, I can see Trump out of the rods of my right eye, crouched like a big angry spider at the Defense Table, not moving.

"By the way," says Shawn. "If he had done that, if he had stayed silent or if, God forbid, he told the truth, do you honestly think that any of the terrible things that have happened to Ms. Carroll in the last five years would have come to pass? If Donald Trump had followed the law and not defamed Ms. Carroll, do you really think that people would have come after her the way they did, calling her a liar? A paid Democratic operative? A fraud? Too ugly to sexually assault? Of course not.

"When the president speaks, the world listens. And as we have seen the statements, the hate mail, the threats that she has gotten, they parrot Donald Trump's words. Causation? There couldn't be clearer proof of causation. If Donald Trump hadn't lied, if he hadn't defamed her, Ms. Carroll's life, it would have gone on. Her career would have continued and she wouldn't be flooded with hate and threats and we wouldn't be here today.

"Ms. Habba said in her opening, and then again today, that Ms. Carroll *likes* her new brand. I have to ask, what brand is that?

"Is it the I-was-paid-to-falsely-accuse-the-president brand? Or is it the I'm-a-whack-job-who-made-up-a-story-to-sell-books brand? They're saying *that's* the brand that Ms. Carroll wants and not the brand that she had back in 2019 before he came after her? The brand of being a writer for the world's largest women's fashion magazine? Or having the longest running advice column in publishing? Writing for *SNL*? Appearing on primetime TV? Being nominated for an Emmy? Of course Ms. Carroll prefers the brand she had before Donald Trump defamed her. Of course she would rather be known as a writer than a liar and a fraud.

"So, yes, this case is about defamation, defamation of a woman who has been sexually assaulted. Defamation by the man who sexually assaulted her. And yet, Ms. Habba faults Ms. Carroll for not being miserable all the time. I guess her argument is that she must not have actually suffered because she's had some happy moments in her life."

"Objection!"

"Overruled."

"And I have to say, this is a bizarre argument. It is like they're suggesting that Ms. Carroll has to show that she has been a broken wreck of a person every single day for the last five years, that she's had no moments of joy or friendships. In the defense's view, every time Ms. Carroll went to a party with friends, or celebrated a victory in her lawsuit against him, or presented a brave face to the public, she was somehow showing that his defamatory statements caused her no harm and this case is just some big conspiracy against him. That makes no sense, and I guess it is totally inconsistent with how each of you has experienced life.

"The defense wants you to decide that the only way Ms. Carroll could have avoided the bad things that have happened to her is by *staying silent*. Meanwhile, the man who did these things to her, the man who sexually assaulted her, he gets to do whatever he wants. According to the defense, he gets to lie. He gets to threaten. He gets to ignore a jury verdict."

"Objection!"

"Overruled."

"He gets to defy the law and the rules of this courtroom. You *saw* how he has behaved through this trial. You've heard him. You *saw* him stand up and walk out of the courtroom while Ms. Kaplan was speaking. Rules don't apply to Donald Trump. He gets to do whatever he wants and use his massive, powerful platform to keep ruining her life. He even believes he gets to testify under oath and lie once again."

"Objection!"

"Overruled."

"Ladies and gentlemen, this is not a campaign rally. It's not a press event. This is a court of law. And it's Ms. Carroll's life. Donald Trump sexually assaulted her. He defamed her. He keeps defaming her. He is not the victim. This is her life. Help her take it back. Make him stop. Make him pay enough so that he will stop. Thank you."

*　　*　　*

The jury is so riled by Robbie Kaplan, Alina Habba, Esq., and Shawn G. Crowley, not to mention all the thrilling jumping up and objecting, and the smoke coming off the top of Trump's head, and His Honor pausing the proceedings to tell the defense—i.e., Mr. Boris Epshteyn, to STOP strolling around the courtroom during summation like a boulevardier in the Belle Époque—that when Judge Kaplan asks the jury members to raise their hands if they would "like a break," or otherwise "we can go right ahead," well, "right ahead" is where the jury wants to go.

Andy the deputy clerk steps forward and makes the official announcement:

THE DEPUTY CLERK: To all the spectators in the gallery: The Court is about to charge the jury. You either must remain seated throughout the duration of this charge or leave at this time.

Marshals, please lock the doors!

THE COURT: Members of the jury, we've reached the point in the trial where you are about to perform your function as jurors.

His Honor instructs the jury—and then, dang!

If he doesn't make us all feel like we are George Washington crossing the Delaware, saying that this court in which we have all been fighting the last two weeks is the oldest federal court in America. The Mother Court!

"This is the very first United States court to hold session under the Constitution. It did so even before the first session of the United States Supreme Court. And since those earliest days in our nation's history—through wars, through economic depressions, through pandemics—jurors like *you* have been asked to decide cases, and your role is just the same as the role of the countless jurors before you."

The Mother Court! The United States District Court for the Southern District of New York, the twenty-seven-floor block of granite and marble, the Daniel Patrick Moynihan Mahogany Extravaganza with its forty-two courtrooms standing tall at the beginning of the Continent. I do not know what time it is in Judge Kaplan's courtroom—I am too tightly wound to ask anyone—but looking back at the *New York Times* reports, the following actions are taking place:

1:43 p.m. The jury retires to deliberate.

1:45 p.m. The spectators, courtroom artists, press, clerks, marshals, Secret Service, etc., etc., shovel whatever larded, starched, butter-fatted, sugared, oiled and fried donuts, cronuts, clubs, heroes, pitas, and pizza they can manage to grab and shove down their gullets for lunch.

2:01 p.m. Maria Cramer of the *Times* spots Robbie Kaplan and Alina Habba Esq. in the Daniel Patrick Moynihan cafeteria on the eighth floor, reporting they are "friendly to each other, smiling and exchanging pleasantries" as they stand in line at the grill counter.

2:01 p.m. Anusha Bayya of the *Times* also notes that the city's marriage bureau is just steps away from the Daniel Patrick Moynihan United States Courthouse, and New Yorkers are celebrating their nuptials with "pops of confetti" and "loud cheers."

2:38 p.m. Jonah Bromwich of the *Times* reports "the mood" inside the press room is "bored and tense."

3:20 p.m. Ben Weiser and J. Edward Moreno of the *Times* publish a profile with the headline: "Judge Lewis Kaplan is known for his intellect and command of the courtroom."

4:14 p.m. Anusha Bayya reports that at 3:58 p.m. security officers divert traffic from Worth Street in front of the courthouse.

4:17 p.m. Jonah Bromwich notes "the courtroom appears to be filling with spectators and some of the lawyers."

4:25 p.m. We have a verdict.

I am back in the courtroom. Not "bored and tense." Jangled. I feel my spleen galloping. To calm myself, I sit down in my chair (*my* chair!) between Robbie and Shawn, and—for about the hundredth time—start running "the list," remembering everyone, trying not to forget a name:

Natasha Stoynoff
Jessica Leeds
Jill Harth
Summer Zervos
Alva Johnson
Kristin Anderson
Amy Dorris
Karena Virginia
Rachel Crooks
Lisa Boyne
Cathy Heller
Temple Taggart McDowell
Karen Johnson

Mindy McGillivray
Juliet Huddy
Jessica Drake
Cassandra Searles

Some say there are forty-seven women. Some say twenty-six. I do not know how many women have accused Trump and I do not know what will happen when I hear the verdict. But I know two things: I cannot remember half of the women's names, but running the list calms me down, and, second, I make Trump—well, I am about to say to myself, "At least I make Trump show up!" But I turn in my chair and see he is gone.

4:37 p.m. Judge Kaplan says, "We will have no outbursts and will maintain entire *decorum* during the proceedings!"

*   *   *

The spectators—such a great many people squished into the pews!—are here for a gala, a spree, a smackdown, a lift-up, nobody is sitting still, everybody is turning and craning and standing and shifting and whispering, the marshals are on alert, my sister Barbie is turning shades of cranberry, my niece Lauren is turning shades of pale blue-chartreuse, clouds of pink dust fly where the artists are wielding their chalk at a frantic pace. Everybody is wound up. Everybody is horribly excited. Everybody looks like they are ready to scream. Robbie Kaplan, Shawn G. Crowley, and I clasp hands. Our neural pathways are *lit*! His Honor, more somber than ever, addresses the jury:

THE COURT: Ladies and gentlemen. I understand you have reached a verdict. Who is the foreperson?

——*The publicist rises. The publicist! Dear God! Robbie, Shawn G. Crowley, and I nearly squeeze one another's hands off. The publicist! Youngish, blond, brilliant blue eyes, very fit, very attractive, wearing a rose-red sweater, and extremely self-possessed. She has paid close, twinkling attention to both sides and all witnesses. I do not know another thing about her, but, Friends, I love her. Shawn G. Crowley loves her. Robbie Kaplan loves her. We all love her and do not know why we love her, we just do. We are gripping one another's hands.*

THE FOREPERSON: It is.
THE COURT: Please hand the verdict to Andy. The clerk will read the verdict.

——*Andy reads the verdict. He cocks his head to the side and reads the verdict again. He hands the verdict up to Judge Kaplan. A long moment as Judge Kaplan reads the verdict, his eyebrows rising about a yard above his glasses.*

THE COURT: Madam foreperson, does the "M" that appears next to various numbers mean—? What does it mean?
THE FOREPERSON: Million.

——*Such a crash of happiness hits me, I am nearly knocked off my own legs.*

THE COURT: Thank you.
THE DEPUTY CLERK: (*Reading*) Did Ms. Carroll prove, by a preponderance of evidence, that:
Question 1.
Ms. Carroll suffered more than nominal damages as a result

of Mr. Trump's publication of the June 21 and June 22, 2019, statements?

Yes.

Compensatory damages: You award, other than for the reputational repair program, **$7.3 million.**

Compensatory damages: You award, for the reputational repair program only, **$11 million.**

——Robbie is on my right and Shawn G. Crowley is on my left, and I feel us lifting off the floor holding hands like in Peter Pan— not the Johnny Depp version, not the Hugh Jackman version, not the Keira Knightly, not the Spielberg with Julia Roberts, but the 1955 live production that I watch, as a child, on NBC television, with Mary Martin.

Question 2.

In making the June 21, 2019, statement, Mr. Trump acted maliciously, out of hatred, ill will or spite, vindictively, or in wanton, reckless, or willful disregard of Ms. Carroll's rights?

Yes.

Question 3.

In making the June 22, 2019, statement, Mr. Trump acted maliciously, out of hatred, ill will or spite, vindictively, or in wanton, reckless, or willful disregard of Ms. Carroll's rights?

Yes.

How much, if any, should Mr. Trump pay to Ms. Carroll in punitive damages?

$65 million.

And like Peter Pan I cannot say that I have ever come down from flying around the courtroom ceiling. You may see me looking like—it may *appear* that I have come down and am walking around smiling outside the Daniel Patrick Moynihan United States Courthouse, for instance, but my heart still flies, Friends, as I bid thee farewell.

The New York Times ✓ @nytimes · Jan 26, 2024

A Manhattan jury on Friday ordered Donald **Trump** to pay $83.3 million to the writer E. Jean **Carroll** for defaming her ever since she first accused him of rape. **Trump** was found liable last year of sexually abusing her in the mid-1990s. https://nyti.ms/3Sgs1DD

Jury Orders Trump to Pay E. Jean Carroll $83.3 Million For Years of Defamation

Michael M. Santiago/Getty Images

EPILOGUE

So. What am I gonna do with the $83 million?

Well, Miss Rachel Harris, chair, International Trust & Estate Planning at Loeb & Loeb, has set up a revocable trust, and the bulk of the money from the trust will go to the E. Jean Foundation. And, since Trump is already mad that he has to pay me the $5 million, uh, pardon me, make that $6 million—it is $6 million with his having to pay 9 percent interest compounded daily. And as Trump is even madder he has to pay me the $83,300,000—excuse me, did I say $83,300,000? Forgive me. If we add in the $5 million, I mean the $6 million, plus the 9 percent compounded deliciously on the $83,300,00, it comes to, let me see . . . well it looks like it comes to around $100 million. Yes. Slightly over $100 million. Now what was I talking about? Where was I? Oh, yes.

What am I gonna do with the $100 million?

I, E. Jean Carroll, pledge to make Trump very, *very* mad by giving most of the $100 million to all things he *hates*. If Trump despises it—women's reproductive rights, voting rights, climate solutions, etc.—*I'm* gonna be giving money to it. And, what's more, each donation I give, I will make public on my Substack (ejeancarroll.substack.com) so we can all feel the joy of making Trump angry.

And why, Friends, is the 9 percent interest continually compounding? Because Trump is continually appealing the two unanimous jury decisions. *And* because Robbie, who has started a new firm, Kaplan Martin, and is filled to the absolute quivering *brim* with piss and vinegar, keeps continually crushing him.

Robbie holding the cases she studied when she crushed Trump's appeal to overturn our win in the first trial.

Indeed, when headlines hit around the world,

> ## *Trump Loses Appeal of Carroll's $5 Million Award in Sex-Abuse Case*

it is the first time many people in *this* country hear the new president has been found liable for sexual assault. And many are astounded.

So, Friends, it looks like we are doing a bit of good here. We prove Trump is a liar. We change the rape law in New York. We show that the Adult Survivors Act is needed in every state. We spark the fighting spirits in old ladies everywhere. We demonstrate that when you go to court, forget the facelift, do the hair and makeup. And when Trump kept bitching about the gun? Miss Havisham and Guffington Von Fluke prove you can sit on a chief of police when he is forced to pay a visit to your cabin.

Picture him, Friends. The young, earnest, freshly starched chief, newly appointed, perched on the very edge of the chaise lounge in my cabin, contending with the dogs, and surrounded by Ms. Robbie Kaplan, Ms. Jessica Bennett of the *New York Times*, Ms. Catherine Bosley, managing director of the Levinson Group, myself, and Ms. Vagina T. Fireball.

A lesser man could not have done it!

The next day I "surrender" my gun. Of course, an hour later I buy a new Mossberg 20-gauge shotgun, perfectly legal in New York. I name her "Aphrodite," also perfectly legal in New York.

I meet the illustrious Anita Hill over Zoom, and, looking at her beautiful face, I burst into tears. *Rolling Stone* gives me their Truth Seeker award, and Hunter S. Thompson rolls in his grave when I accept it. *Time* names me one of the "100 Most Influential People in the World," and just to defy conspiracy nuts with all their crack-brained theories about "the dress not existing"—spread with such fury and vengeance by Trump—I wear a black Donna Karan gown to the celebration. And Ivy Meeropol's stunning documentary about my life and its trials is premiering at Telluride.

Judge Lewis Kaplan files an opinion saying that what Trump did is, in fact, "rape," as commonly understood. Anderson Cooper proves everything Trump continually says about the "famous Andy Cooper tape" is a lie. Joe Tacopina calls Robbie the day after Trump is elected president and says, "I'm so sorry, Robbie."

So, I guess that's about it, Friends.

My work here is done. I didn't try to do too much. I did what I could. I beat Trump twice. I could not have done it without Alina Habba, Esq. Thank you, Alina!!

And now, Friends, I leave you with one of the best things to come out of *Carroll v. Trump*. Shawn G. Crowley and Mike Ferrara got married and look what happened:

Callan Ferrara Crowley meets his Auntie Eeee.

ABOUT THE AUTHOR

E. Jean Carroll is a journalist, the author of five books, including the biography of Hunter S. Thompson, and has written for *Rolling Stone*, *Outside*, *Vanity Fair*, *Esquire*, *New York*, and *The Atlantic*. She was named one of *Time*'s Most Influential People in the World in 2024. She throws the ball for her dogs at her cabin in the mountains in upstate New York.